T0372266

BENEATH OUR FEET

BENEATH OUR FEET

EVERYDAY DISCOVERIES RESHAPING HISTORY

MICHAEL LEWIS &
IAN RICHARDSON

forewords
MACKENZIE CROOK
ALICE ROBERTS

with more than 300 illustrations

Contents

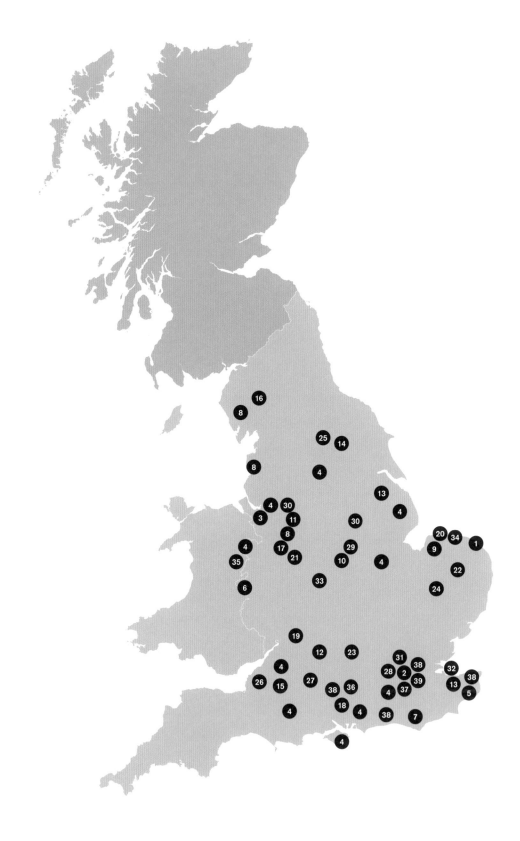

Foreword

Mackenzie Crook

My childhood home was a 1960s terraced house in suburban Kent with a small rectangle of back garden where, aged five in the famously sweltering summer of '76, I decided to dig a hole. A deep hole. Deeper than anyone had ever dared to dig before. By the end of day two I was already eighteen inches down.

I seem to remember I was hoping to find snakes, my rationale being that if you dug a small hole and found worms, if you went deeper you would eventually find snakes.

I didn't find snakes, but I did find cherry pits and short lengths of white clay pipe.

My dad had an old map of the area and showed me that where our house now stood there was once a cherry orchard. The pipes, he said, were the broken stems of tobacco pipes that were probably dropped by the fruit pickers and maybe, because these fragments were so numerous, our garden was where these workers gathered at break times.

I was stunned by this. As far as I was concerned I had found something more exciting

than pipes, pits or even pythons. I had found ghosts. I could see those ancient people sitting in the welcome shade of the fruit trees, smoking their long clay pipes, passing a bottle and laughing and joking right where my paddling pool was now slowly deflating in the sun.

Ever since that summer I have been conscious of those ghosts and I still find clay pipes on an almost daily basis – on beaches, embankments and in beer gardens. I can spot a piece from twenty paces and I have a large jar full of them, each fragment connecting me with a stranger from the past.

As an occasional metal detectorist I am always delighted to find buttons for the same reason: a coin will have passed through many hands and made many transactions, whereas a button adorned the clothing of a particular individual and they would have noticed when it was lost and had to be replaced. Not a dramatic event, but a moment in somebody's life.

My jar of buttons (I also have a jar of buttons) represents so many moments of irritation.

I have found gold twice in my life. The first was a christening bracelet outside a church one Sunday not long after I dug my snake pit. I went with my mum to the village police station and was told to come back in three weeks when, if it had not been claimed, the bracelet would be mine to keep. Luckily for me the owner (presumably a newborn baby) didn't come forward in the allotted time and the treasure was mine.

Forty years later I found another piece of jewellery, this time with my metal detector. About the size of a five-pence coin, squashed and bent, it was a Roman earring or pendant with a milled edge and a design of a long-necked bird. I duly recorded it with the brilliant and dedicated experts at the Portable Antiquities

OPPOSITE My jars of buttons and clay pipe-stems.

BELOW Roman gold jewellery fitting with a long-necked bird, recorded on the PAS database, SF-C9FAB1.

The British Museum's Portable Antiquities Scheme

Scheme, where it was officially declared treasure and offered to museums to purchase.

No museum, large or small, was able to acquire it. So, again, it was mine to keep.

At Sutton Hoo, a king was buried in an immense ship alongside unimaginable wealth. The ceremony would have been spectacular, the barrow a place of pilgrimage, guarded around the clock, and everyone would have known of the treasure buried beneath the mound.

But decades passed, then centuries. And at some point nobody was left who remembered. The king dissolved back into the earth, but his gold and garnets remained and literally nobody knew. Until they were found by Basil Brown.

And there is so much more, beneath our feet, still to be found.

On these small islands every inch of land has been trodden by peasants and kings. This book is about those people who once walked where we now walk and the things they left behind, discarded as rubbish, dropped by accident, or buried and never retrieved.

To see these things in museums is inspiring. But to find them is to time travel.

Mackenzie Crook

Foreword

Alice Roberts

Archaeological artefacts provide us with a different way of engaging with the past. Archaeology isn't the handmaiden of history – it's another source of evidence that can open new lines of enquiry. Artefacts can make us think differently about what we read in historical sources, or shed crucial light on periods for which we have little to no written history. They provide us with evidence about trade and exchange, beliefs and values, technology and fashion. And they also give us a very human, tangible way of engaging with the past – of getting close to the world of those who walked before us in the landscape.

I remember poring over a collection of coins and silver ingots with John Naylor from the Ashmolean Museum and the Portable Antiquities Scheme (PAS). The coins were fascinating – most of them had been minted for the Anglo-Saxon king Alfred the Great (r. 871–899), but a few showed two kings, sitting side by side: Alfred and Ceolwulf II (r. 874–c. 879), the last king of Mercia, now less well known than Alfred. A single penny in the hoard provided

the earliest possible date for its burial, at some time after the late 870s. Perhaps the hoard was buried by Vikings retreating after their defeat by Alfred's army at the Battle of Edington.

The coins gave us astonishing insight into a turbulent period of British history, and a rather more complicated picture than the written chronicles provide. Seated alongside Alfred on these coins, Ceolwulf may have been a more important leader than is suggested by the Anglo-Saxon sources that portray him as a puppet king of the Vikings. And if the hoard had been buried by Vikings, this haul of silver jewellery, ingots and coins might suggest that they had been paid off by Anglo-Saxons – and therefore that the Battle of Edington in 878 was perhaps not quite so decisive as the histories written by the victors claim.

These valuable insights emerged from the ground, and from the past, thanks to the efforts of metal detectorist Jim Mather, who discovered the hoard in a field near Watlington, Oxfordshire, in 2015 (see pp. 150–53). The first object he found was a silver ingot, which he recognised from having seen a similar artefact in the British Museum. When he encountered the mass of silver coins, he realised that he had found something even more important and contacted the Portable Antiquities Scheme. David Williams (Surrey Finds Liaison Officer) came out to excavate the hoard. Back in the British Museum lab, conservator Pippa Pearce was tasked with carefully freeing the silver coins, jewellery fragments and ingots from the soil.

This is just one of the many wonderful discoveries and new historical revelations emerging from the work of the Portable Antiquities Scheme that I've learned about over twelve series of making BBC's *Digging for Britain*. These finds made by passionate, responsible detectorists, mudlarks, fieldwalkers and other public finders have helped to push the bounds

OPPOSITE Kings Alfred of Wessex and Ceolwulf II of Mercia depicted seated together on a silver 'Two Emperors' penny from the Watlington Hoard found by Jim Mather.

BELOW Sam Moorhead and myself examining coins and pottery from the Frome Hoard at the British Museum for *Digging for Britain*.

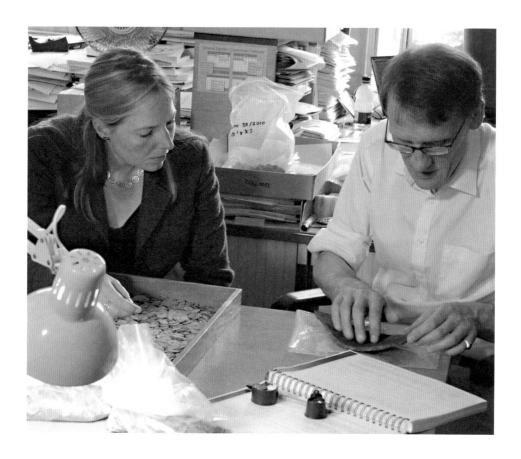

of what we know about the past, revealing the clues buried in the landscapes beneath our feet.

Amazingly, since its inception in 1997, the PAS has recorded more than 1.7 million finds. The earliest find recorded so far, the Happisburgh Handaxe (see pp. 20–23), dates to 850,000 years ago, when Britain (or at least a bit of the land that is now Britain) was inhabited by earlier species of humans. And then there are Bronze Age torcs, miniature Iron Age weapons, thousands of Roman coins (including the Frome Hoard, see above and pp. 98–103), Anglo-Saxon sword fittings, Tudor pendants – the list goes on and on. Some of these wonderful objects – and their intriguing stories – are found within this book.

One of the very first sites I dug on, a Viking Age settlement in Anglesey, was discovered thanks to two metal detectorists, Archie Gillespie and Pete Corbett. They turned up a Viking coin in a potato field and took it to the National Museum of Wales. Detectorists like Archie and Pete, walking over ploughed fields in all weathers, finding these clues, are the citizen scientists of the archaeological world. They haven't hidden their finds away; they've shared them with all of us, and we're all the richer for it. Because the past, as I am so fond of saying – the past belongs to everyone.

Alice Roberts
University of Birmingham

Introduction

Michael Lewis

Beneath our feet is another world, hidden from view, waiting to be discovered. It is a world of the past, where the objects left behind give clues about those who were here before us – who they were, and what their lives might have been like.

Some of the most spectacular artefacts discovered in Britain have been found by members of the public rather than professional archaeologists, most through metal detecting. The excitement in this kind of discovery, besides the thrill of finding things, is that it connects people who have a recreational interest in the past with archaeologists like Ian and myself who study it for a living. We are all working together to understand Britain's long, complex history.

It is estimated that there are around 60,000 recreational metal detectorists in the UK, searching mainly arable land. Undoubtedly some take up the hobby hoping to get rich, but for most detecting is an opportunity to get out into the countryside, to spend time with like-minded people and make interesting discoveries. This is not to say that detectorists don't hope to make the find of a lifetime, but they know that the chances of finding another Staffordshire Hoard (pp. 136–45) are very slim.

Perhaps they will find the occasional Roman brooch or medieval penny after several hours in the soggy rain or burning heat. But most get just as excited by common items such as worn tokens and broken buckles, thrilled to be the first person to hold the object since it was lost or buried. Finds like these provide a tangible link with the past and open up the mind to imagine the people who once owned these objects, what they did with them and how they lost them. Even common items provide important evidence about the past, so it is crucial that detectorists and other public finders exploring past landscapes do so responsibly and record their finds.

Another method of investigating the past is mudlarking – searching rivers and streams for archaeological finds, either by eye or with metal detectors. In the 19th century mudlarks were mainly children sent down to the river to find items of some worth that could help their families survive. The most well-known modern mudlarks are the some 4,000 permit holders licensed by the Port of London Authority to search the foreshore of the tidal River Thames in London. They include members of the Society of Thames Mudlarks, a small organisation set up in the early 1980s, when mudlarking was a niche hobby among metal detectorists, to control who was digging in the Thames mud and to encourage collaboration with archaeologists. As is still the case, members of this Society were given more rights (in terms of where they could dig and how deep) if they followed certain conditions, but all Thames mudlarks are required to report their finds. Now, owing to social media, many more people are aware of mudlarking and tempted to try their hand at it. As with the surge of interest in metal detecting, this has had the positive effect of democratising archaeology, but can also put fragile riverine

OPPOSITE Archaeologists Luke
Barber and Chloe Hunisett
excavating a Roman coin hoard
found by a detectorist near
Petworth, West Sussex. Thanks to
the finder, who knew to stop digging
and report the discovery, the context
of the hoard has been preserved.

BELOW Fieldwalkers in Lanarth,
Cornwall, searching ploughed land
for artefacts.

sites at risk, and increases workload pressure
for the small number of archaeologists
recording these finds.

A similar, albeit smaller, group of public
finders are fieldwalkers, who walk through
farmland, particularly ploughed fields, searching
the ground by eye for worked flints and pottery
or any other signs of human occupation. Some
of these fieldwalkers might be attached to local
archaeology and history societies, but many
work alone. Like metal detecting, fieldwalking
can be used in professional archaeology.
Spotting whether or not a flint has been
worked by human hands is a skill, since many
naturally broken or plough-damaged stones
can superficially look like tools. Identifying
pottery is also a sought-after talent since there
is an abundance of regional and local fabric
types. The knack of the fieldwalker is not only
spotting flint and pottery, but also being able
to identify items of archaeological interest.

Finally, some finds are made completely
by chance, by people out walking or digging
in their gardens. A few of these finds have
turned out to be quite spectacular – such as
the Hackney Hoard (pp. 246–51). Although
chance finds are just as likely to be common or
modern objects, the moment of discovery is no
less of a thrill, and learning about the object
can be a rewarding experience, taking the
finder on their own historical journey.

PUBLIC FINDERS AND PROFESSIONAL ARCHAEOLOGY

People can learn a lot about their finds
through books, the internet and social media,
but ultimately – especially if they find
something unusual, interesting or important –
they will want to connect with a professional
archaeologist based in a museum, university
or working for the Portable Antiquities
Scheme (PAS), which was established to record

archaeological finds made by the public in
England and Wales.

The relationship between archaeologists and
public finders, especially metal detectorists,
is complex. Many archaeologists were hostile
to metal detecting when it first became
popular in the 1970s and 1980s. Professional
archaeology had developed as a scientific
discipline during the late 19th and early 20th
centuries. Before then, particularly in the late
18th and 19th centuries, antiquarians had
investigated sites of archaeological potential
primarily looking for artefacts, as detectorists
and other public finders do today. Now we
see such finds as only part of the picture. For
modern-day archaeologists, context – the
relationship between the physical objects
and the location and arrangement in which
they were found – is even more important
than the finds themselves. Put simply, a single
jigsaw-puzzle piece might be interesting, even
aesthetically pleasing, but its value comes from
it being part of something bigger – the rest
of the jigsaw. Detectorists were once seen as

BELOW Spectacular gold and garnet pendant from a 7th-century Anglo-Saxon woman's grave, discovered by a detectorist in Winfarthing, Norfolk, NMS-E95041 (see pp. 146–49).

already been dislodged by agricultural activity and might otherwise be lost.

Similarly, in London, archaeologists were recognising the benefits of liaising with River Thames mudlarks, who had developed expert knowledge of where archaeological finds were concentrated and the layering of the foreshore deposits. As such, mudlarks (most then members of the Society of Thames Mudlarks) were brought into the archaeological fold to help excavate foreshore sites in London in the 1970s and 1980s, ensuring that more finds were recovered and that sites were better understood.

PUBLIC SEARCHING AND THE LAW

Inspired by these early collaborations, a founding principle of the PAS was that finders and archaeologists should work together. The Scheme came about following the introduction of the Treasure Act 1996, recognising that finds outside its scope still had archaeological value and should be recorded. In Scotland and Northern Ireland all public finds already had to be reported by law, but this was not the case in England and Wales. So the PAS provided a mechanism for recording these finds without the bureaucracy (and associated resources) that were necessary for the mandatory reporting of all archaeological (even ownerless) finds.

depriving archaeologists of pieces of the past by removing finds from their all-important contexts. Worse still, a small number of detectorists were (and still are) looting sites without the landowners' permission, for objects to steal and sell on, thus depriving us of knowledge about these places and, ultimately, limiting our understanding of British history.

Not all archaeologists in the 1970s and 1980s saw metal detecting as entirely bad. The detecting community then, as now, represented a broad spectrum, with a money-motivated 'treasure-hunting' minority at one extreme and, at the other, a small archaeologically aware group who might be regarded as citizen scientists. In some extensively cultivated areas of England, such as Norfolk and Lincolnshire, local archaeologists recognised that metal detecting had a role in locating new sites and understanding archaeological landscapes, so they sought to engage with detectorists, highlighting the importance of recording finds. Here, as in most places where detecting was common, finders were not searching known archaeological sites and removing finds from original contexts, but recovering items that had

Treasure is an intriguing and ancient legal concept. The law in England (and Wales) dates back to at least the 13th century. The Crown (through its agent, the coroner) claimed any precious metal (gold and silver) that was deliberately hidden and its owner unknown. The primary purpose was to claim bullion for the royal coffers, but over time, the archaeological value of finds under what was then known as Common Law of Treasure Trove (a name still used in Scotland) came to be realised, so the law was adapted to enable finds to enter museum collections. But not all

BELOW Archaeologists and metal detectorists working together to excavate the Bronze Age Near Lewes Hoard in Sussex (see pp. 52–55).

finds were protected – and one of the greatest discoveries of 20th-century British archaeology would soon be under threat.

In 1939, archaeologist Basil Brown, under the instruction of landowner Edith Pretty, found the Sutton Hoo treasure – the ship burial and grave goods of a member of the Anglo-Saxon ruling elite of East Anglia, perhaps no less than King Rædwald. The spectacular finds included a cache of gold and garnet objects, and many more made of silver, bronze and other metals, appropriate to accompany a king in the afterlife. Treasure, in every definition of the word – or so one would think! Astonishingly for us today, at a coroner's inquest, the Sutton Hoo finds were deemed not to be 'Treasure' under Common Law of Treasure Trove, since it was not believed that the find had been buried with the intention of recovery. A logical verdict perhaps – since the people who buried these items in a grave clearly intended for them to stay in the ground – but not without consequences. The Crown relinquished all rights to the 'non-Treasure' and Mrs Pretty could then legally do with it what she liked – sell it off, even melt it down. Thankfully she donated the entire assemblage to the British Museum, but had she not, it could have been a travesty for archaeology.

The Treasure Act 1996 (see pp. 253–54) attempted to ensure that a find as important as the Sutton Hoo treasure would automatically end up in a museum. It introduced a more expansive legal definition that did not require the objects to have been hidden with the intention of recovery. The new Act also provided for landowners, giving them rights to claim a reward, normally divided 50/50 with the finder(s). Under the new Act, a find such as Sutton Hoo would be protected, because it contained objects made of precious metal, but it was not until July 2023 that a new 'significance-

BELOW Roman copper-alloy
pennanular brooch from
Denbighshire, LVPL-F9C5E8,
one of the almost half a million
Roman public finds that have been
recorded on the PAS database.

based' definition of Treasure protected
important base-metal finds like the Crosby
Garrett Helmet (pp. 104–09) and the Ryedale
Hoard (pp. 92–97). Even now, archaeologically
important items made from other materials
such as stone, leather and wood are not
protected. As such, the law in England and
Wales, compared to other countries in Europe
(including Scotland), is notably limited in scope.

The approach in England and Wales towards
'portable antiquities' (that is, all archaeological
finds that can be easily transported) is to ensure
that museums can acquire the most important
finds, and that the rest are recorded voluntarily.
This is different from what happens to finds
from archaeological excavations, which are
invariably deposited with museums and other
institutions for storage and possible display,
although the storage and conservation needs
of these 'archaeological archives' are growing

beyond what most museums can cope with.
It can still be challenging for museums to raise
the necessary funds to acquire and conserve
important portable antiquities found by the
public, even those classed legally as Treasure.

THE ROLE OF THE PAS

Public finds in England and Wales are recorded
with the PAS so they can be used to advance
knowledge. This information is published
on the PAS database (www.finds.org.uk) for
anyone to view and learn about the objects.
Each record includes images, a description,
measurements and weight, and the all-
important findspot. Indeed, without a findspot,
items will not be recorded.

A find without a findspot is like a car
without an engine – it might look nice, but it
won't get you very far. It is the findspot that
gives the item its archaeological value, helping

BELOW Self-recorder Tom
Redmayne adding new finds to the
PAS database. The PAS supports
detectorists and other searchers
in recording their own finds.

archaeologists to understand the relationship
between one find and another, and to the wider
landscape. An issue with findspots, however,
is that they are sensitive information – in the
wrong hands they can be used to loot sites.
Metal detectorists, in particular, are keen
that other detectorists do not know where
they search: they may want to search a good
'permission' alone, or only with people they
trust, and they might lose that permission if the
landowner is bothered by lots of prospective
searchers. The PAS therefore only makes
full findspot information available to bona
fide researchers, who have to provide details
of their research, academic references, and
explain why they need full PAS data. Online
the data is made available to no more than a
four-figure National Grid Reference (so within
1 km), and for particularly sensitive finds or
sites this information might be even less precise.
This is enough for most general usage, such as
finding out what has been found locally.

The finds recorded on the PAS database
form a valuable academic resource. This
information is used by archaeologists to help
plan or understand their excavations, and
to identify possible archaeologically sensitive
areas for local government planners in advance
of the building of a new road or housing
estate. PAS data is also used by academics
to understand finds types, relationships and
distribution across larger regions or the whole
of England and Wales, as in the case studies
of miniature weapons (pp. 84–89), vervels
(pp. 218–23) and cloth seals (pp. 240–45).
Importantly, given that many archaeological
excavations these days are in response to urban
development, the PAS database provides a
complementary, mostly rural dataset. It is
probably fair to say that PAS data is essential
for all archaeologists undertaking serious
academic study of finds in a landscape context.

Public searching adds the most value to
archaeology when finders are personally

BELOW Authors Michael Lewis (left), Head of the Portable Antiquities Scheme, and Ian Richardson (right), Senior Treasure Registrar, examining a Bronze Age hoard at the British Museum.

OPPOSITE Roman sceptre-bust from the Ryedale Hoard (see pp. 92–97) on display in the Yorkshire Museum.

invested in the sites they search. If finders have a relationship with the landscape and the communities within it, they are more likely to follow best practice (as outlined in the *Code of Practice for Responsible Metal Detecting in England and Wales*, see p. 256). This does not mean that finders who travel far and wide are inherently irresponsible, but they then need to take extra steps to ensure that finds are recorded. When it is someone else's local history you are uncovering (and also the nation's), there is an ethical responsibility to share this information so it can be appreciated by community residents, archaeologists and planners.

Archaeology is not driven by the goal of finding things, but of answering questions about history and understanding the story of a site. It can be reactive – monitoring, surveying or excavating sites at risk – or carefully planned to explore specific aspects of sites that are already known about. In contrast, metal detectorists (and most other public searchers) are on a quest to find archaeological objects, and their activities are mostly prospective and often random. These differences mean that archaeology and metal detecting complement each other. Detecting and other public searching can identify sites that archaeologists did not previously know about, and archaeology can then provide further information about a findspot, as with the Chiseldon Cauldrons (pp. 78–83), the Frome Hoard (pp. 98–103) and the Vale of York Hoard (pp. 164–71).

When public finders and archaeologists work together, we can learn more about the past. Reporting finds to the PAS ensures that the most important objects end up in museums for everyone to see, and that others are recorded so they can help all of us to understand the archaeology and history of Britain. Beneath our feet, truly, is a world to experience, to get excited about, to learn from and enjoy!

Stone Age

TOTAL FINDS RECORDED ON PAS DATABASE

Palaeolithic: 10,820

Mesolithic: 36,625

Neolithic: 47,552

Early Bronze Age: 3,124

MOST COMMON ARTEFACT TYPES ON DATABASE

Palaeolithic: handaxe, lithic implement, flake, blade, debitage

Mesolithic: lithic implement, debitage, core, blade, flake

Neolithic: scraper, lithic implement, flake, debitage, arrowhead

Early Bronze Age: scraper, flat axehead, arrowhead, lithic implement

TOP 5 COUNTIES ON DATABASE

Palaeolithic: Norfolk, Leicestershire, Hampshire, Suffolk, Buckinghamshire

Mesolithic: Leicestershire, Cornwall, Swansea, Kent, Lincolnshire

Neolithic: Cornwall, Lincolnshire, Norfolk, Leicestershire, Suffolk

Early Bronze Age: Lincolnshire, Norfolk, Cornwall, North Lincolnshire, North Yorkshire

PAS data as of October 2024

1 **Happisburgh Handaxe**
Norfolk

2 **Greenwich Antler Pick**
London

3 **Handbridge Axehead**
Cheshire

4 **Flint Arrowheads**
West Yorkshire; Somerset; Cheshire;
Lincolnshire; Shropshire; Rutland;
Wiltshire; Surrey; Hampshire;
Isle of Wight

FINDS DENSITY

Moderate   High

HAPPISBURGH HANDAXE

'The find led to a decade of fieldwork with remarkable results…[that] pushed back the known occupation of northern Europe from 500,000 to over 850,000 years ago.'
NICK ASHTON, BRITISH MUSEUM

NMS-ECAA52	
OBJECT TYPE Handaxe	
MATERIALS Flint	
DATE Lower Palaeolithic, c. 500,000 BCE	
LOCATION Happisburgh, Norfolk	
DISCOVERY METHOD Chance find while walking on the beach	
COLLECTION Norwich Castle Museum and Art Gallery	
LENGTH 128 mm	
WIDTH 79 mm	
THICKNESS 37 mm	

OPPOSITE The Happisburgh Handaxe, with V-shaped frost fracture visible at the lower edge.

BELOW Opposite side of the handaxe.

HAPPISBURGH

Happisburgh (pronounced Haze-bruh) in Norfolk is a place on the edge. This is as true nowadays as it was in the deep past. Excavations have revealed its windswept sandy beaches to be of great archaeological interest, providing the earliest evidence of human occupation anywhere in Britain. At Happisburgh the oldest human footprints known outside Africa were found, dating to over 850,000 years ago, from a period known as the Lower Palaeolithic. The people who made them were not *Homo sapiens* like us, but *Homo antecessor*, a species that preceded Neanderthals in Europe. They walked upright and were of similar height to modern humans, with a slightly different facial appearance and smaller brains. These people lived in Happisburgh before the English Channel had formed for the first time (*c.* 450,000 years ago), when Britain was physically joined to what would become modern-day France, Belgium and the Netherlands. The footprints were preserved in estuary mud of the River Thames, which flowed much further north than its present course. Archaeologists have even suggested that the 'family' represented by these footprints could have been searching for seafood in the mudflats along the river edge. These people were using flint tools, but, so far as we know, not fire. This in itself is remarkable, since the climate of eastern England at that time was like that of southern Scandinavia today, with long, cold winters. The estuary was dominated by open grassland with pine forest on the hills beyond, and inhabited by mammoths, bison and sabre-toothed cats.

THE HANDAXE

Nearby, on a later site dating to 500,000 years ago, a carefully crafted flint tool known as the Happisburgh Handaxe was found by chance in 2000, by local resident Mike Chambers while he was walking on the beach. The ovate handaxe is made of glossy black flint, which would have been a valued commodity, and is in incredibly good condition for its age. It would have been used unhafted, held in the hand, and had sharp edges that were ideal for cutting meat or even harder

BELOW Artist's reconstruction by John Sibbick of a *Homo antecessor* family using handaxes to butcher carcasses on the beach at Happisburgh.

materials such as wood. It has a likely thermal (frost) fracture at one end.

Palaeolithic objects are not uncommon finds in Britain. At the time of writing, 10,820 Palaeolithic items have been recorded with the Portable Antiquities Scheme. Most are flint or other stone objects, but some fossilised animal bones also have been found and recorded. Norfolk tops the list, with finds described as scrapers, flakes and blades, as well as 213 other handaxes, but the Happisburgh Handaxe, dating to 500,000 BCE, is among the oldest.

Although other flint tools had washed up previously in this area, the handaxe was found in situ, embedded within ancient sediments that had been exposed by the low tide. Thankfully Mike realised that the object was a significant find and reported it to Norwich Castle Museum, which arranged for archaeologists Nigel Larkin and Peter Robins to visit the site and record important information about the context.

IMPORTANCE

Four years after Mike's discovery of the handaxe, the site was investigated by the Ancient Human Occupation of Britain project, which was funded by the Leverhulme Trust and involved archaeologists and other scientists from the British Museum, the Natural History Museum and British universities. It looked at when people had arrived in Britain and what factors had led to their survival or local extinction. Happisburgh was important to that story. Nick Ashton of the British Museum, one of the project leaders, credits Mike's discovery of the handaxe for bringing the area to the attention of archaeologists. 'The find led to a decade of fieldwork with remarkable results. The project not only discovered the human footprints, but also pushed back the known occupation of northern Europe from 500,000 to over 850,000 years ago. It has forced us to reconsider how humans coped with long, cold winters without the use of fire and prompts questions about their abilities to make clothes and build shelters'. For Nick, the Happisburgh Handaxe is a symbol of this globally important research into early human development and evolution.

Mike generously donated his find to Norwich Castle Museum where it takes pride of place in the Natural History gallery and can be enjoyed by all.

BELOW The beach at Happisburgh, with *Homo antecessor* footprints visible on the stone terraces.

BOTTOM Archaeologist Richard Bates examining the footprints near the handaxe findspot.

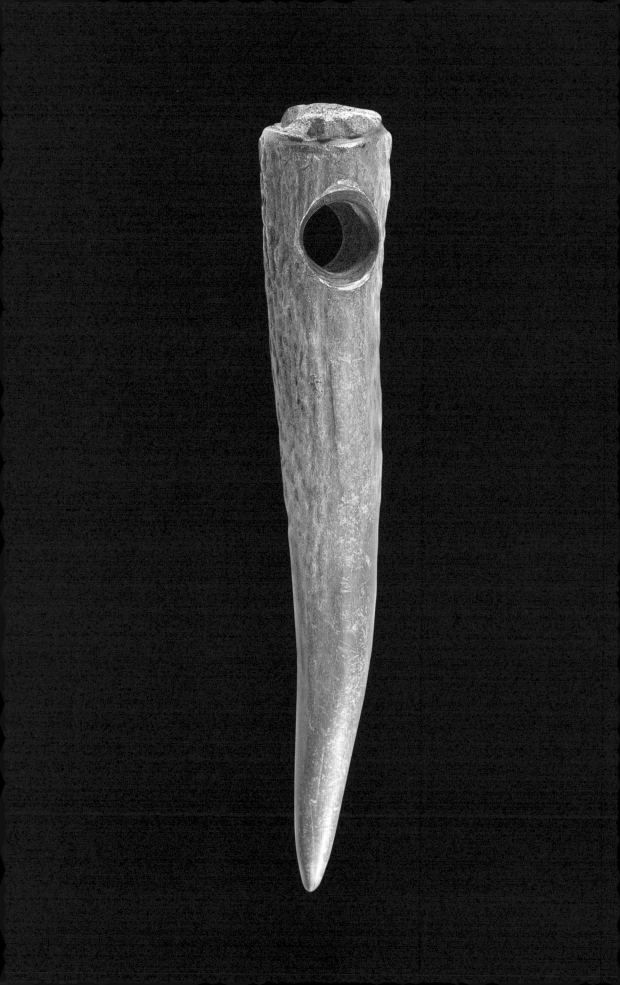

GREENWICH ANTLER PICK

'Picks like this one were used in the construction of structures such as barrows for the dead, in digging ditches and also in mines.'

KATE SUMNALL, LONDON MUSEUM

LON-CC46C2	
OBJECT TYPE	Digging tool
MATERIALS	Antler
DATE	Late Neolithic to Bronze Age, c. 4000–1200 BCE
LOCATION	Greenwich, south-east London
DISCOVERY METHOD	Mudlarking
COLLECTION	London Museum

LENGTH	199 mm
WIDTH	39 mm
THICKNESS	30 mm
DIAMETER	17 mm

OPPOSITE AND BELOW The hole of the antler pick contained the decayed remains of a wooden component.

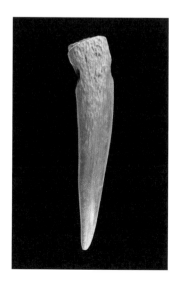

A UNIQUE ARCHAEOLOGICAL RESOURCE

Twice a day the changing tide of the River Thames reveals the foreshore in London, presenting a fresh surface for 'mudlarks' – hobbyists who search the river for archaeological finds – to scrutinise. Low tide uncovers an array of human-made structures of wood, metal and concrete, and artefacts of all materials, spanning thousands of years of use. One thing that mudlarks are certain to encounter is animal bones. Some are from wild or feral animals living in the London area, but most are from domestic animals that have been slaughtered and butchered to feed the city throughout its history. Animal bones, horn and antler were a valuable raw material that could be worked to make many different objects. Antler does not always survive well on land but the anaerobic (oxygen-free) conditions of the Thames mud preserve ancient objects. This was the case with Pete Wakeman's discovery in February 2010 in Greenwich, east London, of a rare pick made from red deer antler.

Pete, who had been a mudlark for a few years by this point, says that on the day he made the discovery the tide was so low that it was 'like someone had pulled the plug on the Thames', exposing the remains of waterlogged ancient tree-branches, roots and twigs – the only time he had ever seen them in the area. Among them, poking up vertically from the thick mud, was the sharp end of the antler pick, already drying in the sun. Pete pulled it upwards, revealing the whole artefact. Although he didn't know exactly what it was, he could tell that it was worked and that it was an interesting piece, so he was excited to show it to Kate Sumnall, Finds Liaison Officer (FLO) for London at the time. One of the conditions of being granted permission to search and pick up objects on the Thames foreshore, via a licence issued by the Port of London Authority as landowner, is that finders have to report all items of archaeological interest for recording to the Portable Antiquities Scheme (PAS) via a FLO, usually at the London Museum. Pete's reporting of this artefact to Kate allowed its significance to be fully realised, and he donated it to the museum.

BELOW The Thames foreshore at Greenwich where Pete Wakeman found the antler pick.

BELOW Neolithic antler digging picks from Grimes Graves, Norfolk.

MANUFACTURE AND DATING

The pick is constructed from a tine (point) cut from the antler of a red deer. It tapers down to a blunt point over its almost 20 cm length. At the thicker base of the pick, drilled through both sides, is a circular hole. When Pete found the pick in the mud, this hole contained a fibrous plug, possibly the remains of the handle, which later analysis showed to have been made of wood. It would have enabled the pick to be used in a chopping or prying motion, akin to a pickaxe. The surface of the antler displays cut marks, evidence of its manufacture with flint tools.

Originally thought to date from the Mesolithic period (*c.* 10,000–4000 BCE), the pick was re-examined by PhD researcher Ben Elliot who suggested that it actually had been made more recently, and that both the form and toolmarks point to a late Neolithic to Bronze Age date (*c.* 4000–1200 BCE).

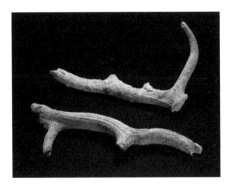

ANTLER TOOLS

Red deer are the largest living mammals in Britain and one of only two deer species native to this island (the other is roe deer). Their antlers were shaped into artefacts from the Mesolithic (for example, the red-deer headdresses found at Star Carr, North Yorkshire, one of which is in the British Museum) through to the Iron Age (a comb-beater found in Danebury, Hampshire, also in the British Museum). The unique properties of antlers – their wide availability, and their hardness combined with the ability to be shaped – made them valuable materials for tools.

Red deer cast (shed) their antlers every year in late winter or early spring. The seasonal appearance and gathering of this resource was part of the natural rhythm of the year and ancient communities knew when and where to find the shed antlers. To prepare the antler and shape it into a practical tool involved many specialist processes, including using a bow drill to make the perforation for the handle. It was time-consuming and required a high degree of skill, but such items – lighter than the stone axes that were employed at the same time (see the Handbridge Axehead, pp. 28–31) and different in shape – came to form a vital part of the prehistoric toolkit.

IMPORTANCE

As Kate (now Curator of Archaeology at the London Museum) explains, 'Picks like this one were used in the construction of structures such as barrows for the dead, in digging ditches and also in mines.' Several antler picks have been found preserved in the flint mines at Grimes Graves, Norfolk. Barrows in Greenwich Park that could possibly be of Bronze Age origin are not far from where this pick was found on the Thames foreshore; it could conceivably have been a tool for constructing them. The pick might have been lost while being used at the water's edge: this area beside the Thames was an important landscape in the Neolithic and Bronze Age, providing access to valuable resources.

Another explanation, suggests Kate, is that the pick 'could have been deliberately placed into the river, perhaps as an offering or to give thanks. Rivers, springs and other watery places have long held great significance to communities and are at the centre of many different beliefs.'

The Greenwich Antler Pick stands out because of the serendipity of its discovery and its remarkable condition. Pete understands that museums are unable to take everything that is offered to them, so he gets a real buzz knowing that his pick (along with a Neolithic axehead he found at Rotherhithe the following year) passed the test and was accepted by the London Museum as a donation; it is now available for others to study and enjoy.

HANDBRIDGE AXEHEAD

'They were clearly very important to the people who owned them. Ground and polished stone axes held a special place in northern European society.'

JAMES DILLEY, PREHISTORIC TOOLS EXPERT

LVPL-2C1556

OBJECT TYPE	Axehead
MATERIALS	Stone
DATE	Neolithic, 4000–2400 BCE
LOCATION	Handbridge, Cheshire
DISCOVERY METHOD	Gardening

LENGTH	170 mm
WIDTH	69 mm
THICKNESS	37 mm

OPPOSITE The axehead is made of polished Cornish greenstone; it would have been fixed to a wooden handle.

BELOW Opposite face of the axehead, and views of one side and both ends.

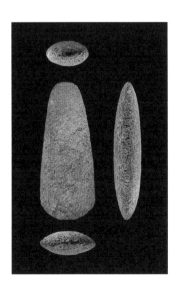

AN UNUSUAL DISCOVERY

Iwan Jones was gardening at home in Handbridge, Cheshire, when he came across an intriguing stone object. It was pointed oval in shape, apparently smoothed down but still slightly rough to hold, and dark green in colour. He showed it to archaeologists who were investigating a local site; they suggested that it might be an axehead made of Cornish greenstone and should be recorded with the PAS.

Iwan subsequently took the object to his local FLO, Heather Beeton at Grosvenor Museum in Chester, for recording. The axehead was complete, made of ground and polished stone, and it dated – incredibly! – to the Neolithic period (4000–2400 BCE). Unfortunately it had suffered some damage, and its original polished surface had largely eroded, leaving behind a roughened surface with multiple areas of additional damage.

The axehead's beautiful form disguises the fact it was seemingly produced as a functional tool. As the term 'axehead' suggests, the Handbridge Axehead would have been mounted on a wooden haft – unlike the Happisburgh Handaxe (see pp. 20–23), which was used alone in the hand. In the Neolithic, these axes would have been utilised for cutting tasks, such as felling trees or shaping wood. Interestingly, there is no evidence that axeheads would have been glued or bound to their handles. It seems that a well-fitting hole in the wooden haft was enough on its own to hold the axehead in place.

THE NEOLITHIC AXEHEAD INDUSTRY

Greenstone is an igneous rock (formed from lava or magma) characterised by its dark green colour, coarse-grained texture and mottled appearance. It was a popular material for axeheads in the Neolithic; almost 100 greenstone examples have been recorded with the PAS. Some have been found as far north as Cumbria and as east as Suffolk, with notable clusters in Lincolnshire and in the south-west. Others have been found even further north, in Scotland, where they are recorded through the Scottish Treasure Trove system.

BELOW Modern reconstruction by James Dilley of a greenstone axe mounted on a wooden handle.

OPPOSITE Cornish greenstone axe factory site in the Polstrong Valley, Camborne.

The main sources of British greenstone are in Cornwall, the Lake District, North Wales and Northern Ireland. Although the Handbridge Axehead has not been petrologically tested (which involves drilling and taking a sample), it is thought that it is from the Cornish 'mines' (so-called Group 1), possibly from the Lizard peninsula. If this is true, the axehead has travelled the whole breadth of England, possibly via Wales. This is incredible, given that Neolithic people would have travelled via trackways on foot, without vehicles or paved roads.

Greenstone mines were not mines as we imagine them today, but rock outcrops that can still be observed in the landscape. Neolithic people would have mined them with hand tools similar to the Handbridge Axehead itself, a process that would have taken considerable time. The silica crystalline structure of greenstone is too coarse to be knapped in the same way as flint, so it was instead 'pecked', which involves bashing the axehead blank with a hard pebble to crush the outer surface. Hundreds or even thousands of strikes were required to peck a blank into the roughout shape before it was polished smooth, which would have taken hundreds of additional hours.

FLINT TO STONE

Since it was easier and quicker to make axes from flint, why bother making them from greenstone? James Dilley (from the company AncientCraft), an expert in re-creating prehistoric tools, explains that ground stone axes made from exotic materials were almost certainly prized over local flint ones, both aesthetically and for their superior performance and durability. 'Unlike the earlier Mesolithic flaked axes', explains James, 'ground stone axes cut into wood more consistently and lasted far longer due to their smooth surfaces and symmetrical profile that distributed shock better.' Because greenstone axes were resource-intensive to produce and were traded long distances, James observes that 'ground and polished stone axes held a special place in northern European society'.

When the first Neolithic people came to Britain they used ground stone axes to fell trees, creating open ground for farming and settlements. As the forests disappeared under the blades of many stone axes, so did the Mesolithic hunter-gatherers who lived within them. All that now remains of this great industry are the axeheads themselves, to be spotted by modern finders with keen eyes.

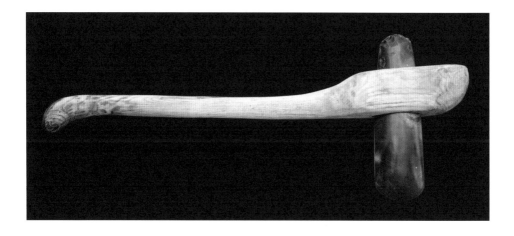

FLINT ARROWHEADS

'There is a lot of flint to be found and it's surprisingly common; just keep your eyes open.'

KEVIN LEAHY, PAS LITHICS FINDS ADVISER

SWYOR-C62A97, SOM-770383,
DENO-8C977B, SWYOR-D25288,
SWYOR-B94A35, LVPL-7D541C,
HESH-3350F2, LEIC-B31DBC,
SOM-853E56, DOR-9DB8FD,
SUR-5F21DB, IOW-FB307D

OBJECT TYPE Arrowhead

MATERIALS Flint and chert

DATE Late Palaeolithic, Mesolithic,
Neolithic and Early Bronze Age

LOCATION Tetford, Lincolnshire;
Whitehill, Hampshire; Heptonstall,
West Yorkshire; Bishops Lydeard,
Somerset; Helsby, Cheshire; Oswestry,
Shropshire; Donhead St Mary, Wiltshire;
Lyddington, Rutland; Corsham,
Wiltshire; Colne Valley, West Yorkshire;
Shere, Surrey; Cowes, Isle of Wight

DISCOVERY METHOD Various

OPPOSITE Barbed-and-tanged Early
Bronze Age arrowhead found on the
Isle of Wight, IOW-FB307D.

BELOW Late Palaeolithic shouldered
point found in Tetford, Lincolnshire,
DENO-8C977B.

FLINT SPOTTING

Arrowheads are among the most immediately recognisable prehistoric flint tools found by the public. For the non-expert, other 'flints' can be hard to identify, especially in knowing their function, or even deciding if they are worked by human hands or not. The FLOs working for the PAS are often shown pieces of flint and stone that their finders believe are ancient tools because they 'feel right in the hand', but have no obvious signs of being worked!

More than a thousand barbed-and-tanged arrowheads have been recorded with the PAS to date. Of these, nearly 400 are late Neolithic and more than 1,000 are Early Bronze Age, most dating somewhere between 2500 and 1500 BCE. As their name suggests, barbed-and-tanged arrowheads have two barbs, which help the arrow stay put when it pierces flesh, therefore making it harder for the victim (human or animal) to remove, and easier for the hunter to retrieve arrows following a kill. The tang enables the arrow to be joined to a wooden shaft. In most instances, the tang would have been inserted into a cut at the end of the arrow shaft and then fixed in place with a binding of sinew and tar. Barbed-and-tanged arrowheads are remarkable feats of engineering, representing a technological evolution of the prehistoric arrowhead.

The earliest arrowheads found in Britain date back as far as the Late Palaeolithic and are extremely rare. One intriguing Late Palaeolithic arrowhead found in Tetford, Lincolnshire (DENO-8C977B), is a shouldered point from around the end of the last Ice Age, *c.* 11,000–8300 BCE.

During the Mesolithic (10,000–4000 BCE), microliths such as those found in Whitehill, Hampshire (SWYOR-D25288), and Heptonstall, West Yorkshire (SWYOR-B94A35), predominate. These tiny flint points or segments snapped from larger blades were probably fitted into arrow shafts. We cannot be certain how all these microliths were used, however, since they may have had multiple purposes.

Most of the arrowheads recorded with the PAS date to the Neolithic (4000–2350 BCE). As with Mesolithic arrowheads,

SWYOR-B94A35

Mesolithic 'geometric' microlith
Heptonstall, West Yorkshire
Late Mesolithic
c. 6500–4000 BCE
Length: 23 mm
Width: 5 mm
Thickness: 2 mm

a. Small size
b. Geometric shape
c. Steep, blunting retouch

SWYOR-D25288

Mesolithic 'obliquely blunted'
arrowhead
Whitehill, Hampshire
Early Mesolithic
c. 9000–6500 BCE
Length: 43 mm
Width: 13 mm
Thickness: 5 mm

a. Steep retouch blunting edge to form
a point

DENO-8C977B

Shouldered point
Tetford, Lincolnshire
Late Palaeolithic
c. 11,000–8300 BCE
Length: 69 mm
Width: 15 mm
Thickness: 4 mm

a. Short, scaled semi-abrupt-low angle
retouch along one edge of tip
b. Additional retouch forming the
'shoulder'

SWYOR-3C3372

Leaf arrowhead
Kirklees, West Yorkshire
Early Neolithic
c. 4000–3000 BCE
Length: 36 mm
Width: 16 mm
Thickness: 3 mm

a. Scaled low-angle retouch on faces
b. Straight original base

LEIC-B31DBC

Neolithic leaf arrowhead
Lyddington, Rutland
Early Neolithic
c. 4000–3500 BCE
Length: 40 mm
Width: 19 mm
Thickness: 3 mm

a. Bifacially worked
b. Pointed base broken off

LVPL-7D541C

Neolithic leaf arrowhead
Helsby, Cheshire
Early to Middle Neolithic
c. 4000–2900 BCE
Length: 33 mm
Width: 21 mm
Thickness: 4 mm

a. Intact 'leaf' shape, with very thin,
transparent edges
b. Cutting edge
c. Pointed base

HESH-3350F2

Oblique arrowhead
Oswestry, Shropshire
Late Neolithic
c. 3000–2300 BCE
Length: 35 mm
Width: 22 mm

a. Two sharp cutting edges
b. Knapped using both direct
and indirect percussion
c. Base trimmed to form platform
d. 'Oblique' arrowhead: one edge
longer than the other

DOR-9DB8FD

Late Neolithic transverse arrowhead
Donhead St Mary, Wiltshire
Late Neolithic
c. 3300–2500 BCE
Length: 37 mm
Width: 36 mm
Thickness: 4 mm

a. No point, chisel-like edge
b. Other edge steeply blunted

SUR-5F21DB

Barbed-and-tanged arrowhead
Shere, Surrey
Early Bronze Age
c. 2500–1500 BCE
Length: 21 mm
Width: 20 mm
Thickness: 4 mm

a. Slightly curved barbs
b. Scaled low-angle retouch covering
both faces
c. Squared tang, slightly damaged

IOW-FB307D

Barbed-and-tanged arrowhead
Cowes, Isle of Wight
Early Bronze Age
c. 2500–1500 BCE
Length: 33 mm
Width: 25 mm
Thickness: 5 mm

a. Straight barbs
b. Invasive, sub-parallel and low angle
retouch
c. Extremely good condition, no
damage

SOM-8F3E56

Group of six incomplete barbed-and-
tanged arrowheads
Corsham, Wiltshire
Late Neolithic to Early Bronze Age
c. 2500–1500 BCE
Length: 33 mm
Width: 23 mm
Thickness: 5 mm

a. Shallow sub-parallel retouch
b. White patina on surface of darker
flint from weathering

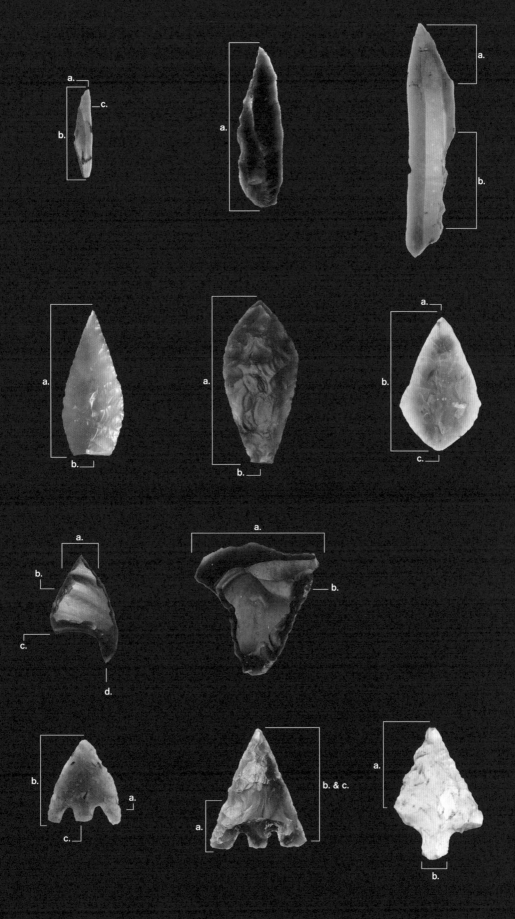

cm

BELOW The 'Amesbury Archer', an Early Bronze Age man buried c. 2470 BCE near Stonehenge in Wiltshire, was interred with eighteen barbed-and-tanged arrowheads and two stone bracers (armguards) to protect his wrist from the bowstring.

those of Neolithic date can come in various forms. Leaf-shaped arrowheads, as their name suggests, have a pointed oval shape. One from Helsby, Cheshire (LVPL-7D541C), is noted for its light brown flint which is increasingly transparent close to its edges, showing off the gentle flaking used to produce it. Oblique arrowheads, such as a dark brown flint 'British type' found at Oswestry, Shropshire (HESH-3350F2), typically have one edge longer than the other. Transverse (chisel-shaped) arrowheads, which have a wide cutting edge instead of a point, are another Late Neolithic form; for instance, one found in Donhead St Mary, Wiltshire (DOR-9DB8FD). Although all these types of arrowhead are also found in the Early Bronze Age (2350–1500 BCE), the barbed-and-tanged arrowhead is the form that is representative of Bronze Age flint work.

PUBLIC FINDS

Many of the prehistoric arrowheads recorded with the PAS have been found by people who have spotted them by chance in the ploughsoil while out metal detecting. This was the luck of Martyn Darricott who was searching arable land at Lyddington, Rutland, when he discovered an Early Neolithic leaf-shaped arrowhead (LEIC-B31DBC). It is finely made in a dark brown flint although part of its tang has unfortunately broken off. Other prehistoric flints are recovered through fieldwalking – that is, by avocational archaeologists who search ploughed fields by eye for pottery and flints. A keen fieldwalker, who regularly looks for archaeology close to where he lives, came across six barbed-and-tanged flint arrowheads in Corsham, Wiltshire

(SOM-8F3E56). Since it is unusual to find so many arrowheads from one place, the group of six has been recorded by the PAS as being of local importance. Another fieldwalker, Russell Irving, came across an impressively crafted leaf-shaped arrowhead of Neolithic date at Colne Valley, West Yorkshire (SWYOR-3C3372); in this case, a translucent light grey flint was chosen by its maker.

Some important arrowhead finds have been made by children, entirely by chance. Marcus Rutherford discovered a beautiful barbed-and-tanged arrowhead in the woods at Shere, Surrey, when he was a child (SUR-5F21DB). It is a lovely specimen, made from a pale grey to light brown flint, and complete, apart from a small break to the tang – although it is of a type technically sub-classed as 'non-fancy'! Another young person, Matthew Boulter, found a barbed-and-tanged arrowhead at school – it was actually discovered within the grounds of Lanesend Primary School, Cowes, Isle of Wight (IOW-FB307D), showing that even in built-up areas hidden history might be beneath your feet.

DISTRIBUTION

Many of the prehistoric arrowheads recorded on the PAS database are incomplete. Barbed-and-tanged arrowheads might be missing a barb or two, and leaf-shaped arrowheads might be missing points. But they all help to paint a picture of the past. The distribution of Neolithic arrowheads recorded with the PAS shows that they are found across the whole of England but are more numerous in the east and south than in the north.

More interesting, however, are the gaps on the map: for instance, a 'channel' running down from the Wash in north-west East Anglia through Cambridgeshire towards London, and another one running west from

London through Berkshire and Wiltshire. A similar picture is observed in mapping Bronze Age arrowheads recorded through the PAS. Kevin Leahy, who is the PAS National Finds Adviser responsible for lithics, thinks that 'our knowledge of arrowheads is strongly affected by where people were making flint tools, but also by where fieldwalkers have been searching. There is a lot of flint to be found and it's surprisingly common; just keep your eyes open when out in the field, and if you find something ensure that the findspot, the most important thing to note down, is marked for recording with the PAS.'

As shown by the collection of flint arrowheads from Corsham, Wiltshire, public flint finders are identifying sites of interest. Some of these sites are new, and others add to existing knowledge, but all are helping to transform our understanding of Britain's prehistoric past. Additionally, as with the flint arrowhead found by Marcus Rutherford in Surrey, finds discovered many years ago can still be recorded with the PAS. The key is whether the find location is remembered, since without a precise findspot these arrowheads have little or limited archaeological value. But when it is known where they were made or used, arrowheads provide a useful addition to the PAS dataset and can advance knowledge.

Bronze Age

TOTAL FINDS RECORDED ON PAS DATABASE

29,840

MOST COMMON ARTEFACT TYPES ON DATABASE

socketed axehead, scraper, spearhead, palstave, awl

TOP 5 COUNTIES ON DATABASE

Norfolk, Suffolk, Lincolnshire, Hampshire, Wiltshire

PAS data as of October 2024

5 Ringlemere Cup
Kent

6 Shropshire Sun Pendant
Shropshire

7 The Near Lewes Hoard
East Sussex

8 Bronze Age Gold Ornaments
Lancashire; Staffordshire; Cumbria

9 East Rudham Dirk
Norfolk

FINDS DENSITY

Moderate   High

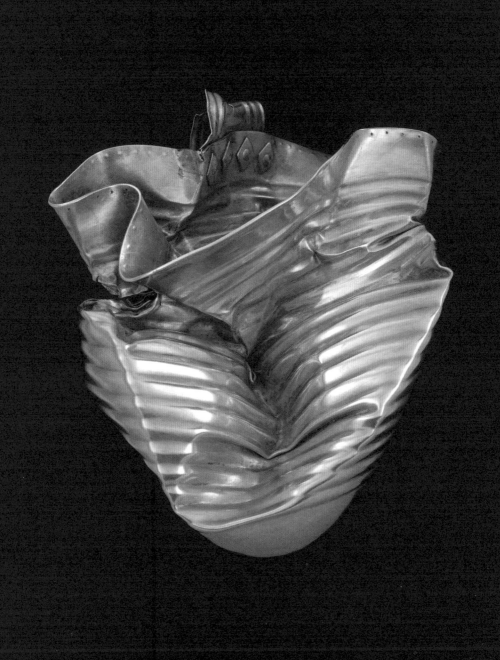

RINGLEMERE CUP

'Although the gold cup was a spectacular find in its own right, it also led to the identification of a previously unknown prehistoric ritual landscape, as well as an exceptionally early Anglo-Saxon cemetery.'

KEITH PARFITT, KENT ARCHAEOLOGIST

PAS-BE40C2	
OBJECT TYPE	Cup
MATERIALS	Gold
DATE	1950–1750 BCE
LOCATION	Woodnesborough, Kent
DISCOVERY METHOD	Metal detecting
COLLECTION	British Museum
LENGTH	112 mm
WIDTH	105 mm
THICKNESS	1 mm

OPPOSITE AND BELOW The Ringlemere Cup has been preserved in the crushed state in which it was found.

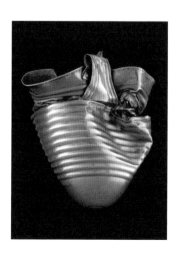

DISCOVERY

Retired electrician Cliff Bradshaw said that he was 'looking for Anglo-Saxons' when he instead discovered one of the most important Bronze Age treasures ever found in Britain. In November 2001 Cliff was metal detecting on a 'friend's permission' (a site obtained by a detecting partner) in potato fields at Ringlemere Farm in Woodnesborough, Kent, concentrating on an area of higher ground that he hoped might be the site of an Anglo-Saxon settlement – a reasonable shout, since he had found early medieval artefacts there on previous outings. He came across a strange metal object that he initially thought was a shiny brass Victorian light-fitting. The item was clearly damaged – it had taken an enormous whack, resulting in a large dent. He decided to take it home and check it out properly. Once the find had been cleaned, Cliff got out his history books and realised, to his astonishment, that it looked just like the Rillaton Cup, a gold vessel recovered in 1837 from a stone cist beneath a cairn on Bodmin Moor, Cornwall – and (so tradition says) later used by George V to store his collar studs at Buckingham Palace. Cliff immediately contacted various experts in Kent, including local archaeologist Keith Parfitt, and reported the cup as potential Treasure to his Finds Liaison Officer (FLO), Michael Lewis. Cliff showed Michael several other objects before he revealed the cup, which he had safely stored in an ice-cream container. Michael was bowled over by the precious metal vessel, especially the quality of its craftsmanship. The verdict was swift and unanimous: Cliff was right! He had found the Ringlemere Cup, a finely made gold Bronze Age vessel for which the only known English parallel is the Rillaton Cup itself.

A team led by Keith, with the landowners' permission, was then set up to explore the findspot. The archaeologists were excited because aerial photography had shown that the site was riddled with ancient features, some likely of prehistoric date. The team included archaeologists from the Canterbury Archaeological Trust and the Dover Archaeological Group, supported by the British Museum. Although their hopes were high that a context for the gold cup might be found, they had

BELOW The Fritzdorf Cup, a Continental gold 'precious cup' with a handle and rounded base, similar to the Ringlemere Cup. It was found near Bonn, Germany, in 1954 and is now in the Rheinisches Landesmuseum Bonn.

BELOW Digital reconstruction of the Ringlemere Cup, created by Stephen Crummy.

little idea how rich the landscape would prove to be. They were about to discover that Cliff had found not only an object of national and even international importance, but an entire site equally so.

GOLD CUPS

The Ringlemere Cup dates to 1950–1750 BCE, in the Early Bronze Age, so it is almost 4,000 years old. It has a flared rim and sub-conical body tapering to a rounded base, which means that the cup cannot stand alone without support, suggesting that it had a specific (perhaps ritual) purpose. The body of the cup has been created by carefully hammering a single piece of gold. It has distinctive corrugated sides with continuous horizontal ribs on the neck and upper body, accented by plain zones above and below and a single row of dots punched from the outer surface just below the rim. A handle, made from a single metal strip and embellished with ridges that match those on the vessel's sides, joins the rim to the main body. The rivets that join the handle to the cup have lozenge plates to make them more aesthetically pleasing. The cup has been crushed, most likely by a plough, particularly on one side. Indeed, Keith was

even able to identify the probably offending farm equipment, showing that if Cliff had not recovered the cup it could have been completely destroyed the following season.

A small number of similar so-called 'precious cups', with unstable bases and usually handles, are known from north-west Bronze Age Europe. There are examples made in silver, and some of similar form in amber and shale. Other gold cups have been found in France, Germany, Switzerland and northern Italy, but the only two from Britain are the Ringlemere and Rillaton examples. The thin gold conducts heat well, which might have made handling and drinking from the Ringlemere Cup an especially sensual experience, tying in with the hypothesis that it had a ritual function. Although it is unknown what type of liquid the cup held, it is possible to imagine that the vessel could have been passed around a gathering and drunk from by each person in turn, like a communion cup in Christian worship 2,000 years later.

Stuart Needham, then Curator of the European Bronze Age Collections at the British Museum, views it as part of a broader European tradition of similar cups. 'I was intrigued by the significance of these widely spread cups made of different precious

a. Handle made from single metal strip
   embellished with ridges
b. Rivets with decorative lozenge plates
c. Punched row of dots
d. Flared rim
e. Corrugated sides with horizontal ribs
f. Rounded base (cup is unable
   to stand upright without support)

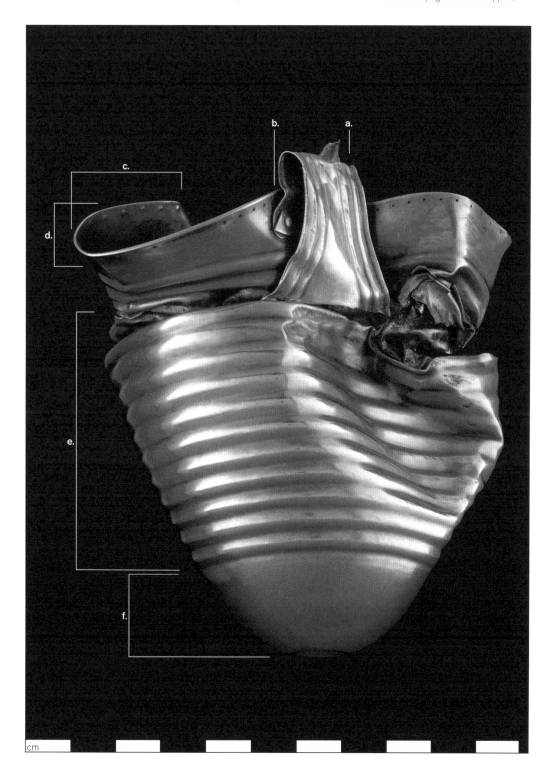

cm

BELOW Antiquarian watercolour by Charles Hamilton Smith of the Rillaton Cup, which was discovered beneath a cairn on Bodmin Moor, Cornwall, in 1837.

BELOW Aerial view of the excavation site at Ringlemere Farm.

materials. While they shared some features in common, all were very individual in their crafting and detailed design. They seemed to be linked by a shared concept rather than being produced by the same set of craft-workers.' For Stuart, the discovery of the Ringlemere Cup gives important hints about cultural and trade links between Britain and the areas of the Continent where other cups have been found. 'Their distribution around the north European seaways links them to burgeoning cross-sea exchange in the Early Bronze Age. The cups could have played an elite ritual role which acted as a bridge between the otherwise distinct cultural groups engaged in this growing network.'

IMPORTANCE

The Ringlemere Cup is now in the British Museum and is one of the prized items of its Bronze Age collection. When not being loaned, it is exhibited alongside its cousin cup from Rillaton (on loan from the Royal

Collection). However, as explained by Keith, who led the excavations at Ringlemere Farm, the Ringlemere Cup is not just a treasure of national importance, but a discovery that dramatically transformed archaeologists' understanding of the landscape around the findspot in Kent. 'Although the gold cup was a spectacular find in its own right, it also led to the identification of a previously unknown prehistoric ritual landscape, as well as an exceptionally early Anglo-Saxon cemetery, all of which combine to make this a crucial new site for the archaeology of Kent.' So Cliff had been right in looking for an Anglo-Saxon site at Ringlemere, but it was only one part of a complex and intriguing landscape that had been occupied for thousands of years.

The site was extensively excavated between 2002 and 2006. It revealed evidence of human occupation as far back as the Mesolithic, and extensive activity in the Late Neolithic when a ditched enclosure was constructed. Around 2000 BCE, a mound was raised within this enclosure, which could have been built as a platform for a timber structure, rather than a burial mound. It seems that the monument was in use for at least 500 years before the Ringlemere Cup was deposited, about 1.5 m south-west of its centre. Besides the main monument, the site has extensive evidence

BELOW Archaeologists uncovered an important prehistoric site at Ringlemere Farm, including this Late Neolithic ditched enclosure and Early Bronze Age mound (possibly supporting a timber structure) where the gold cup had been deposited.

of other prehistoric features, including ring ditches, some being the probable remains of round barrows. As Cliff had anticipated, the excavations also revealed an Anglo-Saxon presence, including a cemetery containing some 60 graves. This evidence shows that Ringlemere was a site of extraordinary significance for many generations of people over a long time.

The random nature of metal detecting is something to consider as a benefit to archaeology. Whatever brought Cliff into those potato fields in Kent – looking for Anglo-Saxons, or just hoping to find anything of some value or interest – without him, archaeologists would have had no reason to venture to Ringlemere Farm; neither the Ringlemere Cup nor the wider landscape context it was buried within would have been discovered; and the additional understanding of the Bronze Age that they have given us would remain unknown. The story of the Ringlemere Cup highlights the value of metal detecting, especially when it is used in conjunction with archaeology.

SHROPSHIRE SUN PENDANT

'This is the most important object from this period – the first age of metal – that has come up in about 100 years. It is internationally significant, reflecting the artistic brilliance of communities from the deep past.'

NEIL WILKIN, BRITISH MUSEUM

HESH-43148A

OBJECT TYPE	*Bulla*
MATERIALS	Gold
DATE	1000–750 BCE
LOCATION	Shropshire Marches
DISCOVERY METHOD	Metal detecting
COLLECTION	British Museum

HEIGHT	37 mm
WIDTH	47 mm
THICKNESS	13 mm (across base); 7 mm (across upper edge)

FIND OF A LIFETIME

In the Shropshire Marches, on the frontier between England and Wales, local metal detectorist Bob Greenaway had long suspected that the area of his searches held special significance for ancient peoples. Over many years he had recovered an assortment of artefacts, dating from the Bronze Age through to the Iron Age, whose presence suggested an ancient spiritual regard for the landscape. Individual items as well as groups of seemingly deliberately buried tools and weaponry pointed to ritual activities in the area.

In late spring 2018, Bob found the most spectacular and rare artefact from the Shropshire Marches to date, when he uncovered the Bronze Age gold 'Sun Pendant' in one of his fields. As he turned back the turf to expose the soil below, the gold caught the sun and sparkled, appearing bright and fresh as on the day it was made. Bob immediately understood that this was an item of immense archaeological significance, despite the sunburst design on one side giving it an 'Art Deco' feel, and took it to his local FLO, Peter Reavill.

Peter recognised that the pendant was from a group of objects called *bullae*, known mostly from Bronze Age Ireland, though rare finds even there. Unlike the Shropshire *bulla*, they are usually heart-shaped. Bob's discovery also revived interest in the only other example known to have been found in Britain, unearthed during the widening of the Mersey and Irwell navigation canal in the 1780s and housed in the personal museum of Sir Ashton Lever, at his home at Alkrington Hall, near Rochdale. Upon Lever's insolvency, his collection (the Leverian Collection) was broken up and sold. The Manchester *bulla* was never seen again!

For Bob, the discovery of the Shropshire Sun Pendant, and shortly thereafter a lead parcel enclosing two Bronze Age gold lock rings (HESH-9EC8BE), was confirmation that the people inhabiting this landscape in prehistoric times regarded it with reverence. Normally a reserved man, Bob has since found himself travelling across the country to speak to period experts and attend publicity events about the pendant and other finds from the landscape. He continues to search for more.

OPPOSITE AND BELOW The two sides of the pendant have different geometric decorations in engraved lines. One side (opposite) bears a stylised sunburst.

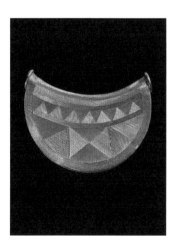

BELOW Bob Greenaway, the metal
detectorist who discovered the
Shropshire Sun Pendant.

BELOW The pendant on display,
in the orientation it would have
appeared when held upwards
towards the wearer's face.

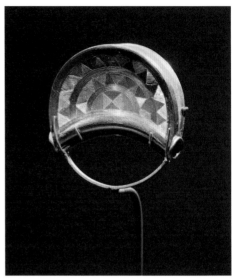

DISPLAY AND NATIONAL TOUR

The Shropshire Sun Pendant forms a shallow
crescent in a rough D-shape, with two flat,
decorated sides on the front and back. Each
displays finely engraved geometric decoration,
with one side representing a stylised sunburst.
At the top is a tube-like form with a gold
collar surrounding the hole at each end
for suspending the pendant from a cord or
necklace; although it resembles a separately
attached tube, this component is just the top
of the pendant, which is hollow throughout.
When on display – first at the Shrewsbury
Museum, then in the British Museum's 'The
World of Stonehenge' exhibition, as well as
the 'Gathering Light' touring exhibition in
Truro, Lincoln, Sunderland and Stornoway –
the pendant has been supported on a mount
with the tube facing down, to better display
the sunburst pattern on one side. But this is
also how it would have appeared to the person
wearing the pendant. The two sides expand
towards the bottom of the object and display
a continuous pattern of thin engraved lines.

The pendant was thoroughly analysed by
scientist Laura Perucchetti and colleagues at
the British Museum who found the metallic
composition to be similar to other known
gold objects from the later Bronze Age.
Their analysis also highlighted the precision
of its finely engraved decoration, which is
remarkable even to modern eyes. Indeed,
the manner in which it was constructed was
tricky to replicate for the modern craftsperson
who made a copy for Shropshire Museums.

WATERY LANDSCAPES

The remarkable condition of the Sun Pendant
allows us to appreciate how it would have been
experienced by the people who made and
used it. We can speculate that the object would
have made an impression on those observing
its wearer, undoubtedly marking them out
as a person of importance, and that it also
would have possessed special significance
for the wearer themselves. The precise details
of the design and its manufacture testify to
the advanced skills of the craftsperson who

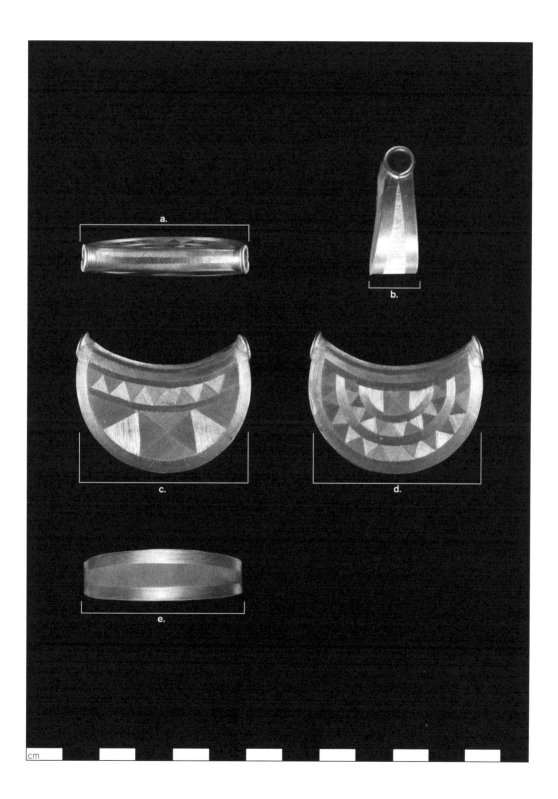

a. Top view: tube-like form with suspension holes at either end
b. Edge view: suspension holes surrounded by rolled collars; the pendant is hollow inside, with invisible seams probably soldered with gold
c. Geometric decoration with central saltire; either side could be visible when worn, possibly at different times of the year
d. Stylised sunburst motif
e. Bottom: decoration of three parallel bands of lines

BELOW An aerial view of the
landscape searched by Bob
Greenaway in the Shrophire
Marches.

OPPOSITE The pendant on display
at the Sunderland Museum and
Winter Gardens.

produced the pendant, and that their society had the capacity to develop and support such craftwork in the first place. Neil Wilkin, Curator of European Bronze Age collections at the British Museum, speaks of the 'humbling' effect of objects like the Sun Pendant, reminding us that 'there are remarkable things that people from deep history could achieve without the aid of modern technology and scientific insight'.

Although easily the most stunning artefact from the Shropshire Marches, the pendant is only one of many objects from the Late Bronze Age and Early Iron Age to be found in this landscape. Others include the aforementioned gold lock rings (with lead wrapping) that seem to have been deliberately deposited by their owners, hoards of axes and spearheads (e.g., HESH-EF00D8) and Iron Age chariot fittings (e.g., HESH-1188AD). In prehistoric times the land was marshy and these waterlogged landscapes may have held special significance for local people. The discovery of the pendant was a catalyst for further professional investigation of the area, and for Shropshire Museums to acquire other artefacts found there, piecing together the story of this special landscape. Bob had found not only one of the most remarkable objects of Bronze Age art in Britain, but also clues about an ancient area whose secrets are only beginning to be revealed.

THE NEAR LEWES HOARD

'One of the most impressive and diverse Bronze Age assemblages found in recent decades. Its striking and highly visible ornaments would have expressed their wearers' identity, status and connections.'

BEN ROBERTS, BRITISH MUSEUM

SUSS-C5D042

OBJECT TYPE Hoard (metalwork and jewellery)

MATERIALS Copper alloy, gold (discs), amber (beads), ceramic (vessel)

DATE 1400–1250 BCE

LOCATION Near Lewes, East Sussex

DISCOVERY METHOD Metal detecting

COLLECTION Lewes Castle and Museum

CONTENTS OF HOARD

3 copper-alloy palstave axes

5 copper-alloy 'Sussex Loop' bracelets

8 copper-alloy finger-rings

4 copper-alloy *tutuli* (bronze cones), and fragments

4 sheet-gold 'appliqué' discs

1 copper-alloy lozenge-headed pin

19 amber beads, and fragments

4 copper-alloy twisted torcs

fragments of copper-alloy coiled spiral ring necklaces

fragments of quoit-headed pins

ceramic vessel

OPPOSITE The hoard, which was buried in a ceramic storage vessel.

BELOW Some of the amber beads and spiral ring necklace fragments.

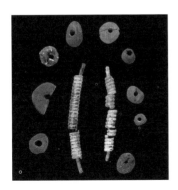

DISCOVERY

One spring day in 2011, on the hills between Lewes and the English south coast, David Lange made an incredible discovery. In an open field, with visibility for miles in either direction, his detector led him to a mostly undisturbed hoard placed in a large ceramic vessel. Its contents illustrated the wide-ranging connections of people in the area during the Middle Bronze Age, around 1400–1250 BCE. David unearthed the majority of the material himself but – being an avid *Time Team* fan – took images as he went along to record the excavation. It would have been preferable if the hoard could have been left in place until professional archaeological support was organised, but this was to come later. David photographed the items, which were stacked on top of one another in the pot, as he removed each layer. Archaeologists Luke Barber (then of Archaeology South-East) and Greg Chunter (then with East Sussex County Council), together with local Finds Liaison Officer (FLO) Stephanie Smith, and Michael Lewis and Ian Richardson from the Portable Antiquities Scheme (PAS) Central Unit, followed up with a small-scale excavation of the site. They were able to locate the original cut into the chalk subsoil in which the vessel was buried, along with some additional amber beads that David had missed.

The hoard is a fascinating mixture of bronze tools and ornaments, amber beads and thin gold sheets, all contained within a ceramic pot when they were buried. In total, there were three copper-alloy palstave axes, five copper-alloy 'Sussex Loop' bracelets, eight copper-alloy finger-rings, four copper-alloy *tutuli* (bronze cones, with fragments), four sheet-gold 'appliqué' discs, one copper-alloy lozenge-headed pin, nineteen amber beads (with fragments), four copper-alloy twisted torcs, as well as fragments of coiled spiral ring necklaces and quoit-headed pins. Within the excavation area, the archaeologists also found the remains of a ditch or trench close to where the hoard had been deposited, consistent with the placement of several other known major hoards from the Middle Bronze Age.

The burying of large collections of ornaments and tools in the ground in the Middle Bronze Age seems to have been done

BELOW Michael Lewis and David
Lange (finder of the hoard)
discussing the amber beads
found during the archaeological
excavation.

away from the areas where the small farming
communities were living in their roundhouses.
It also occurred separately from the burial of
the dead. Even though the types of ornaments
in the Near Lewes Hoard would have been
worn extensively, they are rarely found in
cemeteries where the typically cremated
remains of the deceased were placed in urns.
This site was evidently chosen deliberately, as it
provides a vantage point across the small valley
below and helps mark a territorial claim to
the landscape.

REGIONAL CONNECTIONS

Some of the items in the hoard are known to
have been widespread across Britain and north-
west Europe. But some are only known in this
part of southern England, and others had never
before been found in Britain. The palstave axes
are the most common artefacts in the group.
Others like them have been found throughout
Britain south of the Humber, sometimes singly
but often in hoards alongside other artefacts. An

interesting example is the find from Henstridge,
Somerset (DOR-813231) of a single palstave axe
alongside a complete copper-alloy rapier bent
over itself in a figure-8 shape.

The impressive and distinctive 'Sussex
Loop' bracelets are so called because past
discoveries pointed to them having been
produced almost exclusively in the area
between Lewes and Brighton; for example,
a bracelet in the collection of Brighton
and Hove Museums found at Falmer Hill,
Brighton, in 1918. Recently, however, they
have appeared outside the Sussex region,
including two in a hoard found in Ockham,
Surrey, in 2013 (SUR-B41DB6). The five in
the Near Lewes Hoard are each made from
a single rod (three round-sectioned and two
lozenge-sectioned) twisted over on itself. The
round-sectioned bracelets retain a remarkably
smooth surface.

The copper-alloy spiral rolls threaded
through the necklace are known from only
two other hoards in Britain – one from West

BELOW One of the five copper-alloy 'Sussex Loop' bracelets found in the hoard.

Ashling near Chichester and another more recently found in Hambledon, Hampshire (HAMP-BDF5DF) – all within the same 20-km radius. The photographs taken by David show that the amber beads were on the same necklaces as the spiral rolls. The amber beads would have travelled from the Baltic Sea area. Along with the gold sheets, previously known only in central and southern France, they convey the far-off connections of the hoard. These gold sheets, reminiscent of the foil tops on glass milk bottles, are decorated with three embossed concentric circles incised with parallel dashes. The bronze torcs in the hoard are typical of those found across Britain, Ireland and near continental Europe. The person who buried the hoard therefore had both local roots and international connections, at least as part of a network, stretching across the English Channel and into western and northern Europe.

Ben Roberts, then Curator of European Bronze Age collections at the British Museum, who studied the hoard, says that it is 'one of the most impressive and diverse Bronze Age assemblages found in recent decades. Its striking and highly visible ornaments would have expressed their wearers' identity, status and connections', in both their immediate area and further afield. Recent genetic analysis by Ian Armit and Lindsey Büster shows close connections between members of Middle Bronze Age communities in southern England and France.

The hoard was acquired by Lewes Castle and Museum in 2014. Research into the hoard and preparation for its display involved cutting-edge image capturing and visualisation. The items were scanned by the Cultural Informatics Research Group at the University of Brighton using a combination of Structured Light Scanning and a Mini-Dome device to take a series of high-resolution images from multiple angles. These images were then digitally combined to create visual diplays to amaze museum visitors.

BRONZE AGE
GOLD ORNAMENTS

'There's only one thing that comes out of the ground looking like gold, and that's gold.'

MALCOLM BAGGALEY, DETECTORIST

LVPL-F7196A, DENO-A4D394, LANCUM-C6B5FC	
OBJECT TYPE	Armlets and dress fittings
MATERIALS	Gold
DATE	c. 2100–700 BCE
LOCATION	North Turton, Lancashire; Ellastone, Staffordshire; St Bees, Cumbria
DISCOVERY METHOD	Metal detecting
COLLECTION	Tullie and the Beacon Museum (LANCUM-C6B5FC)

LVPL-F7196A	
WIDTH	61 mm
DIAMETER	86 mm (external)

DENO-A4D394	
LENGTH	127 mm
DIAMETER	56 mm (terminals); 8 mm (bar, max.)

LANCUM-C6B5FC	
LENGTH	82 mm
WIDTH	69 mm
DIAMETER	12 mm

OPPOSITE The Ellastone gold 'dress fastener', DENO-A4D394, moments after its discovery in Staffordshire by metal detectorist Jonathan Needham.

BRONZE AGE BLING

Items of personal adornment dating to the Bronze Age can be as enigmatic as they are beautiful. Some are relatively common, like small solid gold (or gold-covered copper-alloy) penannular rings, more than 200 of which have been recorded with the PAS. They were formerly called 'ring money' but are now believed to be decorative rather than currency, and were most likely worn on the body through a piercing or in the hair. They are fairly standard in appearance and form, though some are plain, while others are embellished with a striking 'tiger-stripe' surface pattern. Mary Cahill (former Keeper of Irish Antiquities, National Museum of Ireland) has suggested that the gold may have been applied to the surface of copper-alloy examples to reduce skin irritation for their wearers; like modern gold-plating, it was also decorative.

Gold bracelets, armlets and similar ornaments from the Bronze Age are much rarer finds and more varied in their construction and appearance. It is not absolutely certain how all of them were used or worn. Some are relatively robust and heavy, others light and delicate. But as a group, they show that a connection with the metalworking tradition in Ireland was maintained in Britain throughout this long period of several thousand years. Three exceptional examples illustrate this well:

THE NORTH TURTON ARMLET (LVPL-F7196A)

This gold armlet was found by detectorist Lee Whitfield in Lancashire in October 2020, just before the second COVID-19 lockdown. It was wedged between two rocks, about half a metre below the surface and covered in soil. Lee's first impression was that it was a piece of rubbish, possibly a tin can. A section from the main body broke off in the process of extracting it from the soil. Lee realised that the object was something much more important, so he got in touch with Alex Whitlock, one of the two FLOs for Lancashire and Cumbria, and then deposited it for safekeeping with Bolton Museum. He had hoped to organise a visit to the site but the COVID-19 lockdown intervened and made that impossible.

BELOW The North Turton armlet, LVPL-F7196A, discovered by detectorist Lee Whitfield in Lancashire in 2020.

Although in two pieces, the Early Bronze Age (*c.* 2100–1900 BCE) armlet is mostly complete. It is formed from sheet gold with no visible seams, and decorated with an embossed pattern of curved lines and lentoid-shaped bosses. X-ray fluorescence (XRF) analysis of the armlet at the British Museum revealed that the metal was approximately 83–85% gold, 15–17% silver, and the rest copper, which is consistent with other Bronze Age armlets of this sort.

The North Turton armlet is of a type known as 'Needham Type 3', following the classifications of Stuart Needham, former Curator of Bronze Age Collections at the British Museum. These armlets are rare finds, with thirteen examples known from Britain and Ireland, of which only six are made of gold. Others include a more damaged example from Bewholme, East Yorkshire (YORYM-80ADC9, acquired by Hull Museum), found in 2016, and two others from Lockington, Leicestershire, discovered in a barrow in 1994 alongside ceramic potsherds and a copper-alloy dagger with wooden scabbard. The Lockington armlets (now in the British Museum, 1996,0901.1-2) are complete and virtually undamaged. Examples from Ireland include a now-lost gold armlet from Whitfield, Waterford, and copper-alloy ones from Lough Gur and Luggacurran.

Stuart has suggested that in armlets of this type, the folded-over rims may have been a design feature to add strength, or possibly to grip an inner layer of leather worn to reduce chaffing. Neil Wilkin, Stuart's successor at the British Museum, is of the opinion that 'the armlet is clearly a prestige item designed to impress those who saw its wearer'.

THE ELLASTONE GOLD 'DRESS FASTENER' (DENO-A4D394)

Jonathan Needham took up metal detecting in early 2020 when his partner (now his wife) purchased a detector for him for Valentine's Day. After some time spent learning the ropes and not finding much of interest, he connected online with fellow hobbyist Malcolm Baggaley, who helped him to adjust the settings of his machine to focus on more promising signals, and the two became detecting buddies. One weekend in early May 2023, the two visited a field that Jonathan had secured permission to search in Ellastone, Staffordshire. At lunchtime on a damp muddy day Jonathan found what he first thought was a light yellow drawer handle – not unlike the 19th-century antiquarian William Wilde's description of similar Bronze Age 'dress fasteners' from Ireland as resembling 'the handle from a chest of drawers'. After a closer look, Malcolm told Jonathan, 'There's only one thing that comes out of the ground looking like gold, and that's gold.' After uploading images to a Facebook group for help with identifying the object, Jonathan quickly learned it was ancient and immediately rang up his local FLO, Meghan King (Derbyshire and Nottinghamshire). Less than 24 hours later he was meeting her at Derby Museum to hand over the find.

Jonathan's find was a D-shaped gold ornament with a curved semicircular bar or bow connecting two cone-shaped terminals.

Unlike some other examples of the type, the surface of his ornament is undecorated. It dates from the Late Bronze Age, specifically from a period known as the Ewart Park phase (800–700 BCE) in England and the Dowris phase (800–600 BCE) in Ireland. The precise function of this type of ornament is uncertain, but it is called a 'dress fastener' because it could have been used to hold together two pieces of cloth, like the folds of a cloak, by passing the terminals through 'buttonholes'. Although resembling a bracelet (the area enclosed by the bar and terminals is the size of a small wrist), it seems too uncomfortable to have been worn that way. The artefact exhibits a high degree of artistic and technical expertise in its manufacture.

Relatively few ornaments of this particular type are known from Britain. They are far more common in Ireland, where more than 60 have been recovered, most recently in 2013 during the construction of a house in Ballycullen, South Dublin. Prior to that, one found in Cave Hill, Belfast, was reported in 1993. In Scotland, another was unearthed in the 1970s on the Isle of Skye and is now in the collection of the National Museums Scotland – apparently in this instance the finder thought that they had found the bells from an old-fashioned alarm clock and ended up pulling the terminals apart! They only recognised it as ancient a decade later.

These items are so rare in Britain that when they do appear they are a strong indicator of an Irish connection. In addition to the Ellastone 'dress fastener', Jonathan reported that he had also unearthed nearby a pair of Bronze Age copper-alloy palstave axeheads, of a later style normally associated with North Wales. Although these palstaves did not appear to be related directly to the deposition of the earlier 'dress fastener', they are evidence of a local connection to North Wales, which had links to Ireland via sea trade and might explain the presence of the Irish-style dress fastener here in Staffordshire.

Analysis of the Ellastone dress fastener at the British Museum demonstrated a metallic content consistent with other gold objects from the Late Bronze Age. When metals scientist Laura Perucchetti examined it under the digital microscope, she was able to see toolmarks that showed that the two cup-like ends had been raised and shaped through hammering in a similar process to most other known examples (except those of very large size, which had separately attached terminals).

ST BEES GOLD ARMRING (LANCUM-C6B5FC)

This was another chance find that almost ended up being cast aside! The finder, care worker Billy Vaughan, unearthed the massive (311 g) solid bar with overlapping ends while metal detecting by the windswept Cumbria coast. He was intrigued by it, but assumed

BELOW Finder Billy Vaughan re-creating the moment he found the gold armring from St Bees.

OPPOSITE Four views of the gold armring from St Bees, Cumbria, LANCUM-C6B5FC.

it was probably just a modern component, possibly from a paraglider (the area is a popular spot for flying them). Thankfully, something made him put it in his finds bag anyway, and he later decided it could be something older so telephoned Lydia Prosser (FLO for Lancashire and Cumbria at the time), who took it in. When Lydia was able to confirm the age of the object, Billy was blown away. After handing in the armring for the Treasure process, he had a friend make a replica for him out of bronze so he could 'keep' his find of a lifetime!

The armring dates to the Late Bronze Age and is made from a solid heavy gold bar, circular in section, and bent into an oval spiral, with the ends overlapping slightly. Most of the outside surface that would have been visible when the ornament was worn is covered in shallow indented dots, tightly clustered. The outer edge of this decorated surface is smoother and the punched dots are much shallower, suggesting that it was indeed worn as a piece of jewellery, rather than having been made for another purpose.

Paralleled by Irish bracelets from the Tullydonnell Hoard in Co. Donegal and Tremblestown Castle in Co. Meath, the only similar example in Britain is a longer (but slightly lighter) one discovered in 1994 by a detectorist in The Lee, Buckinghamshire. Like the St Bees arming, it is decorated with punched dots over its entire surface and is formed from a solid bar that has been wound back on itself – twice, in this case. In the state in which it was found it could not have been worn as a bracelet, except by a very small child for whom it would have been much too weighty. Were these bracelets deliberately reshaped before being cast away or buried, to end their function definitively? The phenomenon of 'killing' an object prior to deposition has been observed in other Late Bronze Age artefacts such as swords and dirks (see pp. 62–65).

NEW KNOWLEDGE

These Bronze Age gold ornaments give fresh insight about the people who made and used them, and deepen our understanding of British and Irish connections throughout the Bronze Age. But they also raise further questions. Were the objects made in Ireland and transported to Britain, or were they made by goldsmiths based in Britain who had knowledge of Irish metalworking? These gold ornaments also have a tangential but important benefit to archaeology because their 'wow' factor gets more people interested in learning about the past and archaeology. At the time of writing, the Ellastone and North Turton finds are both going through the Treasure process and will hopefully be acquired by local museums. The St Bees bracelet has thankfully been acquired jointly by two museums in Cumbria – Tullie in Carlisle and the Beacon Museum in Whitehaven – and is now on shared display.

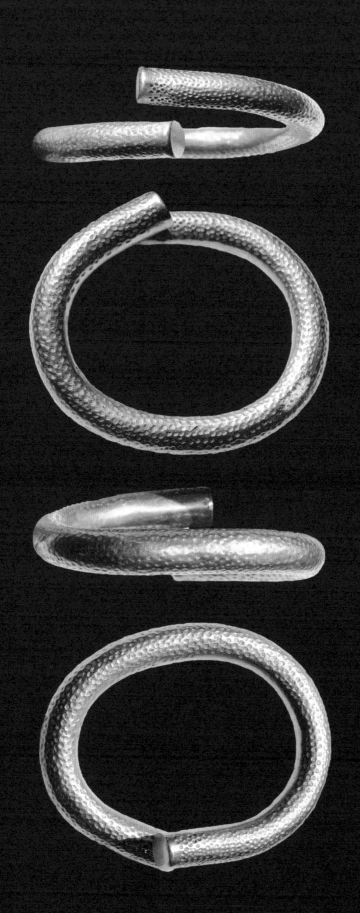

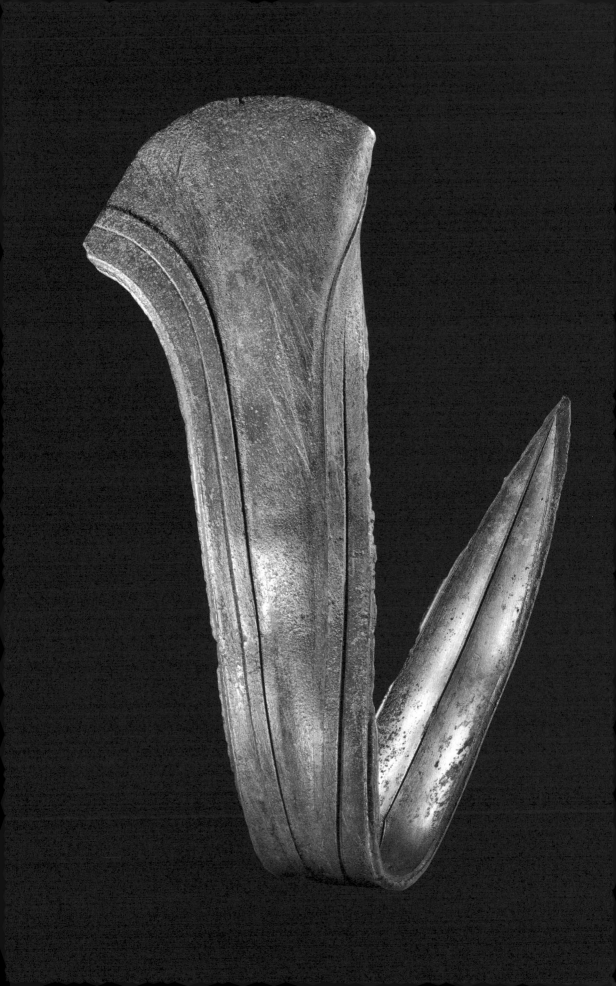

EAST RUDHAM DIRK

'It's absolutely incredible to have a find like this twice in a lifetime.'

ANDREW ROGERSON, ARCHAEOLOGIST

NMS-C7EEF3

OBJECT TYPE Ceremonial weapon

MATERIALS Copper alloy

DATE *c.* 1500–1350 BCE

LOCATION East Rudham, Norfolk

DISCOVERY METHOD Chance find while ploughing

COLLECTION Norwich Castle Museum and Art Gallery

LENGTH 685 mm (if straightened)

WIDTH 175 mm

THICKNESS 8 mm

DISCOVERY

Some of the most remarkable finds made by the public have come to light not through metal detecting, but ploughing. In 2003 a Norfolk farmer (who wishes to remain anonymous) was cultivating land at East Rudham when a large bronze object, sword-like in shape and bent back on itself, came up with the farm machinery. If straightened, the object would be 68.5 cm long, and it weighs almost 2 kg, so an impressive piece. What had been discovered was a ceremonial dirk dating to *c.* 1500–1350 BCE, which puts it in the Middle Bronze Age.

Such items are extremely rare and this was only the second example to be found in Norfolk. The first was discovered in 1988 at Oxborough, just 25 km (16 miles) south-east of East Rudham. It was another chance find, made by Geoff Allen while out walking – he almost fell over its butt end, which was protruding from peaty soil in woodland beside a tributary of the River Wissey. In the case of the East Rudham Dirk, the finder did not immediately realise its significance. The mysterious object remained in the farm office for some years, occasionally being used to prop open the door, and was reportedly almost thrown away in a skip before a friend suggested that it might be of some age. Only then was it brought along to the PAS in Norfolk, causing more than a little surprise for Andrew Rogerson, Senior Archaeologist in Norfolk County Council's Historic Environment Service, and his colleagues.

DIRKS

Dirks are short swords designed to be wielded easily with one hand. Essentially they were used for stabbing, much like a dagger. They are not common metal-detector finds, though almost 80 examples dating to the Bronze Age have been found in England and Wales and recorded with the PAS, along with a few others recovered in archaeological excavations. Unlike the East Rudham Dirk, most of these were fragments or severely damaged. Only the blades of these weapons normally survive, as the hilts would have been made of organic materials such as wood, horn or bone.

OPPOSITE The East Rudham Dirk after conservation at Norwich Castle Museum and Art Gallery. The bending was probably done intentionally to 'kill' the weapon before deposition.

The PAS database shows that such dirks have been found across England and Wales, but not in all parts. Notable gaps are in south-west England and central-west and north-west Wales, which may be significant in understanding these objects, although the reasons for the gaps are currently unknown. Most are 'everyday' weapons, dwarfed in size by the much larger and rarer so-called 'ceremonial dirks' from East Rudham and Oxborough. For example, a complete dirk from Bentworth, Hampshire (HAMP-9AE0D7), is only 12.6 cm in length, and another, from Llangors, Powys (NMGW-C6BDCC), is 16.9 cm long.

PRODUCTION AND DISTRIBUTION

Besides the two Norfolk 'ceremonial dirks', the other four known examples all come from north-west continental Europe, at Plougrescant (Brittany) and Beaune (Burgundy) in France, and Ommerschans and Jutphaas in the Netherlands. All six are very alike in style and execution, albeit with slight differences in size and form, so archaeologists have suggested

that they might have been produced by a single workshop, from which they were distributed to fulfil their (unknown) ceremonial duties. The place of production is unknown, but were it in Britain the nearest sources of copper and tin would have been Wales (for the copper) and Cornwall (for the tin). For Tim Pestell, Curator of Archaeology at Norwich Castle Museum and Art Gallery, 'the dirks are important because they highlight direct or indirect links between people across parts of Europe, suggesting that they shared similar beliefs to need or want such gigantic abstractions of normal dirks. This is a far more intense and shared experience than simply the ownership of big objects.' Tim thinks the fact that the East Rudham Dirk had been 'ritually killed' (bent before deposition) 'provides further insights into these beliefs at the dawn of metalworking'. We don't know exactly what these beliefs were, but all the dirks lack rivet holes for the attachment of handles and have intentionally blunt edges, so they never acted as functional weapons. Furthermore, as Andrew has noted, 'where the details of these

BELOW Archaeological illustration by Jason Gibbons of the East Rudham dirk, including a reconstruction of how it would have looked before it was bent.

BELOW The Oxborough Dirk, another large ceremonial dirk, found in Norfolk by walker Geoff Allen in 1988.

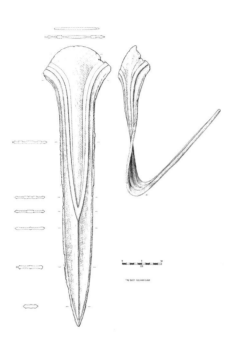

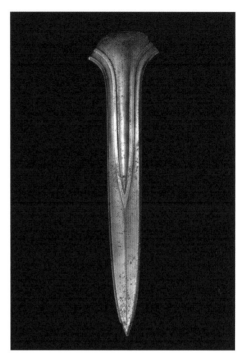

finds were recorded there are strong associations with water, rivers and fens'. Other Bronze Age objects are also found in such places (see, for example, the Shropshire Sun Pendant, pp. 46–51), strongly suggesting they were ritually deposited, perhaps as an offering to gods. That said, the East Rudham findspot is on quite high and dry ground!

Andrew, whose team had previously recorded the Oxborough Dirk, never thought that he would see a second example from Norfolk. 'It's absolutely incredible', he said in the press, 'to have a find like this twice in a lifetime.' Who knows – perhaps there are other examples that have been found, or are waiting to be found, in Norfolk or elsewhere. At least it provides a salutary reminder not to throw away anything you find buried in the ground until you are sure it isn't important – and if in doubt, ask someone!

ENDNOTE

Even though the Norfolk dirks are impressive and rare, when found they were not protected by law, because they were not made of a precious metal – though changes to the Treasure Act 1996 on 30 July 2023 now protect items of outstanding regional or national significance regardless of metallic composition. In 1994 the Oxborough Dirk was sold at Christie's in London and (following an export licence block) later acquired by the British Museum with support from the National Art Collections Fund (now the Art Fund). The acquisition of the East Rudham Dirk was arranged as a private sale, with financial support from the National Heritage Memorial Fund and the Friends of Norwich Museums. This resulted in Norfolk Museum Service buying the object for display at Norwich Castle Museum and Art Gallery.

Iron Age

TOTAL FINDS RECORDED ON PAS DATABASE

78,129

MOST COMMON ARTEFACT TYPES ON DATABASE

coin, brooch, vessel, harness fitting, hoard

TOP 5 COUNTIES ON DATABASE

Norfolk, Kent, Essex, Hampshire, Suffolk

PAS data as of October 2024

10 The Hallaton Treasure
Leicestershire
11 Leekfrith Gold Torcs
Staffordshire
12 Chiseldon Cauldrons
Wiltshire
13 Miniature Weapons
Kent; Lincolnshire

FINDS DENSITY

Moderate   High

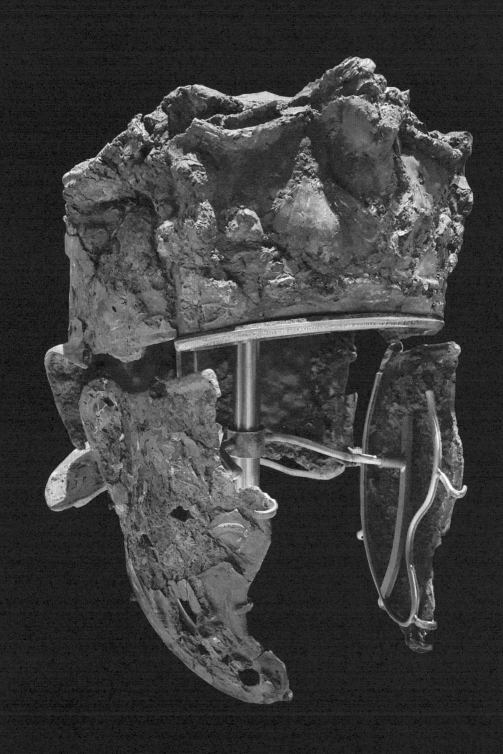

THE HALLATON TREASURE

'Most archaeologists only ever see Iron Age coins in a museum, but I got to excavate thousands of them.'
VICKI SCORE, ARCHAEOLOGIST

IARCH-D4642F

OBJECT TYPE Hoard (including coins and helmet fragments)

MATERIALS Silver and gold (coins); iron (helmets)

DATE Late Iron Age, c. 50 BCE–50 CE

LOCATION Hallaton, Leicestershire

DISCOVERY METHOD Fieldwalking and metal detecting

COLLECTION Harborough Museum

CONTENTS OF HOARD

c. 5,000 Iron Age coins

c. 350 Roman coins

1 Roman cavalry helmet and fragments of others

1 silver bowl

silver ingots

20 fragmentary brooches

1 tankard

animal bones (mainly pig)

OPPOSITE Roman cavalry helmet (after restoration) buried with the hoard; it is iron and silver gilt, with a woman's face flanked by lions on the brow guard.

BELOW One of 22 silver coins made c. 50 CE that were excavated from the same soil block as the helmet.

THE DISCOVERY THAT KEPT GROWING

Some finds are made when someone is searching land that they've never been on before. Others result from dedicated long-term investigation of an area by people with a connection to the landscape – like the Hallaton Fieldwork Group, a community archaeology organisation founded in the 1990s that explored the historic countryside around the local parish in Hallaton, Leicestershire, mostly through systematic fieldwalking. By the year 2000, its members had identified some promising areas to the south-west of Hallaton where concentrations of Iron Age and Roman potsherds were turning up. One of their number, Ken Wallace, who was also a keen metal detectorist, brought in his machine to assist the group in their exploration, focusing on some fields where animal bones had been found in addition to the ceramics. Within a short time, he discovered more than 200 Iron Age silver coins in the ploughsoil. Ken knew the importance of recording their exact findspots, and that is what he did, revealing concentrations of coins that indicated intentionally buried hoards.

For some, these coin hoards alone would be the find of a lifetime, but for Ken and the Hallaton Fieldwork Group they were just the beginning. Ken reported the coins to Peter Liddle, Keeper of Archaeology at Leicestershire Museums. This led to a professional excavation by the University of Leicestershire Archaeology Service (ULAS), assisted by the Hallaton group, and the eventual recovery of one of the most important collections of material from the late Iron Age and early Roman conquest period in Britain (c. 50 BCE–50 CE).

In total, over several years of excavations, the team recovered c. 5,000 Iron Age silver and gold coins, the most ever found at a single site in mainland Britain, mainly in discrete intentional hoarded groups. They also recovered more than 350 Roman coins, large amounts of animal bones (almost all pig), Roman cavalry helmets and assorted other artefacts, including a silver bowl, silver ingots, the remains of 20 brooches and a tankard.

The coin deposits consisted of at least sixteen separate hoards, mostly located around an archaeological feature

BELOW Conservator Marilyn Hockey micro-excavating one of the Roman helmet cheekpieces from a soil block at the British Museum.

BELOW Cheekpiece 1 with pig bones and coins in soil. Its decoration (not visible here) shows a victorious Roman emperor on horseback trampling an enemy.

identified as an entranceway (see below); several were associated with the helmets. Together these pointed to a site of ritual significance that was actively used during the transition from the late Iron Age through to the Roman conquest period.

The coin hoards were brought to the British Museum in soil blocks where they were micro-excavated by conservators, and then catalogued and studied by Ian Leins, Curator of Iron Age and Coins at the time. The helmets, so fragmented and corroded that archaeologists initially thought they had found a 'rusty bucket', were also carefully lifted in one piece, encased in protective plaster of Paris, for painstaking conservation by Marilyn Hockey and her colleagues, which took more than ten years. The end result was a restoration, from hundreds of tiny fragments, of 80% of one helmet bowl and several cheekpieces. One cheekpiece was decorated in high relief with an image of a Roman emperor on horseback trampling a barbarian, and a brow piece had a three-dimensional female goddess emerging from it.

MORE THAN A 'HOARD'

The Hallaton site rises above and looks out to the south over the Welland Valley in south-east Leicestershire. Such commanding views over the landscape are typical of known Iron Age temple sites like Hayling Island, Hampshire, and Harlow, Essex.

The first excavation on the Hallaton site was a targeted 2-m² trench centred on an area in which metal detecting had yielded positive signals; this square was then expanded to a larger trench, 11 m × 9 m, in which six hoards of Iron Age coins were found. Subsequent excavations, eventually encompassing approximately 1800 m², revealed the presence of a boundary ditch and entranceway to the east. This made it possible to see that many of the coin hoards had been placed deliberately inside the entranceway.

The coins consisted of a range of denominations from a number of Iron Age groups of people, but most were silver units tradditonally acribed to the Corieltavi, a tribe from what is now the East Midlands. There

BELOW Gold quarter stater,
one of only three known examples,
c. 10–40 CE. It is inscribed 'CVNO'
on one side (right) and 'DVBN' on
the other, evidence for a political
alliance between the leaders
Cunobelin and Dubnovellaunos.

BOTTOM Analysis of the huge
quantity of pig bones suggested
that they were ritual offerings,
buried mostly whole with only
a choice cut removed.

were also three gold quarter staters – the only three known anywhere – inscribed 'CVNO' on one side and 'DVBN' on the other, in an apparent political demonstration of a connection between the eastern ruler Cunobelin (*c.* 10–40 CE) and another leader, possibly Dubnovellaunos; a contemporary leader by that name issued coins in Essex and Kent.

Another important coin, one of the earliest Roman coins ever found in Britain, was a Republican *denarius* dated to the early 2nd century BCE. The site also contained scattered later coinage through to the end of the Roman period. Most of the stratified Roman coins, from deliberately placed hoards, were from the late Republic and early Imperial periods and displayed minimal signs of wear, showing that they had been used in the ritual activities associated with the late Iron Age. The unstratified coins of later date were more heavily worn and were probably casual losses rather than ploughed-out deposits, demonstrating that the site had been occupied throughout the Roman period, as also suggested by the remains of 1st- and 2nd-century Roman brooches found during the investigations, even if the ceremonial aspects of its use had disappeared or changed.

The animal remains were key in interpreting the significance of the site. Almost all (97%) of the bones recovered during the excavations were from domesticated pigs or wild boars, a proportion that was much higher than a typical Iron Age occupation site. The bones at the bottom of the pits were articulated, meaning that they had been buried with flesh still on them. These were then covered with disarticulated bone fragments, which could be interpreted as post-meal remains, with some placed in pits to the east of the entrance to the enclosure, and others laid out in a layer around the pits. Jennifer Browning of ULAS,

in her analysis of the faunal remains, reports that one volunteer excavator described seeing 'a pavement of bones'. The bones in the pits showed very little sign of being gnawed (for example, by dogs or rats) indicating that the pits had been sealed shortly after the animal remains were placed in them. The bones comprising the right front quarter of many of the pigs' remains were missing in the excavated area, indicating that there was something important about that portion of the pig, perhaps the favoured cut for a sacrificial offering; these missing joints might have been buried in another unexcavated area around the site, or removed further afield. Archaeologists also recovered the remains of three dogs deposited in two locations. The most complete skeleton, of an adult dog, was deliberately

BELOW Some of the nearly 5,000 Iron Age gold and silver coins. They represent the largest group of coins from a single site in mainland Britain and were buried in sixteen groups, interpreted as ritual deposits.

OPPOSITE TOP The Roman helmet and helmet cheekpieces on display at Harborough Museum.
OPPOSITE BOTTOM Fieldwalkers from the Hallaton Fieldwork Group searching near the findspot.

placed on its right side in the entranceway feature, with the partial remains of another dog in the same area. The meaning of these canine remains is a mystery.

All of this evidence emphasised that the Hallaton site was one of ritual significance beyond simple feasting or animal sacrifice. Among the artefacts possibly associated with the ritual site were fragments of 20 brooches, metal components of a tankard, a small silver bowl which had no parallels among Iron Age material in Britain, and silver ingots, possibly from coins that had been melted down. The remains of the Roman cavalry helmets were found in a clear deposit with coins that allowed them to be dated to around 50 CE, making them some of the later pieces to have been deliberately buried at the site.

IMPORTANCE AND LEGACY

More than 20 years after its discovery, the Hallaton Treasure remains a testament to best practice and demonstrates how collaboration between members of the public, archaeologists and museum professionals can ensure that as

much as possible is learned from a find. 'It was an amazing experience,' says archaeologist Vicki Score, who directed the excavation and led the research into the site. 'Most archaeologists only ever see Iron Age coins in a museum, but I got to excavate thousands of them'. The number and variety of the Iron Age coins from the site, and the precise information captured about their findspots, were vital to understanding wider aspects of their deposition. Detailed analysis of all the coins found at Hallaton, both in contained hoards and loose in the plough soil, showed similar profiles to other groups of coins from around England recorded by the Portable Antiquities Scheme (PAS) and reported under the Treasure Act. Since the Hallaton coins are almost all believed to have been deposited within discrete hoards before they were damaged by the plough and dragged across the site, other similarly dispersed collections of coins could also be deliberate deposits – from a single hoard or perhaps a series of separate groups intentionally placed in the same location.

The Hallaton Treasure still impresses in the sheer bulk of material, particularly coins, that were unearthed. Important hoards consisting of single deposits of Iron Age coins have since been found in Wickham Market, Suffolk (SF-65D096; 850 coins), and Baddow, Essex (ESS-DBEBD6; 933 coins), but they are still dwarfed by the thousands of coins recovered in aggregate from the Hallaton site. The Hallaton Treasure is now one of the star attractions of Leicestershire County Council Museums, through the generous support of funders, and takes pride of place in Harborough Museum. Regular conferences are held in Leicestershire to present research into various aspects of the hoard. And the Hallaton Fieldwork Group carries on with their important information-gathering in the local area.

LEEKFRITH GOLD TORCS

'The survival of these objects reminds us what
a fractional picture we have of Iron Age societies
in most areas of Britain.'
JULIA FARLEY, BRITISH MUSEUM

WMID-FD08D9

OBJECT TYPE Jewellery hoard

MATERIALS Gold

DATE Iron Age, c. 400–300 BCE

LOCATION Leekfrith, Staffordshire

DISCOVERY METHOD Metal detecting

COLLECTION Potteries Museum and
Art Gallery

CONTENTS OF HOARD

Complete gold torc with thistle-shaped
terminals

Complete gold torc made from a pair
of twisted wires

Broken gold torc with small thistle-
shaped terminals

Gold bracelet

OPPOSITE The three gold torcs and
gold bracelet found by detectorists
Mark Hambledon and Joe Kania.

BELOW Detail of terminal decoration
on the largest complete torc.

NECK RINGS AND MORE

Torcs – large metal ornaments worn (or assumed to have
been worn) around the neck – have been found in Britain and
Ireland dating back to at least the Middle Bronze Age, but are
particularly associated with Iron Age peoples. One of the most
famous representations of a torc is on a Roman marble statue
known as 'The Dying Gaul', thought to be based on a Greek
original from the 3rd century BCE; the otherwise naked subject
wears a simple twisted torc with two flared terminals. A large
hoard of Iron Age torcs found between the 1940s and 1990s
in Snettisham, Norfolk (and now in the British Museum and
Norwich Castle Museum and Art Gallery), contained an array
of different forms, sizes and metals; some of the torcs were
decorated in the characteristic La Tène artistic style. Compared
with examples from the Bronze Age, however, Iron Age torcs,
especially complete ones, are rare finds in Britain, particularly
outside of East Anglia. This made the finding of the Leekfrith
torcs all the more interesting.

In December 2016, Mark Hambledon and Joe Kania
decided to take their metal detectors to a pasture in the lightly
populated parish of Leekfrith, 15 km north-east of Stoke-on-
Trent, Staffordshire. They had last searched this field 20 years
previously, a decade after the farmer had stopped ploughing it,
and, finding nothing, had done little detecting there since.
On this occasion, however, they found four gold items that
added greatly to the information known about this part of the
West Midlands during the Iron Age. The first complete gold torc
was found at the crest of a small hill. Mark and Joe then located a
second torc, a fragment of a third, and a complete gold bracelet
in a line running down the hill (they found a further fragment,
the missing piece of the third torc, at a later date). Mark and Joe
quickly realised that these were important objects and contacted
Teresa Gilmore, Finds Liaison Officer (FLO) for Staffordshire
and the West Midlands, with the news. Teresa immediately
set the wheels in motion to progress the case, and within a few
days had organised an investigation of the findspot by local
archaeological colleagues to take place in the new year, scientific

analysis and photography of the finds. She even
persuaded the coroner to pencil in an inquest,
in advance of formal paperwork about the find!

The torcs and bracelet were taken in at
Birmingham Museum and Art Gallery, where
Pieta Greaves undertook scientific analysis of
them. Julia Farley, then Curator of Iron Age
Collections at the British Museum, went there
to see them in person in order to produce her
report for the coroner. The Potteries Museum
and Art Gallery in Stoke-on-Trent then secured
special permission from the Department for
Culture, Media and Sport to put the items on
display immediately following the coroner's
inquest, making this one of the shortest
windows between discovery and display of any
Treasure find. According to Deb Klemperer
(then principal curator at the Potteries
Museum), this month-long display led to a
noticeable increase in museum visitor numbers.

ILLUMINATING A MYSTERIOUS AGE

The torcs and bracelet are believed to have
been deposited together in the ground, and
then knocked by the plough and dragged
down the slope at some point before the field
was given over to pasture. They share visual
similarities but each is unique.

The first and largest neck torc found (almost
15 cm in diameter and weighing 230.6 g) is a
gold rod with 'thistle'-shaped terminals. The
body is plain except for a stamped decoration
of three circles in several locations near the
juncture between each terminal and the main
body. The terminals themselves have a series
of light grooves running around them, and
flat faces. The second torc, also complete and
nearly the same size (though lighter in weight, at
42.1 g), is made of two equally sized gold wires
twisted around each other in a uniform pattern.
The wires are joined together at each end to

IRON AGE

BELOW Detail of the 'three peltas' decoration on the bracelet terminals.

BELOW Coroner Ian Smith and British Museum curator Julia Farley examining the torcs.

make a small 'thistle'-shaped terminal and then these terminals are bent so that they can be hooked onto one another, making a clasp for the torc. The broken third neck torc resembles a small version of the first torc (weighing 63.2 g).

Perhaps the most aesthetically appealing item in the group, and the most useful in dating it, is the gold bracelet. The band is made of four gold wires: two are large hollow rods that spiral around each other, with two smaller wires (each twisted on itself to give a rope-like effect) in the grooves between them. The hollow rods form solid, flat terminals, which are decorated with a sophisticated design of three 'peltas' (an elongated crescent with the ends looping back on themselves), each made from an applied wire, with the negative space filled with chased or engraved decoration.

The Leekfrith torcs, especially the thistle-headed examples, closely resemble Continental types dated from the 5th to the early 3rd century BCE; a few have been found in Britain, though more commonly in bronze than gold. The bracelet is closely paralleled in form, if not decoration, by an example from a grave in Waldalgesheim in south-western Germany that dates to the late 4th century BCE. Assuming that the Leekfrith torcs were made around the same time, they present a picture of what is now the West Midlands in the Middle Iron Age as a place with international connections and access to sophisticated dress and craftsmanship. Detailed analysis of the metals showed that their composition was consistent with other gold ornaments believed to have been manufactured in Britain. They could have been made locally in the West Midlands, inspired by European styles, or could have belonged to someone who had immigrated from the Continent or travelled there. As Julia noted in her report on the hoard, 'the survival of these objects reminds us what a fractional picture we have of Iron Age societies in most areas of Britain'. Staffordshire is one of the few places in England, outside of East Anglia, where small concentrations of Iron Age gold torcs have been recorded. But most of these are potentially later in date (from the 2nd and 1st century BCE), and the information we have from earlier times is sparse. The discovery of the Leekfrith torcs casts the West Midlands in a new light as a dynamic place with early Continental connections. Perhaps the later development of a local style of 'cushion terminal' torcs represents a long tradition of gold working in this area, rather than simply imitating the developments in East Anglia.

The torcs remain on display in the Potteries Museum, for all to see.

CHISELDON CAULDRONS

'Placing so many cauldrons together may have brought a significant event or a series of events to a close.'
JODY JOY, ARCHAEOLOGIST

TREASURE CASE NO.	2005 T178
OBJECT TYPE	Cauldron hoard
MATERIALS	Bronze and iron
DATE	3rd–4th century BCE
LOCATION	Chiseldon, Wiltshire
DISCOVERY METHOD	Metal detecting
COLLECTION	British Museum

CONTENTS OF HOARD

11 complete cauldrons

6 fragmentary cauldrons

2 cattle skulls

OPPOSITE Teams from Wessex Archaeology and the British Museum excavating one of the eleven complete cauldrons.

BELOW Archaeological drawing by Alexandra Baldwin reconstructing one of the cauldrons.

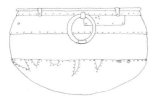

DISCOVERY

Peter Hyams says he wasn't much interested in history at school, as many metal detectorists say of themselves, but later in life, through his hobby, he actually made history! In November 2004, the semi-retired electrician was searching on arable land in Chiseldon, Wiltshire, when he came across a few pieces of bronze sheet and what looked like a crumpled can. Initially it wasn't clear what the objects were or how old they might be, so Peter reached out for help. Peter recalls that the first responses from archaeologists were not helpful, but he persisted and subsequently gained the support of local archaeologist John Winterburn. Following an initial survey of the findspot, John organised an excavation by the Chiseldon Local History Society. Working in inclement conditions, the society's volunteers revealed at least three vessels, fragments of bronze sheet and some iron rings, all within a pit cut into chalk. Realising that professional excavation was needed, John, to Peter's dismay, halted the proceedings. Katie Hinds (then Wiltshire FLO) also visited the site and took away with her some of the fragments of the bronze sheet to show to her colleagues. At this time it was thought that the vessels might be Anglo-Saxon, but it was useful to be sure before excavation continued. By this time Peter was also doing his own research. He had seen Oxford-based archaeometallurgist Peter Northover on television and reached out to him, believing he might be able to help date the metal finds. He was right! By May 2005, Peter Northover's preliminary examination of some vessel fragments suggested that they were sheet bronze and likely prehistoric in date. What Peter Hyams had discovered was part of a hoard of seventeen Iron Age cauldrons, eleven substantially complete, the others less so.

TREASURE!

On learning that the vessels might be prehistoric, and therefore legally classed as Treasure under the 2002 Designation Order to the Treasure Act 1996 (a change in law made to protect prehistoric base-metal hoards, instead of only gold and silver objects), Katie approached Wessex Archaeology to undertake

further investigation of the findspot. This was
directed by Andrew Fitzpatrick, with the British
Museum supporting the investigation and
providing two of its conservators, Alexandra
Baldwin and Simon Dove, who proved crucial
given the complexity of the find.

The excavation in June and July 2005 took
place in difficult conditions. The cauldrons
were full of soil, tightly packed within a
circular pit (approximately 2 m in diameter
and 65 cm deep), and some of them had
fused together. Furthermore, some cauldrons
had been deposited upside-down and others
the right way up. One of the cauldrons had
even been damaged deliberately before it was
placed in the ground. Removing the cauldrons
from the pit was therefore a very complicated
and time-consuming process.

They were left encased in the surrounding
soil and lifted in blocks, bandaged in plaster
and clingfilm to keep them intact. These
soil blocks were then taken to the British
Museum where the cauldrons were micro-
excavated in the conservation lab. However,
the Museum was unable to work on them
until their legal status was clear. As Treasure,
their ownership rested with the Crown until
they could be acquired by a museum – in this
case the British Museum itself. This process
was delayed because the finder contested the

(independent) Treasure Valuation Committee's
assessment of the cauldrons' value: £800. This
might seem a small amount for something of
such enormous archaeological interest, but a
finder's reward is based on the condition of the
items as found, and in this situation the very
high, albeit necessary, conservation costs would
outstrip any probable open-market value of
the cauldrons. The micro-excavation was then
delayed further because the British Museum
needed to raise funding for the conservation
work and conduct a pilot study to ascertain
how long this work would take. Finally,
between 2010 and 2014, thanks to funding
from the Leverhulme Trust, Alexandra, this
time joined by Jamie Hood, began work
revealing the cauldrons within their soil blocks.

Two cattle skulls were found with the
hoard and had been buried at the same time
as it. Radiocarbon dating showed these to
be from the 3rd or 4th century BCE, giving
a date for the deposition of the hoard. The
archaeologists examining the cauldrons had
initially believed the vessels to be from the 1st
or 2nd century BCE. The style of decoration
– for instance, the 'cattle head' mount from
Cauldron 2 – had previously been identified
as dating from the 1st century BCE. The simple
form of the cauldrons, with globular bowl and
iron rim and handles, had also always been
assumed to be characteristic of vessels of the
1st and 2nd centuries BCE because objects like
them had been found in well-dated graves and
settlements from this period. The date from
cattle skulls suggested that the cauldrons were
actually several centuries older, questioning
these hitherto long-held assumptions about
Iron Age artistic styles and object forms.

Alexandra and Jamie were at first unsure
about how much information they could
glean from the cauldrons since they were
in such a poor state of preservation.

The conservation process was painstakingly slow, not least because the objects were prone to deteriorating once the soil that protected them was removed. Nonetheless, details of manufacture, such as marking-out lines and hammer blows, were still visible in the metal, allowing the conservators and archaeologists to understand how the cauldrons had been made. The Iron Age craftworkers had used sophisticated techniques such as quenching of iron components, and had worked with extremely thin bronze sheets, which required great skill to hammer out evenly. Another important discovery in the laboratory was the preservation of food residues, otherwise rarely found on prehistoric metal vessels. These residues showed that the cauldrons had been used to cook both meat and vegetable dishes, such as stews, gruels and porridges.

A fieldwalking and geophysical survey of the area surrounding the location of the hoard was undertaken by Wessex Archaeology in 2010 as part of the 'Celts and Romans in North Wiltshire Project', a community project funded by the Heritage Lottery Fund. It revealed occupation as far back as the Late Neolithic (some 4,500 years ago) and evidence of a Romano-British (effectively late Iron Age) settlement. At the hoard site, degraded pottery and animal bones suggested the presence of a nearby Iron Age settlement at the time the Chiseldon Cauldrons were buried, and it was overlooked by at least two previously known Iron Age hill forts, at Barbury Castle and Liddington Castle on either side of the River Og, and possibly another at Chiseldon itself.

REMAINS OF A GREAT FEAST?

The Chiseldon assemblage was important because never before had so many complete prehistoric cauldrons been found together in a single deposit. This offered archaeologists new

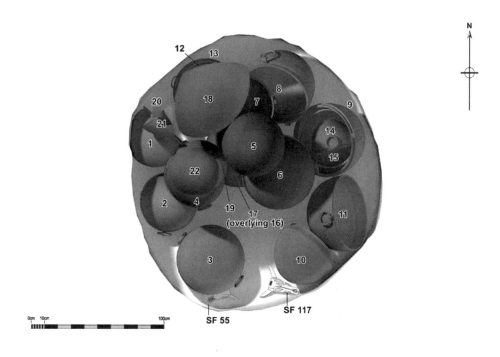

BELOW AND BELOW RIGHT
Micro-excavation of the cauldrons
in the lab by Alexandra Baldwin.

OPPOSITE Fields near the findspot
at Chiseldon.

insights into life during the Middle Iron Age,
particularly around the preparation and eating
of food. As Jody Joy (then Curator of the
European Iron Age at the British Museum),
who led the study of the Chiseldon Cauldrons,
explains, 'Until recently, there has been little
understanding of such vessels, including their
function, date and typology, simply because
most finds of such vessels in the past lack an
archaeological context.' Jody's comment refers
to the many 'antiquarian finds' in museum
collections that were dug up by amateur
enthusiasts without detailed records of where
they were found or what had been found with
them – so it was key that Peter stopped digging
and sought professional archaeological help.
'Because we can date this burial to the 4th
or 3rd century BCE, we now know such vessels
were used some 100 years earlier than we
previously thought. This is important because
it coincides with a period of the remodelling
of hill forts in the Wessex region [broadly
much of south-west England], and at a time
when hoarding as a practice was hitherto
almost unknown.' It suggests that the burial
of the cauldrons provides important new
insight into wider social changes in the
Middle Iron Age.

Also important for Jody were the food
residues on the cauldrons, as evidence not

only of what Middle Iron Age people in the
area ate, but also that 'they had the potential
to mass produce and serve food for feasting,
perhaps for many hundreds, if not thousands,
of people'. However, Jody points out that in
the Chiseldon assemblage 'there is limited
evidence for bowls and other utensils', and
their absence suggests that the hoard might
be 'symbolically representative of such a mass
feast [rather] than providing the physical
remains of such an event'.

This leads to the question of why the hoard
was buried. If it is not simply the residue of
a 'Celtic knees-up', then the arrangement
of the cauldrons and cattle skulls clearly
had some special meaning. Perhaps, as
Jody thinks, 'placing so many cauldrons
together may have brought a significant
event or a series of events to a close, and
it is likely the relationships of the people
involved and the choice of the burial site
were also important'.

Although we will never know the full story,
Peter's find of a few bits of copper alloy one
autumn day in the Wiltshire countryside has
opened up fascinating new insights into the
ancient past, radically changing our thoughts
about the people who lived in and around
Chiseldon during the Iron Age.

MINIATURE WEAPONS

Enigmatic collections of tiny metal weapons and tools, possibly buried as sacred offerings in the late Iron Age and early Roman era

SUR-1C249A, LIN-B1B742, LIN-B14EE4, LIN-B0BAF5, LIN-B08E07, LIN-AE62A0, LIN-ADC107, LIN-9DE863

OBJECT TYPE Weapons and tools (miniature)

MATERIALS Lead alloy and copper alloy

DATE Late Iron Age to early Roman, *c.* 100 BCE–100 CE

LOCATION Hollingbourne, Kent; Nettleton, Lincolnshire

DISCOVERY METHOD Metal detecting

OPPOSITE One of six miniature spearheads found in the 1970s in Nettleton, Lincolnshire, LIN-AE62A0.

BELOW LIN-AE62A0, actual size.

SMALL THINGS

An oddity of prehistory is the production of miniature objects, many mimicking much larger items, including tools and weapons. To date, the PAS has recorded about 600 of them; two-thirds are attributed to the early Roman period, though many date from the late Iron Age.

Some of these miniature objects even hark back to metalwork that was produced in the Bronze Age. At Hollingbourne, Kent, metal detectorist Mariusz Ciepluch found a lead-alloy miniature palstave (SUR-1C249A), which he donated to Maidstone Museum. Although the palstave is an axehead type that is typically Middle Bronze Age in date, no Bronze Age material was found in the immediate vicinity of his search. Instead, much of the local material culture was Iron Age, including many coins and even some dress accessories. There was also evidence of Roman occupation, again including coins, but also brooches, strap fittings and flue tiles. This suggests that the miniature palstave is also of Iron Age or Roman date.

At Nettleton, in the Lincolnshire Wolds, at least 30 miniature copper-alloy objects have been found within relatively close proximity to one another. All are believed to date to the late Iron Age or early Roman period, between 100 BCE and 100 CE, although that is now being re-evaluated, with some scholars suggesting that certain miniature weapons are more likely to be of the Late Bronze Age. The Nettleton finds were detected by Michael O'Bee in the 1970s and recorded in 2007 with Adam Daubney, then Lincolnshire FLO.

Adam remembers that he was 'flabbergasted by the discovery', as it was unusual for someone to find so many miniature objects in one area. The items included miniature axes, of which one (LIN-B1B742) seems to imitate a late Iron Age to Romano-British iron axe form, akin to a type also known in the Bronze Age. Another miniature weapon (LIN-B14EE4) was of particular interest as it is completely made in copper alloy, whereas the full-size weapon it depicts would have had a metal axehead and a wooden handle (haft). Also recovered on this site was a miniature sword blade (LIN-B0BAF5). Intriguingly this has two

BELOW The landscape around
Nettleton, Lincolnshire.

OPPOSITE Diagram comparing two
of the miniature shield fragments
to a full-size Iron Age shield.

holes along its blade, perhaps for suspension, suggesting that this object may have been worn, or (even) mounted. Another sword (LIN-B08E07) was complete, with a handle and pommel. Besides a total of four miniature swords, Michael also discovered six miniature spearheads. One (LIN-AE62A0) has a lozenge point, with the shaft formed from rolled metal; both the point and shaft are decorated with simple lines. Given that the spearheads have sockets, they could have once been mounted on miniature wooden shafts.

The most interesting finds at Nettleton, however, were 22 miniature shields, some fragmentary, all unique. One (LIN-ADC107), found in two parts, is decorated with a central circular boss, formed of a dome and two raised concentric circles surrounding it, set on a large lozenge panel. Other decoration can be seen on the shield but is much harder to make out. Intriguingly, this shield has two lozenge holes on either side of the boss, and also a small circular perforation beside one of them. These might suggest that it once had a miniature grip. Other shields have

larger piercings, which could be evidence for them having been mounted onto something else, or even being 'ritually killed'. Another of the shields (LIN-9DE863) was once hexagonal in plan with oval sides, but half the object is missing. Of interest is its decoration, which includes punch marks resembling horseshoes or torcs, or perhaps inspired by the crescent motifs on some late Iron Age coins.

RITUAL ACTIVITY

The group of miniature items found by Michael at Nettleton clearly points to a site of some significance. Julia Farley, formerly Curator of the European Iron Age at the British Museum, argues that 'a conventional interpretation of the site might be that it was a shrine or temple and that the objects were ritual offerings, but it is also important to see the finds within a wider landscape and social context'. Importantly, this site, like others where miniature objects have been found, occupies a very distinctive position in the landscape, lying on a crest at the highest point of this upland region, commanding dramatic

LIN-9DE863
Miniature shield fragment
Copper alloy
Nettleton, Lincolnshire
400 BCE–100 CE
Length: 40 mm
Width: 23 mm
Thickness: 1 mm

a. Miniature shield rim

LIN-ADC107
Miniature shield fragment
Copper alloy
Nettleton, Lincolnshire
400 BCE–100 CE
Length: 55 mm
Width: 28 mm
Thickness: 1 mm

b. Miniature central boss

The Battersea Shield
Full-size Iron Age shield found
in the River Thames and now in
the British Museum
350 BCE–50 CE
Length: 777 mm
Width: 357 mm

a. Shield rim
b. Central boss

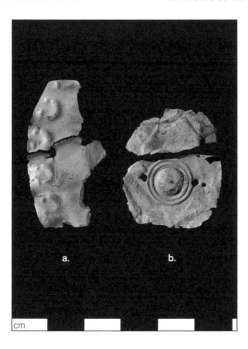

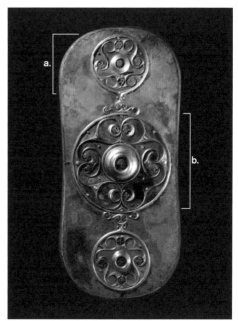

views across the surrounding landscape. Excavations at Nettleton in the 1990s revealed a series of prehistoric and early Romano-British enclosures. Led by archaeologists Steve Willis and David Dungworth, this excavation showed the area to be an important late Iron Age centre, with evidence for both settlement and ceremonial activities. Miniature objects were not recovered as part of this fieldwork, but an Early Bronze Age flat axe was found redeposited in an Iron Age context, maybe 1,000 years after the axe was made. This suggests that Iron Age people were deliberately curating and replicating earlier metalwork, intrigued by the existence of ancient objects and clearly considering them important.

Significantly, Julia believes that there were well-established traditions involving the deposition of full-sized metalwork, often weaponry, at riverine sites in some parts of Bronze Age and Iron Age Britain.

These practices predate the production and deposition of miniature metalwork in the late Iron Age which, though clearly related, are notably different. Intriguingly, in contrast to the deposition of full-size weapons, normally restricted to watery sites and graves, miniature items were often deposited close to settlements. During the late Iron Age, the nature of settlement sites was also changing, with many becoming larger or more densely inhabited. In eastern England there was a movement to new landscape zones for such 'ritual' offerings. Julia interprets the miniature weapons as symbolic representations of full-sized objects that distilled their qualities and associations, but could be employed within these changing settlement patterns affecting Iron Age society. If this is right, then the 600 or so miniature objects recorded with the PAS have great potential to help identify new sites and provide further insights into prehistoric settlements and beliefs.

LINCOLNSHIRE

LIN-B08E07
Miniature sword
Nettleton, Lincolnshire
Copper alloy
400 BCE–100 CE
Length: 49 mm
Width: 9 mm
Thickness: 3 mm

LIN-AE62A0
Miniature socketed spearhead
Copper alloy
Nettleton, Lincolnshire
400 BCE–100 CE
Length: 27 mm
Width: 8 mm
Diameter: 5 mm

LINCOLNSHIRE

LIN-B1B742
Minature socketed axehead
Nettleton, Lincolnshire
Copper alloy
1000 BCE–100 CE
Length: 21 mm
Width: 9 mm
Thickness: 6 mm

LIN-B0BAF5
Minature sword
Copper alloy
Nettleton, Lincolnshire
400 BCE–100 CE
Length: 27 mm
Width: 6 mm
Thickness: 1 mm

KENT

SUR-1C249A
Miniature palstave axehead
Hollingbourne, Kent
Lead
800 BCE–400 CE
Length: 39 mm
Width: 14 mm
Thickness: 7 mm

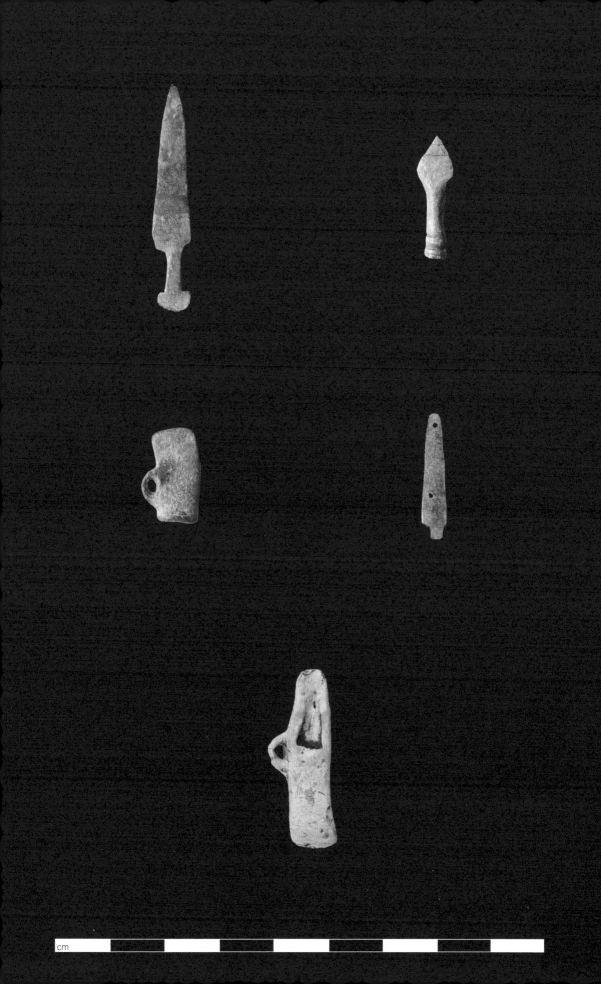

Roman

TOTAL FINDS RECORDED ON PAS DATABASE

832,116

MOST COMMON ARTEFACT TYPES ON DATABASE

coin, brooch, vessel, finger-ring, hoard

TOP 5 COUNTIES ON DATABASE

Suffolk, Norfolk, Lincolnshire, Wiltshire, Monmouthshire

PAS data as of October 2024

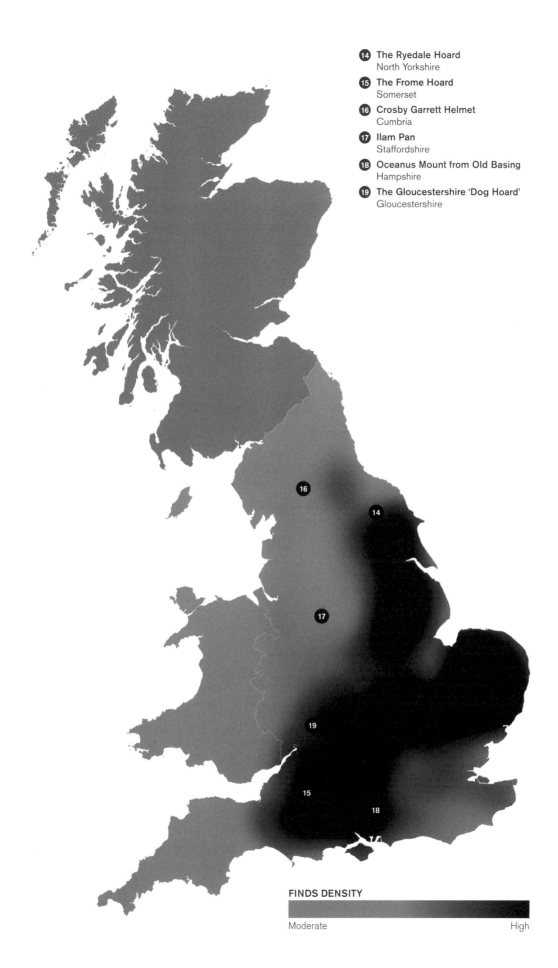

14 The Ryedale Hoard
North Yorkshire

15 The Frome Hoard
Somerset

16 Crosby Garrett Helmet
Cumbria

17 Ilam Pan
Staffordshire

18 Oceanus Mount from Old Basing
Hampshire

19 The Gloucestershire 'Dog Hoard'
Gloucestershire

FINDS DENSITY

Moderate   High

THE RYEDALE HOARD

The riddle of a strange grouping of Roman bronze sculptures and a surveyor's plumb bob

YORYM-870B0E	
OBJECT TYPE	Hoard (metalwork)
MATERIALS	Copper alloy
DATE	c. 200 CE
LOCATION	Ryedale, North Yorkshire
DISCOVERY METHOD	Metal detecting
COLLECTION	Yorkshire Museum

CONTENTS OF HOARD

sceptre-head in the form of a bust

horse and rider figurine

horse head (possible key handle)

plumb bob

Sceptre-head

HEIGHT	130 mm
WIDTH (max)	78 mm
DEPTH (max)	51 mm

Horse and rider figurine

LENGTH	74 mm
HEIGHT	87 mm
WIDTH (max)	30 mm

Horse head

LENGTH	52 mm
HEIGHT	18 mm
WIDTH	30 mm

Plumb bob

HEIGHT	73 mm
DIAMETER	41 mm

OPPOSITE The Ryedale Hoard, clockwise from top left: male bust sceptre-head; horse and rider figurine; plumb bob; horse head, probably from a key handle.

PANDEMIC DISCOVERY

In May 2020, towards the end of the first national COVID-19 lockdown, when people from different households were first permitted to mix outside again, James Spark and Mark Didlick met up to go metal detecting in Ryedale, near Ampleforth, North Yorkshire. There, roughly 20 km north of York, they made a remarkable discovery. After searching most of the day with nothing to show for it, they decided to try one last field. Within 10–15 minutes, James found 'some horsey thing'. Over a cup of tea in the field before heading home, Mark looked at the item more closely and thought it had some age to it, so they walked back to the same area to search it again more carefully. After getting a strong signal they unearthed what seemed to be a scrap of tin and put it aside. They kept digging and revealed, to their amazement, a small bust 'staring straight at them'. Then, from the same hole, they pulled out a large conical item.

James and Mark were taken aback by the strange group of finds but didn't know what to make of them or how old they were. That evening they sent photos to a friend whose father is an archaeologist; he thought that they appeared to be Roman in date. Early the next day Mark and James made another sweep of the area and located one further item, the bronze foresection of a horse figurine. Confident that little more was to be found, they contacted the Finds Liaison Officer (FLO) for North and East Yorkshire, Becky Griffiths. Becky shared the news with her manager, Andrew Woods (Senior Curator, Yorkshire Museum) and the items were deposited with Amy Downes, FLO for South and West Yorkshire, who, together with John Pearce at King's College London, undertook the initial research on them. The nature of the artefacts and the fact they were found together raised questions about both their primary uses and the reason for their deposition.

AN ECLECTIC COLLECTION

The four items are made predominantly of copper alloy, with a smooth dull-green patina. The first find – what James described as a 'horsey thing' – is actually a horse and rider figurine.

The rider, probably a representation of the god Mars, once wielded a spear with his right arm, which is raised and bent at the elbow; his left arm is held in front of him and his hand grips the horse's mane. The second and most striking find is a hollow male bust with curly hair, a slightly forked beard, oversized oval eyes (with hollow irises that would have originally been set with coloured material) and a prominent nose with wide nostrils. It appears to be a representation of a Roman emperor, probably Marcus Aurelius (r. 161–80 CE). The small bit of metal that the finders had assumed was a scrap of tin is actually a separate back plate for the bust. The third item is a solid conical plumb bob, weighing a substantial 282 g. From the flat top emerges a mushroom-shaped knop or lug, the stem and top of which are pierced with circular holes to allow suspension from a cord. The fourth piece of the hoard is thought to be the remains of a key, the handle of which is a bronze sculpture of the front of a horse with its front legs extended; an iron stub projecting from the back was probably the shaft of the key.

These are impressive pieces, very carefully and skilfully made, and with a commanding aesthetic, especially the bust of the emperor. It is reminiscent of another bronze bust found in Brackley, Northamptonshire (BERK-E24C84, now in the collection of the Ashmolean Museum), which was called Ol' Blue Eyes by the archaeologists who first studied it because of its striking blue glass irises. The size and hollow form of the Ryedale emperor bust, and the presence of a detached back plate behind the head, mean that it is most likely to have topped a sceptre or staff, suggesting a ceremonial use. A more schematic bronze bust sceptre-head, of the god Mars, was found in Wickenby, Lincolnshire (NLM-5FBEB7), in 2003, but they are quite rare pieces on the Portable Antiquities Scheme (PAS) database. The horse and rider figurine, cast in one piece, is more complete and finely executed than the majority of the 23 others recorded with the PAS (often argued to be local British representations of the god Mars), if not matching the beauty and quality of a superb two-piece version found in Cambridgeshire in 2006 (SF-99E3E4). The Ryedale Hoard is the furthest north that both a horse and rider figurine and a sceptre-head have been found. The plumb bob, a weight used in building works to define a straight vertical line, is massive compared to most of the other 41 from the Roman period recorded with the PAS, although it should be noted that a number of these are described as only 'probably' Roman in date. Exactly when the hoard was buried is uncertain, though taking the probable association of the sceptre-head with Marcus Aurelius as a guide, deposition could have occurred around 200 CE.

RITUAL ACTIVITY?

The diverse nature of the pieces of the Ryedale Hoard makes it seem unlikely that they were household possessions buried together for safekeeping. John Pearce thinks it is possible, though unlikely, that they were a collection of bronze scrap stored as potential raw material to be reused for making new pieces. However, another explanation is that they were left as part of a ritual activity. Indeed, the sceptre-head of Marcus Aurelius, probably a component of priestly regalia, recalls a much larger (950 mm tall) and more life-like hollow bust of his adoptive father Antoninus Pius (r. 138–161 CE) that was found in 1857 with other bronze artefacts in Willingham Fen, Cambridgeshire, and interpreted as a ritual deposit; it is now in the collection of the Cambridge University

BELOW The Roman bronze
Piercebridge Ploughman, found
in County Durham, shows the ritual
cutting of a furrow to mark a town
boundary. The Ryedale Hoard
may have been connected
to a similar ritual.

Museum of Archaeology and Anthropology. The Ryedale bronzes also somewhat parallel a hoard found in a pottery vessel in the early 1920s at Felmingham Hall, Norfolk, and now in the British Museum. That hoard is a collection of bronze figurines and busts representing a blend of Roman and native British deities, along with other instruments, such as a bronze rattle, with potential ceremonial function. A hollow-eyed, curly-haired bust of Jupiter in that hoard resembles the Marcus Aurelius sceptre-head from Ryedale and is roughly the same size. The Ryedale horse-handle key may have been included not because of its function but because of the equine motif, which the depositor might have felt naturally complemented the horse and rider figurine of Mars, thus pleasing that deity.

So it seems plausible that the Ryedale bronzes could have been brought together for a ritual or religious reason – but what was it? One possible answer lies in the most generic of the artefacts, the plumb bob. Martin Henig (Oxford University) suggests that 'the plumb bob was always a key object for demarcating sacred space accurately'. It is therefore possible that the findspot of the Ryedale bronzes was such a sacred space and that the burial of the bronze objects marked the dedication of a shrine. The presence of the ceremonial sceptre-head, and the horse and rider figurine that may represent Mars, support this idea. The role of plumb bobs as a component of the Roman survey instrument, the *groma*, suggests another possibility. John points out that such instruments were crucial to reorganising landscapes after Roman conquests – for example, in creating new towns or laying out new rural estates. The Roman survey process had a strongly ritualised dimension. A bronze figurine in the British Museum, known as the Piercebridge Ploughman from its 19th-century findspot at Piercebridge, County Durham, shows an unusual plough team – a bull and cow – making the ritual cutting of a furrow to form a town's new symbolic boundary. Perhaps the plumb bob

was offered to the gods to make sure that a new division of nearby countryside was pleasing to both the emperor (a quasi-divine figure) and the god Mars whose responsibilities included not only war but also defending farms and fields.

A HAPPY ENDING

For Andrew Woods, the Ryedale Hoard is of 'national significance' and especially important because most Roman collections come from urban centres, whereas this find provides insight into rural activity. However, when the Ryedale Hoard was found in 2020, it fell outside the then-current legal definition of Treasure, so the landowner and finders were able to keep all of the bronze objects and decide their fate. It was hoped that the York Museums Trust would be able to negotiate a private treaty sale, but the hoard was put in an auction and sold to a private buyer for £185,000. Thankfully a consortium of supporters led by American benefactor Rick Beleson, the Art Fund and other private donors, helped to finance the sale of the pieces from the private buyer to York Museums Trust, and the hoard eventually went on display at the Yorkshire Museum. For their part, finders Mark and James were very happy to see the material safe in a public collection.

In an innovative exhibit, the museum introduced the public to the mystery of the burial of the hoard, presenting the different scenarios for the assemblage and deposit of the items and inviting visitors to decide which was most likely. Andrew has been impressed by the popularity of this display and is looking forward to continuing to learn more about these enigmatic objects. He is grateful that their acquisition by the museum means they will be seen by millions of visitors for decades to come. The discovery has permeated the arts throughout the local area; Mark relates how his daughter's school uses the story of the Ryedale Hoard in their spelling lessons. It illustrates that the discovery and museum acquisition of important archaeological material are not the end, but the beginning.

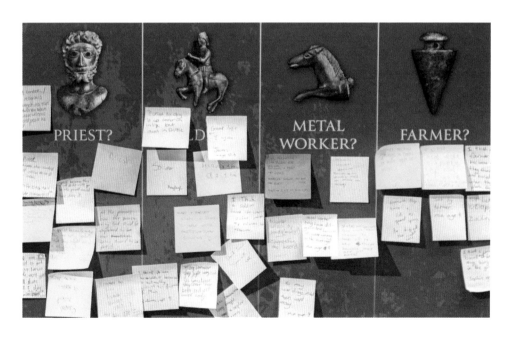

THE FROME HOARD

'A massive find changes everything.'
SAM MOORHEAD, PAS NATIONAL FINDS ADVISER

SOM-5B9453

OBJECT TYPE Hoard (coins)

MATERIALS Copper-alloy and silver (coins); earthenware (vessel)

DATE post *c.* 290 CE

LOCATION Frome, Somerset

DISCOVERY METHOD Metal detecting

COLLECTION South West Heritage Trust (Museum of Somerset)

CONTENTS OF HOARD

52,498 copper-alloy coins

5 silver *denarii*

Black-burnished ware vessel

ROMAN COINS AND HOARDING

The most commonly recorded artefacts on the PAS database are Roman coins. They were produced and deposited in huge quantities in antiquity, and therefore have been recovered subsequently through metal detecting in large numbers, making them important pieces of information in the archaeological record. Under the pre-1997 common law of Treasure Trove, for finds to be classed as Treasure there had to be a reason to believe that they had been hidden with the deliberate intention of future recovery. Coin hoards from all periods were seen as obvious examples of this practice, put in the ground for safekeeping and for some reason (displacement, death, forgetfulness) never recovered by their original owners. But sometimes, as Sam Moorhead (former PAS National Finds Adviser for Iron Age and Roman coins) argues, the discovery of a massive hoard, like the Frome Hoard, 'changes everything'.

AN OPERATION ON AN INDUSTRIAL SCALE

In April 2010, Dave Crisp was searching a field near Frome, Somerset, with his metal detector when he received an 'iffy' signal. It was in the same area where he had found some late Roman silver *siliquae* from an unrelated scattered hoard two days earlier, so he had reason to be hopeful that something similar would turn up. He opened the ground with his spade and reached into the hole. After digging a considerable depth, he began to find sherds of pottery and a few corroded bronze Roman coins. It was at this point that he took the crucial step of stopping digging and calling for assistance. He filled in the hole and placed a horseshoe under the turf (to assist in relocating it later) before taking careful note of the findspot. He then contacted his local FLO, Katie Hinds (based in Wiltshire). Dave's actions are a prime example of a detectorist following best practice, enabling the important archaeological work on the hoard that followed.

Katie swiftly contacted the Somerset FLO, Anna Booth, and together they visited the site with county archaeologist Bob Croft and local archaeologist Alan Graham, who would

OPPOSITE Archaeologist Alan Graham excavating the Frome Hoard.

Below The pot, already broken, was dismantled in situ so archaeologists could excavate the coins in layers.

Below The coins in the hoard, all copper alloy except for five silver *denarii*, date from the latter half of the 3rd century, a time of upheaval in the Roman Empire.

thereafter lead the excavation. Over three days, with the help of volunteers and Dave himself, they peeled back the earth to reveal a massive black ceramic vessel filled to the brim with coins. Already damaged by compaction from tractors, and much too heavy to lift out of the ground without collapsing on itself, the pot was carefully taken apart and the hoard was excavated in layers over two days. The contents of each layer were bagged separately and boxed for transport to the British Museum by Sam and Roger Bland, then head of the PAS.

Once the hoard was at the British Museum, conservator Pippa Pearce galvanised her colleagues to undertake a massive cleaning operation. The coins were all given an initial wash and dry that allowed the majority to be identified for the Treasure process, which stipulates that items should be valued in the condition in which they were found. After that, Sam, Roger and colleagues Richard Abdy and Eleanor Ghey in the Department of Coins and Medals at the British Museum sorted through the coins, separating them by emperor according to excavation layer, to enable the report for the coroner to be written. They determined that there were approximately 52,500 coins in the hoard, making it the second-

largest Roman coin hoard from Britain, and the largest ever found within a single pot!

The state of preservation of the coins varied depending on where they were in the pot – those at the bottom had been below the water table and were heavily corroded – and whether they were debased silver (made predominantly of copper alloy, as the vast majority were) or good silver. The hoard was declared Treasure and acquired by the Museum of Somerset as the result of a major fundraising campaign led by Steve Minnitt, then Head of Museums at the South West Heritage Trust. It then became important to produce a detailed catalogue of the coins and so the British Museum's conservation department undertook further work to prepare them for full recording. This sounds simple enough, but it took two conservators working full-time for a year and a half, with additional assistance from all the Museum's other metal conservators, to complete around three-fifths of the hoard (*c.* 30,000 coins). The base metal coins had a high degree of corrosion that was best tackled through a combination of precisely timed and formulated acid baths and mechanical cleaning under the microscope (not to be tried at home, as any miscalculation can destroy an object!). This was critical work because it allowed enough of the corrosion to be removed to make many of the previously illegible coins decipherable.

CARAUSIUS AND CRISIS

The earliest coins in the Frome Hoard are debased silver radiates, so called for the type of crown (known as a radiate) worn by the emperors depicted on the coins, of the 250s–60s CE, particularly those from the reigns of Valerian I (253–60), Gallienus (253–68) and Claudius II Gothicus (268–70). During the 3rd century, the Roman Empire experienced upheaval that saw the creation of a breakaway 'Gallic Empire' focused on the western provinces of Gaul and Britain between 260 and 274 CE. The largest groups of coins within the hoard are from this period, with over 9,300 radiates of Victorinus (269–71) and more than 23,000 for Tetricus I (271–74) and his son Tetricus II (272–74).

A later period of usurpation saw Carausius (286–93) and his successor Allectus (293–96) seize power in Britain before the province was returned to Roman control by the future emperor Constantius I (293–306) in 296 CE. The latest coins in the hoard are of Carausius, with 854 identified examples that include five silver *denarii* (the only good silver coins in the hoard). This is the largest number of Carausian coins known from any hoard to date. Importantly, they indicate that the hoard could not have been buried before Carausius' reign – indeed, the latest coins date to only midway through his reign, *c.* 290/91 CE. It is therefore plausible that the Frome Hoard was buried for safekeeping by an individual in Somerset, a prosperous grain-producing region, to protect their wealth at a time of unrest.

A SACRED SPRING

The physical arrangement of the Frome Hoard tells a different story, however. The pot was so large that it would have been impossible to carry it full of coins without the vessel walls breaking from the weight, so it must have been placed in the ground first and the coins added afterwards. If it had been a savings pot, a kind of 'piggy-bank', you might expect to see the oldest coins towards the bottom and the most

BELOW Finder Dave Crisp assisting with the excavation of the hoard, checking for any stray coins left behind in the hole.

BELOW Sam Moorhead, former PAS National Finds Adviser for Iron Age and Roman coins, and television presenter Alice Roberts examining coins from the hoard.

recent ones towards the top as the pot was gradually filled. This is not the case: the coins are extensively mixed, with the Gallic coinages comprising approximately two-thirds of each layer. The majority of Carausius' coinage was located at the centre of the vessel, and his silver *denarii* were seemingly positioned deliberately with the last additions at the top of the hoard. This suggests that the coins were deposited in a single act, probably from multiple containers, and that the Carausius coinage was added halfway through the process.

Furthermore, examination of the findspot revealed that the hoard had been deposited on boggy ground close to an ancient watercourse and spring – wet enough that in more recent times the landowner had installed drains to keep the land dry for agricultural use. This led Sam and Roger to wonder whether the pot of coins had been a votive offering to the gods, deposited by a group of people or the wider local community. Britain has many deposits of metalwork from the Bronze Age, Iron Age and Roman periods that seem to have been ritually

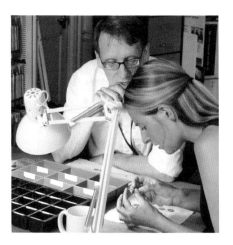

placed in watery areas (see the Shropshire Sun Pendant, pp. 46–51). Is the Frome Hoard another form of this practice?

Increasingly, evidence suggests that this may be the case. Andrew Brown (National Finds Adviser for Iron Age and Roman coins at the British Museum) is creating a detailed catalogue of the coins, helping to confirm the initial observations of the composition and stratigraphy of the hoard. Frome 'changes everything' not just because of the sheer scale of the finds, but because it has helped to inform the processes that archaeologists follow in discovery, excavation and conservation of similar hoarded assemblages, interpreting them beyond simple stores of monetary wealth.

None of this would have been possible had Dave Crisp not followed best practice and stopped digging when he did. His actions were a high-profile example to other detectorists of the benefits of waiting for archaeological support when an important hoard or artefact is located in the ground. Since the discovery of the Frome Hoard, many more hoards have been left by detectorists in situ for archaeologists to excavate, or removed intact in their original container for micro-excavation in a conservation laboratory.

BELOW The hoard included many coins of Carausius (r. 286–93), who broke Britain away from the Roman Empire, but it may have been a votive offering rather than personal wealth hidden during political unrest.

BOTTOM Frome, Somerset, was a proseperous grain-producing region in the 3rd century CE.

CROSBY GARRETT HELMET

'Nothing could be more chillingly evocative of the ruthless power of the Roman army than to meet the gaze of the mask's immobile human face.'

RALPH JACKSON, BRITISH MUSEUM

LANCUM-E48D73

OBJECT TYPE Cavalry helmet

MATERIALS Copper alloy

DATE 3rd century CE

LOCATION Crosby Garrett, Cumbria

DISCOVERY METHOD Metal detecting

HEIGHT 407 mm (base of chin to top of griffin)

WIDTH 225 mm

DEPTH 263 mm (tip of the nose to the back of the helmet)

OPPOSITE The Roman cavalry parade helmet probably depicts a Trojan wearing a Phrygian cap.

BELOW Detail of the griffin mount on the peak of the helmet. The empty mount below the vase may have held a gemstone.

A MOMENTOUS FIND

The word 'treasure' has two meanings. It can describe artefacts in the general sense – as rare, irreplaceable, expertly made or aesthetically appealing – or (usually capitalised as Treasure) it can refer to a very specific legal category of archaeological find that can be claimed by the British state. Confusingly, an item can be 'treasure' in one sense of the word, but not the other. Some nationally important finds have fallen outside the legal definition, leaving them unprotected. The Crosby Garrett Helmet was the preeminent recent example of this.

The copper-alloy Roman helmet was discovered in May 2010 by a father-and-son team of metal detectorists (who wish to remain anonymous) in eastern Cumbria – a surprise find, after they had searched the area nearby with very little to show for their efforts. It was unearthed in several pieces: the nearly intact visor (face-mask) was lying face-down, with the crumpled bowl of the helmet lying inside, and at least 68 other fragments scattered around it, including a griffin figurine. The helmet was obviously something incredibly special but since it was not precious metal, it fell outside what was then the legal definition of Treasure, so its fate was now in the hands of the landowner and finders. Quite early on it was evident that there was an intention to sell it. Luckily, under the condition of confidentiality, the landowner allowed for a geophysical survey and excavation of the findspot. This was organised by Stuart Noon, then FLO for Lancashire and Cumbria. The excavation revealed a few further scraps of metal likely to be from the helmet, some 4th-century CE coins and late Roman ceramics, but it was difficult to interpret the stratigraphy of the helmet's burial because the ground had been disturbed too much during its removal. The geophysical survey showed that the area was a rural settlement that had most likely been in use during both the late Iron Age and Roman periods.

The owners of the helmet made contact with the auction house Christie's which agreed to offer it for sale. Sally Worrell (National Finds Adviser for Roman and Iron Age artefacts for the Portable Antiquities Scheme) and Ralph Jackson (former

Curator of Romano-British collections at the British Museum, who has sadly now passed away) were shown the discovery by the finders and were able to photograph and record the pieces quickly before they were taken away. Before the auction, Christie's organised the helmet's restoration by a metalworker using hand tools. The pieces were tacked together in such a way that the joins were visible (so as not to give the appearance that the helmet was found undamaged), but other empty areas required filling in with fresh metal. This reconstruction went beyond normal museum practice for the presentation of fractured pieces, and it also restricted the opportunity for longer-term in-depth scrutiny of the pieces in a lab setting, which might have revealed more about the origins, construction and use of the helmet.

As the date of the auction approached, Tullie museum in Carlisle mounted an unprecedented campaign of fundraising and public appeals to be in a position to buy it, eventually raising £1.7 million, much of it from public subscriptions. The museum approached members of the antiquities trade in an attempt to arrange a private sale, but the owners were determined that the auction should go ahead. Ultimately the helmet was sold at to a private buyer for £2.33 million in October 2010.

DESIGNED TO DAZZLE

The helmet is an example of a headpiece worn during cavalry demonstrations or games, and was not designed to be used in battle. The complete helmet was made in three pieces: a face-mask (visor) which would have covered the entire face of the wearer, the bowl, and the griffin figurine on its peak. Before it was sold, PhD student Ruth Fillery-Travis was allowed brief access to the helmet and conducted an X-ray fluorescence test of the pieces using a handheld scanner, revealing that most of it was 82% copper, 10% zinc and 8% tin, and that the face-mask had a tin wash. The griffin, however, was 68% copper, 18% tin, 10% lead, and 4% zinc, showing that it had been made separately.

The face-mask has a hauntingly realistic and androgynous, almost feminine appearance. The tin-washing on the face would have provided a striking contrast to the luscious curls of yellowy bronze hair framing it, and to the bowl with its tall 'Phrygian' (or soft-peaked) cap. The bowl is connected to the face-mask via a hinge at the base of the front, held in place by two rivets decorated with a concentric circle design. At the back, a row of moulded bronze hair-curls escapes from the cap at the base of the neck.

The griffin (a mythological beast, half-eagle and half-lion) sits on a curved mount, fixed to the peak of the helmet. One of its front paws

BELOW The Ribchester parade helmet, found in Lancashire in 1796 and now in the British Museum.

OVERLEAF Eastern Cumbria, the region where the helmet was found. Cumbria was difficult terrain for the Roman soldiers stationed there.

rests on a two-handed jar (*kantharos*) above an empty setting that most likely would have featured a jewel. An incised flower motif appears at the centre of the rear of the bowl, and a smaller flower motif is on either side of the griffin.

Roman military archaeologist Mike Bishop posits that the helmet is meant to be a representation of a Trojan, and that features such as the decoration on the rivets point to a date of manufacture in the 3rd century CE.

PRESERVING THE PAST

Examples of this type of helmet are known from both Europe and the Middle East. In Britain, however, the only closely comparable finds are the Ribchester Helmet, found in Lancashire in 1796 and now in the British Museum, and a group of more fragmentary parade helmets from Newstead, Roxburghshire, found in 1905 and now in National Museums Scotland. These examples are dated to the late 1st or early 2nd century CE; the Crosby Garrett Helmet is the only 3rd-century helmet that has been found in Britain. Its intricate detail and striking countenance convey the time and investment that the Romans put into military demonstrations and sporting events, even on the fringes of its empire. In Ralph's view, 'In its completeness and its iconography, it is one of the finest surviving cavalry sports helmets from the Roman world. But more than that, it is a face from the past, and nothing could be more chillingly evocative of the ruthless power of the Roman army than to meet the gaze of the mask's immobile human face.'

Thankfully, the owner of the Crosby Garrett Helmet has allowed it to go on public show on several occasions, including in the 'Bronze' exhibition at the Royal Academy in 2012, at Tullie in 2013, at the British Museum alongside the Ribchester Helmet in 2014, and again in the British Museum 'Legion' exhibition in 2024. But the fact remains that it is not in a public collection, and therefore not avalible for everyone to see whenever they like.

The public outcry about the fate of the Crosby Garrett Helmet proved to be the catalyst that convinced the UK government to expand the definition of Treasure to better protect important discoveries of this calibre. In 2023 the UK Arts Minister Lord Parkinson signed into force new legislation that introduced a new 'significance-based' class of Treasure for finds that are more than 200 years old, made of metal and provide 'exceptional insight' into an aspect of national or regional history, archaeology or culture. Perhaps this is the greatest legacy of the Crosby Garrett Helmet: that future finds of its importance will now be given the protection they need to become part of public collections and available to all.

ILAM PAN

'If the vessel was made for Draco, perhaps it was some sort of retirement gift. It seems likely that he was in the Roman army and certainly knew Hadrian's Wall very well – especially if he helped build it!'

SALLY WORRELL, PAS NATIONAL FINDS ADVISER

WMID-3FE965	
OBJECT TYPE Vessel	
MATERIALS Copper alloy with enamel	
DATE 2nd century CE	
LOCATION Ilam, Staffordshire	
DISCOVERY METHOD Metal detecting	
COLLECTION British Museum, Tullie and the Potteries Museum	
HEIGHT 47 mm	
DIAMETER 90 mm	
THICKNESS 2 mm	

OPPOSITE The Ilam Pan is missing its handle and base but is otherwise intact.

BELOW Part of the dedicatory inscription to a person named Aelius Draco, with enamelled 'Celtic-style' curvilinear decoration.

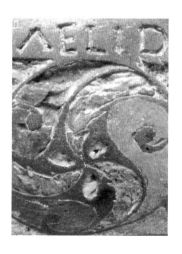

DISCOVERY

In June 2003, Kevin Blackburn was metal detecting with Julian Lee near Ilam, Staffordshire, when he came across an important Roman object. Kevin took his find to Birmingham Museum, where it was subsequently studied and recorded by Sally Worrell (PAS National Finds Adviser for Prehistoric and Roman Objects) with the help of other experts. They identified the 'Staffordshire Moorlands Pan' (later known as the Ilam Pan) as a type of Roman handled vessel sometimes called a *patera* or *trulla*.

This is not the only example recorded with the PAS. Another interesting group of Roman pans (WILT-92B052) was subsequently found at Kingston Deverill, Wiltshire, in February 2005. This group consisted of three larger pans and two wine strainers discovered by detectorist Paul Bancroft, who reported the find to Katie Hinds, the local FLO, but left the vessels in situ, thus preserving crucial contextual information; the hoard was subsequently excavated by Wessex Archaeology. One of the pans was stamped 'P.CIPI.POLIBI', for Publius Cipius Polibius, a well-known maker of such vessels in Capua, close to modern Naples and the Roman city of Pompeii, at the end of the 1st century CE, thus helping to date the find. This vessel (now in the Salisbury Museum with the rest of the hoard) was used to heat liquids, while the strainers were used to remove sediment from wine.

A UNIQUE PAN

All that survives of the Ilam Pan is its copper-alloy bowl; the pan's handle, which probably would have been of flat 'bow-tie' form, and base are missing. The distorted body of the vessel has a gentle convex form, with a slightly turned-out, rounded-edged, rim at the top and a raised 'foot-ring' stand at its base. Traces of solder survive where the handle and base would have been fixed to the body. The bowl of the pan is beautifully decorated with 'Celtic-style' curvilinear ornament, consisting of eight roundels in turquoise and blue enamel, enclosing swirling six-armed 'whirligigs' centred on a three-petalled motif, inlaid with alternating yellow, red and possibly purple

BELOW Fragment of a similar Roman pan with an enamelled inscription naming forts along Hadrian's Wall; it was found by a detectorist in Basildon, Essex, ESS-5945F8.

BELOW Finders Julian Lee and Kevin Blackburn with the Ilam Pan.

enamel. Between the roundels are eight pairs of hollow-sided triangles inlaid with either red or turquoise enamel. Much of the enamelling survives, which would have looked spectacular, albeit quite gaudy to the modern eye, against the original golden colour of the metal. The Ilam Pan might have been a dipper or ladle, or even a drinking cup; the presence of enamel suggests that it was not for heating, straining and infusing as in the case of the Kingston Deverill pans.

What makes the Ilam Pan so special, however, is its unbroken and unpunctuated engraved inscription of 56 letters inlaid with turquoise enamel. This inscription lists four forts, located in the western part of Hadrian's Wall: Bowness (MAIS), Drumburgh (COGGABATA), Stanwix (VXELODVNVM) and Castlesteads (CAMMOGLANNA). Intriguingly, the fort of Burgh-by-Sands (*Aballava*), which is located between Drumburgh and Stanwix, is not named. The pan's inscription also incorporates the name of an individual, 'AELI DRACONIS', preceded by the words 'RIGORE VALI', although experts disagree on whether 'AELI' is part of Draco's name or not. It is not clear whether the words 'RIGORE VALI AELI DRACONIS' come before the name of the forts or after. In short, the inscription on the Ilam Pan has generated lots of debate among archaeologists and historians.

A RETIREMENT GIFT?

It is now thought that 'RIGORE VALI' may be translated as 'the line of the wall', which makes sense since the pan names forts on Hadrian's Wall. Furthermore, Aelius Draco might be the surveyor of the Wall himself, and perhaps the vessel was even made for him. Roman specialists David Breeze and Christof Flügel have recently proposed that the pan's inscription translates as 'The line of the wall, (the work of) Aelius Draco, was drawn from *Maia* [an alternative Roman place-name for *Mais*] to *Coggabata*, (from there) to *Uxelodunum* (and from there) to *Cammoglanna*', and also that the pan could have been made at Carlisle between approximately 122 and 140 CE. Draco is an uncommon Roman name of Greek origin, which suggests that this individual came from the Greek-speaking part of the eastern Roman Empire. Sally thinks 'If the vessel was made for Draco, perhaps it was some sort of retirement gift. It seems likely that he was in the Roman army and certainly knew Hadrian's Wall very well – especially if he helped build it!'

Only three other vessels with similar inscriptions naming forts on Hadrian's Wall are known. One is the Rudge Cup (on display at Alnwick Castle), which was discovered near Froxfield, Wiltshire, in 1725, down the well of a Roman villa. Another pan, now in the Musée de Picardie, was discovered in Amiens, France,

BELOW Complete Roman pans with
intact base and handle (left and
right) in the Kingston Deverill Hoard,
discovered by detectorist Paul
Bancroft in Wiltshire in 2005.

OVERLEAF Ruins of Hadrian's
Wall near Sycamore Gap in
Northumberland.

in 1949. A further fragment, from Basildon, Essex (ESS-5945F8), was recorded by the PAS in 2016. Between them, the pans name seven forts, but the Ilam Pan is the first to include Drumburgh and is the only example to name an individual as well. Also intriguing is that the Ilam Pan celebrates a symbol of Roman conquest (Hadrian's Wall) juxtaposed with a local decorative style (curvilinear motifs and enamels). It is a classic example of the Roman army in Britain appropriating local craft skills and artistic styles.

How the Ilam Pan came to be in the ground is a mystery, but the circumstances around the deposition of the Kingston Deverill Hoard may give a clue. The archaeological excavation of the Kingston Deverill findspot showed that the hoard had been buried deliberately. A nearby Romano-British temple on Cold Kitchen Hill, a place perhaps marking the border between two Iron Age tribes – the Belgae to the north and the Durotriges to the south –

might suggest that the hoard was buried as an offering to the gods. Similarly, the Ilam Pan is from a landscape setting with possible ritual significance, near where the River Manifold rises from an underground stream, and where other possible votive offerings have been found. Alternatively, since the Kingston Deverill Hoard was found close to a Roman road, this could indicate that it was buried for safekeeping by someone travelling on that road who never came back for it. Whatever the case, it is possible that both finds were deposited by individuals connected with the Roman army and that therefore such pans, by association, have a military connection.

At the time it was found, the Ilam Pan did not meet the legal definition of Treasure, so it was by no means certain that it would end up in a museum for all to enjoy. Thankfully, however, it is now shared by the British Museum with Tullie in Carlisle and the Potteries Museum in Stoke-on-Trent.

OCEANUS MOUNT FROM OLD BASING

Depicting the god Oceanus – a Titan and embodiment of the world ocean – this is one of the finest pieces of figural bronze work from Roman Britain

SUR-77CBD4	
OBJECT TYPE Furniture fitting	
MATERIALS Copper alloy	
DATE 1st century CE	
LOCATION Old Basing, Hampshire	
DISCOVERY METHOD Metal detecting	
COLLECTION British Museum	
LENGTH 119 mm	
WIDTH 90 mm	

OPPOSITE The face of the god Oceanus on what was probably a Roman furniture fitting.

BELOW Finder Rossen Iantchev's photo of the fitting when he unearthed it on a metal-detecting club outing.

A FACE FROM THE PAST

It is remarkable when an artefact is unearthed so well preserved that it seems to have been 'made yesterday'. Finds with special resonance are those featuring human faces, which seem to come to life as they stare back at a viewer for the first time in hundreds or thousands of years. The Oceanus mount from Old Basing is striking for both reasons: well-preserved despite being copper alloy, and incorporating a richly detailed face of a Roman god. It was discovered by Rossen Iantchev, who moved to the UK in the late 1990s from Bulgaria and took up metal detecting in 2019. Ross found the mount on an outing of the Soil Searchers metal-detecting club near Basingstoke in superb September weather in 2020. He described how, after finding a silver *denarius* below the surface, he waved his detector in the hole before backfilling it and got another signal. Figuring it was another coin, he dug further down, cleared away some loose soil and then 'saw an amazing bearded face looking back' at him. After getting assistance from a fellow detectorist to lift it out carefully, Ross contacted Simon Maslin (FLO for Surrey) and brought the object to him for recording. It was such an interesting and unusual piece that Simon was keen to consult with colleagues, including John Pearce at King's College London who helped to confirm that the fitting was a survivor from the Roman world.

MYSTERIOUS FUNCTION

The object is a teardrop-shaped convex mount or appliqué; its bearded face in moulded high relief measures 90 mm high by 70 mm wide. Because the piece is so well-preserved, it is possible to see all of the original details of the decoration, allowing it to be identified as the Greco-Roman divinity Oceanus. The wide-open eyes stare straight outward, with hollowed pupils that may once have held a gemstone or other colourful material. Seaweed fronds represent the god's moustache, beard and eyebrows, and extend in an extra line from the corners of the nose to below the ears, creating a mask-like effect. Among the voluminous locks of the head hair are two sea creatures

BELOW Emperor Carausius, a former naval commander, issued coins in late 3rd-century Britain with Oceanus depicted on the reverse.

BELOW Detail of Oceanus on a Bacchic platter from the 4th-century Mildenhall Hoard.

rising like horns, but they are missing just enough detail to be entirely sure what they are – different representations of Oceanus show a variety of animals coming from his head. Behind the ears, dolphins are swimming down in the direction of the chin.

Attached horizontally at the back of the mount is a strip of copper alloy, about 120 mm long and broken at both ends; it is decorated with an incised swirling foliate pattern inlaid with white metal. The strip was part of a larger object, but it is not certain what that object was. Classical archaeologist Norbert Franken at Johannes Gutenberg-Universität, Mainz, suggests that the mount may not originally have been designed to be fixed onto the strip, given that it obscures the strip's decoration. Richard Hobbs, Curator of Romano-British Collections at the British Museum, consulted with several experts about what the fitting might originally have been attached to, and believes that it could have adorned an item of furniture, such as a washstand.

DECORATION WITH MEANING

In ancient Greek mythology, Oceanus was one of the Titans (the pre-Olympian gods), among the few who kept his freedom after Zeus and the Olympian gods overthrew Chronos and took power as the ruling pantheon. As the name suggests, Oceanus was the embodiment of the world ocean beyond the Pillars of Hercules (the Straits of Gibraltar) and was believed to encircle all of the inhabited world.

The Romans were great borrowers of the beliefs and artistic traditions of other peoples, and famously adopted the Greek gods into their theology. As a representation of an elemental force, Oceanus' image appears in many different contexts across the Roman Empire, including on coins and mosaics. The image of Oceanus resonated particularly strongly in the Roman concept of Britain, given its separation from the rest of the empire by the English Channel and North Sea, themselves parts of that world ocean. Certainly for Carausius (r. 286–93) – the former naval commander who formed a breakaway empire based in Britain

BELOW Oceanus depicted on the
4th-century mosaic from Withington,
Gloucestershire.

and, possibly with the assistance of stormy weather in the Channel, defeated an invasion force assembled by Emperor Maximian – Oceanus was a force to keep on side, as shown on some of his coins.

One of the most striking depictions of Oceanus from Roman Britain is as the central figure of the silver Bacchic platter from the Mildenhall Hoard, a collection of 34 pieces of silver tableware found by a farm labourer in Suffolk in 1942 and now in the British Museum. That hoard is dated to the second half of the 4th century CE and the Oceanus figure on the platter, like the Old Basing mount, features dolphins emerging from his beard, at either side of his chin, and in place of his ears. Although the Old Basing mount is thought to be several hundred years older, it makes for a fitting complement to the Mildenhall Hoard. When the Oceanus mount was acquired by the British Museum in 2021 it was therefore put on display in the same case as the Mildenhall objects, behind the platter.

Martin Henig, professor of archaeology at Oxford University, has suggested that the mount from Old Basing was made in the 1st century CE, given its comparable quality to bronzes from Campania, noting also an Oceanus-influenced temple pediment at Bath of similar date. He also drew a parallel with a bronze plaque with a Maenad (in Greek mythology, a female follower of Dionysus) in high relief and with silver eyes, found in Pompeii and published by John Ward-Perkins and Amanda Claridge in their catalogue for the 1976–77 Royal Academy exhibition 'Pompeii AD 79'.

But the fitting really stands out because of its craftsmanship. Martin believes it is one of the very finest pieces of figural bronze work from the earlier centuries of Roman Britain. He compares it in quality to an *askos* (pitcher-like flask) handle of Flavian date (69–96 CE) that features an exceptionally fine satyr head, from Alec Down's excavation of Fishbourne Roman Palace in Sussex.

Thankfully the Old Basing mount has survived in remarkable condition for almost 2,000 years. It is now available on display in the British Museum for the appreciation of all.

THE GLOUCESTERSHIRE 'DOG HOARD'

A mysterious buried cache of hundreds of pieces of Roman metalwork and bronze sculptures, nearly all broken – perhaps deliberately so

GLO-BE1187	
OBJECT TYPE	Hoard (metalwork)
MATERIALS	Copper alloy
DATE	4th century CE
LOCATION	Gloucestershire
DISCOVERY METHOD	Metal detecting

CONTENTS OF HOARD
1 complete dog figurine
20 fragments of hollow-cast statue
1 dodecahedron fragment
1 folding skillet-handle fragment
1 face with curly hair (from a vessel?)
1 face of a figurine
2 animal paws (feet from chests or boxes?)
2 fragments of a thick copper-alloy box
3 escutcheons or mounts (lion-head, human-head and bull's-head)
1 circular escutcheon with notches
4 fragments of an inscribed plaque
1 possible vessel handle terminal
3 bracelet fragments
1 possible tweezers fragment
4 chest or box handles
1 D-shaped buckle
3 domed sheet copper-alloy items
1 furniture fitting with large ovoid foot
10 bell-shaped casket mounts
25 cup or bell-shaped furniture studs
1 disc-shaped furniture fitting
1 hinge
1 spoon
1 coin of Crispus, minted Trier, 321–24 CE
4 fragments of copper-alloy slag
Sheet copper-alloy vessel, box and furniture fragments, all folded

OPPOSITE The complete dog figurine from the hoard.

REMARKABLE DISCOVERY

One Sunday in August 2017, metal detectorists Pete Cresswell and his brother-in-law Andrew Boughton made a remarkable discovery: a cache of hundreds of pieces of Roman metalwork, totalling over 5 kg in weight and nearly all broken, perhaps deliberately so. The hoard was found undisturbed, with the objects seemingly deposited within specific layers. This suggested to archaeologists Penny Coombe and Martin Henig (who wrote about them in the journal *Britannia*) that some pre-depositional sorting might have occurred. The objects had been buried in a pit, probably in a bag of organic materials that had since decomposed. Sadly, much of the hoard's archaeological context was lost in the process of it being dug up. Nevertheless, the finders soon realised the significance of what they had found and contacted Kurt Adams, their local FLO. Kurt, impressed by the nature of the find, took it in to be recorded on the PAS database. The hoard did not qualify as Treasure, so there was no obligation to report the discovery and therefore no certain route by which the objects might have been acquired by a museum.

BROKEN FINDS

The hoard contained many items, but the stand-out piece is a stylised dog figurine, elongated and in standing pose. The figurine is sometimes referred to as 'the licking dog', since its tongue protrudes from its mouth as if the animal is panting. Its head is notably large and tilted upwards as if to receive the attention of its owner, and its large ears point forward, bringing the figurine to life. The shoulders of the animal are decorated with a panel containing rows of half-ovals, each infilled with a series of chevrons bisected by a central vertical line, giving the appearance of leaves or feathers. According to John Pearce, professor of Roman archaeology at King's College London, this stylisation of its features gives the dog an affinity with other Romano-British art, which draws on Iron Age precursors. Otherwise, decoration is limited to picking out

BELOW A complete Roman
dodecahedron, found in
Much Hadham, Hertfordshire,
BH-692011. The function of
these dodecahedrons is still
a mystery to archaeologists.

OPPOSITE Some interesting
fragmentary copper-alloy items
from the hoard, clockwise from
top left: dodecahedron, human
face, inscribed plaque, bull's-head
escutcheon and draped bearskin.

certain features, like its eyes, mouth and paws.
The dog has drilled holes in both its front paws,
presumably to attach it to a base. Whether it
was displayed on a stand, or something else
(for instance, a piece of furniture), remains
uncertain, as does its relationship to the
other objects in the hoard, most of which are
too fragmentary to determine their original
function. Close to the dog's shoulder decoration
are another two holes (one on each side) that
could have been for attaching the object to
other figures, so they could stand together on a
base. On the underside, in the area of the dog's
stomach, there is a large square opening, of
unknown purpose.

Twenty fragments from other large bronze
statues were found with the dog. Penny and
Martin describe them as important additions
to the corpus of large bronzes from Roman
Britain. They include fragments from a life-
size statue of the goddess Diana hunting; it
is possible that the dog was one of Diana's
hunting hounds in the same piece or group.
Another fragment depicts a draped bearskin;
this was likely part of a support for the Diana

statue, rather than worn by the goddess herself,
and in John's view one of the most vivid
surviving images after the dog, because it is
of an opposing art tradition, looking to the
Classical world rather than the Celtic Iron Age
past. Also found was a fragment of a human
face, showing one side of the head and an eye,
and another with an eye that looks like it is a
representation of an animal, possibly another
dog. Further fragments included part of a
dodecahedron (an item of unclear function,
though not unheard of among metal-detecting
finds), part of a skillet handle, and an animal
paw, which is probably the foot from a chest or
box. Indeed, fragments from a thick copper-
alloy box were also retrieved, as well as four
handles. Escutcheons (or furniture mounts)
in the form of a bull's head, a lion's head and
a human head were also found, and another
that was circular. Other furniture fragments
included a foot and leg, a large ovoid foot,
studs, a hinge and many fragments of metal
plate, some decorated, others not. John thinks
that four fragments of an inscribed plaque
reading '[…]V[?]MCONLA[…]' could be
from a statue base or even a chest, though its
inscription is hard to decipher: it might refer
to the collection of money by a corporate body
(a *conlatio*). Also found were items associated
with personal adornment, including bracelet
fragments and a D-shaped buckle, and some
possible tweezers.

On the surface of it, the hoard represents
an eclectic group of objects. It could be
either a cache of scrap materials from many
sources or a collection that has been more
carefully curated. Included within the hoard
was a copper-alloy *follis* of Crispus, dated to
321–24 CE and minted in Trier. This coin,
along with other items in the hoard, suggests
a burial date in the last three-quarters of the
4th century CE.

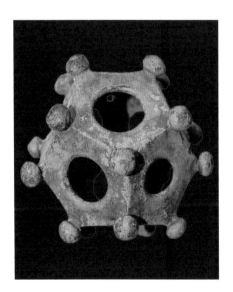

BELOW Remains of the late 3rd-/ early 4th-century Lydney Park temple complex in Gloucestershire.

BELOW The hoard contained twenty fragments of a hollow-cast statue. They could be from a temple votive sculpture that was intentionally smashed when the local inhabitants converted to Christianity.

LICKING DOGS

For Kurt, the dog figurine was the 'most amazing' item within the hoard and 'a unique discovery for British archaeology'. In the Classical world dogs were sometimes believed to be able to cure human ailments. From the 5th century BCE onwards, pilgrims flocked to healing temples associated with the Greek god Asclepius, such as one at Epidaurus, where dogs were kept to lick the affected parts of afflicted people. At the late 3rd-/early 4th-century Roman temple complex at Lydney Park, Gloucestershire – that is, in the same region and roughly of the same era as the Dog Hoard – representations of dogs in stone and bronze were found. Perhaps the Dog Hoard related to that temple, or another one yet to be discovered. However, the archaeologists who have studied the hoard believe that the key to interpreting it is the fragmentary 'hunting Diana' (*Diana venatrix*) statue, which suggests that the dog could be one of her hounds. As such, it might even be possible to interpret the broken-up box fittings (together with the coin) as evidence of money boxes from a shrine.

As was suggested tentatively for the Ryedale Hoard (see p. 95), there is a tradition of interpreting such metalwork hoards, especially when items have been purposefully damaged or broken, as founders' hoards – collections stashed by metalworkers who intended to recycle them for raw materials. The question then, is why bury them in the ground instead of simply piling them up somewhere? Perhaps burying metal was an easy way to store it and keep it safe from loss or theft, or to protect it from corrosion by the elements. But it is also possible, as is now thought of many Bronze Age hoards, that the burial of such collections of metal items had ritual significance. It is certainly intriguing that the dog alone was not damaged or broken up. By the time of the hoard's deposition in the 4th century CE, however, Roman Britain was already partly Christian. The hoard might then represent the destruction and spoliation of a temple as part of this process of Christianisation – perhaps, as Penny and Martin suggest, during the reigns of Magnus Maximus (r. 383–88) or Theodosius I (r. 379–95). Even if the objects resulted from such an 'iconoclastic' event, they might still have been deposited to store them for later recycling, or even for safekeeping, as attested elsewhere in Roman Britain. So the reasons for the burial of the hoard remain a mystery, one to which we might never know the answer.

BELOW For unknown reasons, the
dog was the only item in the hoard
that was left intact.

SALE

Given that the Dog Hoard was not legally
protected as Treasure, the finders and
landowner decided to sell the whole hoard.
In 2019 it was put on the open market by
Christie's auctioneers with an estimate
of between £30,000 and £50,000. Since
no museum in Gloucestershire was able to
bid for the hoard, staff at Bristol Museum
and Art Gallery agreed at very short notice
to try to buy it. Curator of Archaeology
Kate Iles sought a second opinion on the
valuation, submitted funding applications with
input from Senior Curator Gail Boyle, and
appointed an experienced agent to bid on the
museum's behalf. On 3 July, the 'Gloucester
Licking Dog Hoard' (lot 104) was sold to
a private buyer for £120,000 (plus buyer's
premium). Although this was the same amount
of money that the museum had raised, sadly
their agent could not go any higher to outbid
the successful buyer. It was a devastating blow.
Gail said, 'I hoped that we had raised enough
money to buy the Dog Hoard for everyone to
enjoy, but we knew it was a gamble that might
not pay off.' Although the hoard was loaned
to Bristol Museum and Art Gallery to enable
further research, it sadly remains in a private
collection and is not currently available to be
seen by the public.

Early Medieval

TOTAL FINDS RECORDED ON PAS DATABASE

67,606

MOST COMMON ARTEFACT TYPES ON DATABASE

brooch, coin, strap end, pin, stirrup

TOP 5 COUNTIES ON DATABASE

Norfolk, Lincolnshire, Suffolk, East Yorkshire,
North Yorkshire

PAS data as of October 2024

20 The Binham Bracteate Hoard
Norfolk

21 The Staffordshire Hoard
Staffordshire

22 Winfarthing Pendants Burial
Norfolk

23 The Watlington Hoard
Oxfordshire

24 Drinkstone Æstel and Others
Suffolk

25 The Vale of York Hoard
North Yorkshire

FINDS DENSITY

Moderate   High

THE BINHAM BRACTEATE HOARD

Bracteates are associated with Germanic and Scandinavian cultures of the Migration Period during and after the decline of the Roman Empire

BM-8BD5F0, LVPL-511952,
LVPL-5146E4, LVPL-43ADD1,
NMS-8381A4, NMS-D18CC1

OBJECT TYPE Hoard (jewellery)

MATERIALS Gold, gilded copper alloy, silver

DATE 6th century CE

LOCATION Binham, Norfolk

DISCOVERY METHOD Metal detecting

COLLECTION Norwich Castle Museum and Art Gallery

CONTENTS OF HOARD (TO DATE)

6 gold bracteates

1 gold bracelet

1 gilded copper-alloy bracelet

1 silver brooch

OPPOSITE AND BELOW B-type gold bracteate found as part of the Binham hoard in 2011, NMS-8381A4.

MYSTERIOUS FIND

In-situ hoards – those discovered in their original location and with all or most of their contents still in place – are exciting finds for archaeologists. Yet much of the open land in Britain, especially in southern and eastern England, is used for agriculture and anything deposited in cultivated fields is susceptible to being damaged or dispersed by farm machinery, crop chemicals and natural erosion. In these settings, metal detecting is particularly well-suited for locating elements of a hoard that have been strewn across the landscape. If findspots are carefully recorded by detectorists and other searchers over a long period of time, this can allow the hoard to be pieced back together, and possibly some of its valuable contextual information to be recovered.

So it was with a hoard of Anglo-Saxon gold bracteates (disc pendants) and associated material found in a field in Binham, Norfolk. The first bracteate was found in 2004 by Dennis O'Neill who was in the area on a family holiday. Dennis remembers that the ground was so hard that he had to chip away at it to reveal the pendant at a depth of 5 cm. Not knowing what it was, he put it in his finds bag to look at later. He then shared photos of it with his detecting club, who told him what it was and advised him to get in touch with the Portable Antiquities Scheme (PAS) in Norfolk, which is part of Norfolk County Council's Finds Identification and Recording Service. The bracteate went through the Treasure process and was eventually acquired by Norwich Castle Museum and Art Gallery. Dennis then invited his club mates Glenn Lister and Cyril Askew to join him in searching the area in subsequent years, and more items from the hoard were located in 2009, 2011 and 2013. In 2014 the three friends assisted in a formal archaeological investigation of the site organised by Tim Pestell (Curator of Archaeology, Norwich Castle Museum and Art Gallery) during which the latest bracteate from the hoard turned up. This is characteristic of metal detecting, in that searching the same area year after year, particularly following recent agricultural work, can turn up new material that has come to the surface or that has simply been

BELOW One of the A-type bracteates, NMS-8381A4, had been deliberately folded prior to deposition.

OPPOSITE The non-bracteate items in the hoard.

missed in previous outings. Over time, items that had been impressive in and of themselves when discovered in ones and twos eventually combined to form the largest collection of 6th-century gold in Britain.

DISC PENDANTS

The hoard consists of six gold bracteates, two bracelets (one gold, one gilded copper alloy) and a silver brooch. The bracteates range in size from 68 mm diameter, the largest yet recorded from Britain (LVPL-43ADD1), to one (BM-8BD5F0) that is 44 mm in diameter. They were made from blank gold sheet discs that were stamped using metal dies cut with the design in reverse. Unsurprisingly, given their relative thinness (less than a millimetre) and having been found in ploughsoil, all of the pendants have suffered a degree of damage. Most have lost their suspension loops. The 2013 bracteate (LVPL-511952) appears to have been crumpled intentionally prior to being deposited, and likely also suffered subsequent damage in the soil, but was otherwise complete, even retaining its attachment loop. It had been produced from the same die as the bracteates found in 2009 (LVPL-43ADD1) and 2011 (NMS-8381A4). The

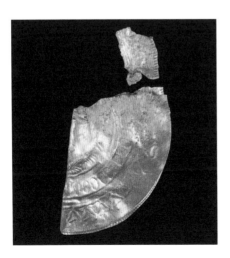

decoration on the latter was interpreted using X-ray, because this pendant had been folded in half, apparently deliberately and carefully. Archaeologists did not want to damage the bracteate by unfolding it, or lose evidence that might show how and why it had been folded.

Bracteates are categorised according to their designs and the Binham examples are of those described as 'A' and 'B' types, three of each. A-type bracteates show a human face, ultimately deriving from Roman coins with the face of a 4th-century emperor. B-types show a human figure, often accompanied by animals. The central decoration on the Binham A-type bracteates, all from the same dies, has a male bust in profile, with a pronounced nose, mouth and round eye, and a hairstyle with a diadem crown and central jewel motif in the form of a spiral. The man's costume, with stylised folds and brooch, is close to Roman models, but differs from Roman coins in that the details appear as contour lines instead of shown in relief. In front of the face is a line branching into two ends, possibly representing a two-headed snake. Surrounding the head are characters, including Latin letters and runes, which do not form any meaningful words. On each pendant, the central image is surrounded by two or four concentric zones decorated with triangular or S-shaped individual stamps.

The three B-type bracteates have a central scene within a geometric border that has been produced using identical dies. They all depict a sword-wielding male figure facing right. He is engaged in combat with a beak-headed quadruped, his left hand raised against its jaws and a sword clasped in his right hand behind his head. Vertical lines give the impression of a helmet. There are four runes above his left hand, the central two of which were probably damaged on the die. There is a further beak-headed quadruped behind and below the

NMS-D18CC1 (top)
Brooch
Silver
Length: 13 mm (max)
Width: 34 mm (max)

LVPL-43ADD1 (centre)
Bracelet (in two pieces)
Copper alloy
Length: 40 mm / 47 mm
Width: 10 mm / 10 mm
Thickness: 2 mm / 10 mm

LVPL-5146E4 (bottom)
Armlet
Gold
Length: 67 mm
Height: 54 mm
Width: 11 mm

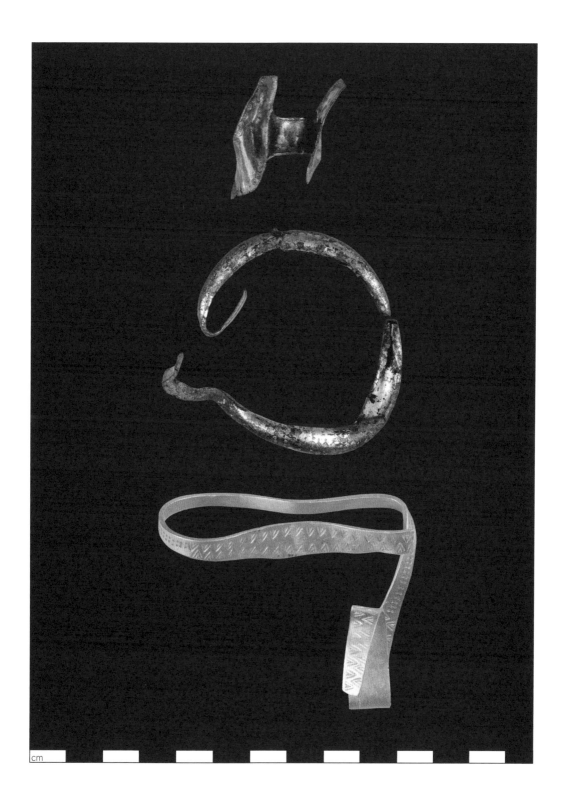

LVPL-43ADD1
A-type bracteate
Gold
Diameter: 68 mm
Thickness: 1 mm

BM-8BD5F0
B-type bracteate
Gold
Diameter: 44 mm

LVPL-511952
A-type bracteate
Gold
Diameter: 50 mm
Thickness: <1 mm

NMS-D18CC1
B-type bracteate
Gold
Diameter: 50 mm
Thickness: <1 mm

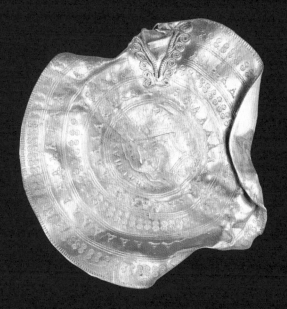

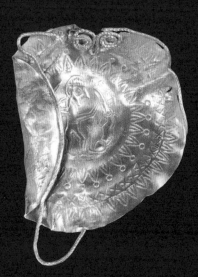

cm

warrior's sword arm and behind his right leg. The 2014 example (NMS-D18CC1), which is larger than the other two, has an additional outer ring of triangular punched decoration. The gold foils on all three are surrounded by the remains of a twisted gold-wire border, whereas the three A-type bracteates instead have small incisions along the edge that appear to imitate twisted wire.

The decoration of both of the bracelets is consistent with an Anglo-Saxon date, matching the bracteates. The silver sheet, probably a brooch fragment, is also decorated in an Anglo-Saxon style, with designs of concentric circles around its outside edge. All three objects are now twisted out of shape.

NORTHERN EUROPEAN TIES

Bracteates have been found across Denmark, Sweden, Norway, Poland, northern Germany, the Netherlands, eastern England and northern France, both individually and in groups. They are associated with the cultures along the coasts of the North Sea and the Baltic Sea during the late Roman and Migration periods and date from the mid or late 5th century to the mid 6th century. Worn as pendants, they appear to be amuletic, with imagery referencing aspects of religion and mythology. The runic inscription on the Binham B-type bracteates is not straightforward to read or interpret, both in the formation of some of the runic characters themselves and their meaning. John Hines at Cardiff University has suggested that they could be translated variously as 'wet' (referring, perhaps, to a drink, as is suggested by an inscription alluding to mead and ale on another bracteate from England), or as a form of the verb 'to know', or as the expression 'to bear witness'.

Bracteates found in graves, and thus assumed to have been buried with their owners as dress accessories, do not normally show signs of deliberate damage prior to deposition. This is in contrast to the bracteates (and gold bracelet) from this hoard which, like some examples from

BELOW Finders Glenn Lister, Dennis O'Neill and Cyril Askew with archaeologists Tim Pestell and Phil Emery.

hoards in Scandinavia of similar date, appear to have been damaged deliberately before being buried, ending their function as items of jewellery. This intentional damage, and the fact that the Binham bracteates were buried together, suggests some sort of ritual 'sacrifice' connected to practices that early Anglo-Saxons may have brought from their ancestral lands in continental Europe. The Binham hoard therefore provides a rare and interesting insight into shared beliefs between East Anglia and Scandinavia during the formative period of early Anglo-Saxon England.

Several other gold bracteates have been recorded in England, including others from north Norfolk such as an A-type bracteate from Shouldham Thorpe (NMS-DF6591), but none were found in hoards like at Binham. The diligence of Dennis, Glenn and Cyril in noting precisely where each bracteate was found enabled both the follow-up excavation and better understanding of the objects' relationships to each other, which made it

possible to state with confidence that they were from the same hoard. In collaboration with Charlotte Behr at University of Roehampton, Tim argues that the hoard may be evidence that Binham was a previously unknown high-status centre in the 6th century because geographical concentrations of bracteates elsewhere in England – Suffolk and Kent, for instance – are associated with high-status and royal sites. The Binham B-type bracteates are near-identical to an example from what was later an East Anglian royal palace complex at Rendlesham, while another bracteate from Rendlesham was made with the same die as one found at Eastry, Kent, also a later royal site.

The Binham hoard elements were acquired over time by Norwich Castle Museum and Art Gallery, and went on display together at the exhibition 'Anglo-Saxon Kingdoms' at the British Library in 2018–19. Dennis, Cyril and Glenn still return to Binham every year, looking for more elements of the hoard, though without further success to date.

THE STAFFORDSHIRE HOARD

'Hold now, O earth, the possessions of earls, now that the heroes cannot.'

BEOWULF, LINES 2247–48A (LAMENT OF THE LAST SURVIVOR)

WMID-0B5416; WMID-399670

OBJECT TYPE Hoard (metalwork, weaponry and jewellery)

MATERIALS Gold, silver, copper alloy, garnet

DATE Mid-7th century CE

LOCATION Hammerwich, Staffordshire

DISCOVERY METHOD Metal detecting

COLLECTION Birmingham Museum and Art Gallery and the Potteries Museum and Art Gallery

WOW!!!!!!

Like most Finds Liaison Officers (FLOs), Duncan Slarke, then FLO for Staffordshire and the West Midlands, was used to people getting excited about the archaeological importance of their finds. In July 2009, he was contacted on behalf of detectorist Terry Herbert and urged to come to Terry's house immediately and take a look at what he had discovered. Duncan was prepared to be let down. But as soon as Terry opened the door and started to show him the array of material, Duncan knew that this was a discovery of huge significance. Over a period of five days, in a field in Hammerwich, Staffordshire, Terry had recovered hundreds of gold and silver objects and fragments that he recognised as Anglo-Saxon. Duncan's feelings on first seeing them were summed up by the email that he sent to colleagues at the PAS Central Unit:

> WOW!!!!!! Found Staffs, and this is not all of it, over 200 items – pictures from finder. Any initial thoughts? Thinking nationally important. Assume that it's a hoard rather than associated with burial. Will talk to the landowner to sound him out about excavation. Probably more there but the finder gave up on the point of excavation and contacted me. I have collected.

When Roger Bland (Head of the PAS at the time) heard the news he took direct control of the response, aware that the find was truly remarkable. He convened an emergency meeting with Birmingham Museums Trust, the Staffordshire Historic Environment team and Historic England. A full 'rescue' excavation was then undertaken by the Birmingham University Field Archaeology Unit with funding from English Heritage. During this excavation, which lasted a month, more than 1,600 additional objects were found, many close to the surface. Other tiny fragments were found when soil blocks collected by Terry were later excavated in the lab.

As part of the Treasure process, Kevin Leahy (National Finds Adviser for the PAS) and his wife Dianne were given the vital

OPPOSITE AND OVERLEAF A small selection of the spectacular gold and silver items in the Staffordshire Hoard. The complete hoard totalled 4,600 artefacts.

BELOW Archaeologists from
Birmingham University Field
Archaeology Unit excavating the
findspot of the Staffordshire Hoard.

BELOW Silver-gilt cheekpiece from
a high-status helmet, decorated with
interlaced animals.

task of compiling a summary list of all of the
objects for a report for the coroner and eventual
use in the valuation of the material. Over
marathon sessions at Birmingham Museum
and Art Gallery and then the British Museum,
Kevin and Dianne weighed, measured,
described and catalogued each of the objects –
using a paper raffle-ticket book to assign each
find a unique 'K-number' in their database.

'THE POSSESSIONS OF EARLS'

Kevin and Dianne's work quickly revealed
the broad nature of the material in the hoard.
It contained 4,600 pieces, including 600
'significant items' of high-status gold and silver
dating from as late as the mid-7th century.
Many were parts of sword hilts, and almost
all of them were damaged. There were an
unexpected number of sword pommels, 78 in
all (62 gold and 16 silver), some with filigree,
others with cloisonné cut gemstone decoration
(usually garnet) or interlaced animal motifs.
Thirteen gold sword 'pyramid' mounts
(thought to have decorated the leather straps
that held swords in their scabbards) sported a
similar array of filigree, gemstone and animal
decoration. Also present were a large number
of plain gold and silver components of sword
hilts, as well as five small gold and garnet
fittings in the shape of animals. Although
gold and garnet hilt fittings from a *seax* (a type

of short bladed weapon) were also among
the hoard, there were no iron sword or knife
blades present at all, demonstrating that the
hoard's owner(s) had deliberately collected
only the precious metal components of
these weapons, presumably for their intrinsic
worth rather than their aesthetic appeal. The
precious fittings had been too damaged in the
process of removal from their original weapons
to be useful as spare parts to 'kit out' less flashy
swords and knives.

Portions of at least one high-status helmet
were contained in the hoard. Among the items
initially discovered by Terry was a silver-gilt
cheekpiece with the interlaced animal
decoration from the right side of a helmet.
The partner cheekpiece was found in a further
controlled survey of the area by archaeologists
with a team of detectorists in 2012. In the soil
blocks recovered in 2009 and micro-excavated
by conservators were thin, fragmentary sheets
of silver-gilt foil featuring scenes of armed
warriors; these would have formed the outer
portion of the bowl of the helmet.

BELOW Modern replica
reconstruction of the helmet
from the Staffordshire Hoard.

The conservation team (led by Pieta Greaves, now of Drakon Heritage) also determined that several silver-gilt metal strips with grooves contained traces of natural adhesives, so are thought to be the channel in which a horse-hair crest would have been fixed to the top of the helmet. Birmingham Museums Trust and the Potteries Museum and Art Gallery commissioned a reconstruction of the helmet along with an artistic interpretation, which gives a good impression of the striking visual impact it would have made on anyone who beheld its wearer.

Not all the goods present in the hoard were weapons and armour, however. Some of the most impressive of these are likely Christian in nature. There are five cross-shaped objects of varying sizes and shapes. The largest cross, 115 mm tall and made of sheet gold weighing 140 g, is believed to be from an altar or used in processions; it is now bent. It was set with five large garnets, several of which were found in the folded arms of the cross. A large gold 'pectoral' cross (which might have been worn suspended over the chest) is decorated with gold filigree and a central garnet. An intriguing gold strip, probably an arm from another cross, displays the only inscription in the hoard, a Latin rendering of a passage from Numbers 10:35 in the Old Testament, translated by Richard Gameson (Durham University) as 'Arise, O Lord, and may your enemies be torn apart and those who hate you will flee from your face'. Also among the objects in the hoard is a curious gold and garnet disc featuring a central column topped by a chequered black and white millefiori glass gem. Leslie Webster (former Keeper of Prehistory and Europe at the British Museum) argues, based on manuscript illustrations, that this object is a decoration for a priest's headdress.

In addition to the military and Christian material, the hoard contains two groups of strips and mounts, one set in gold and sumptuously embellished with garnets, the other silver with black niello inlay. Another imposing artefact, not obviously military or religious and weighing an impressive 62 g, is a gold mount in the shape of two stylised eagles clutching a fish. Smaller flat gold and silver-gilt mounts in the form of fish, birds and horses are also present, along with six gold snakes each made from a single metal rod.

Though it is impossible to know the precise date that the hoard was deposited, based on the style of the artefacts present and incorporating other factors like the calligraphy of the writing on the inscribed strip, experts estimate it was buried sometime in the mid-7th century. However, some of the items appear to be even more ancient than this, and were probably already antiques or 'heirlooms' at the time they were buried – for example, a silver sword pommel depicting a bearded man, thought to be a 6th-century import from Scandinavia.

THE HOARD AND MERCIA

Anglo-Saxon England in the 7th century was not unified under one ruler, but divided into several independent kingdoms, which were often in conflict with one another. The Staffordshire Hoard was found in what was the Midlands kingdom of Mercia, which (sometimes in alliance with native British kings) enjoyed military success against its rival Anglo-Saxon kingdoms in the early and mid-600s under the pagan king Penda. Penda met his end in 655 at the Battle of Winwaed against the forces of Oswiu of Northumbria (*c.* 612–70), after which Mercian rule passed to his son Peada (d. 656) who had been baptised as a Christian two years earlier.

The discovery in Mercia of a hoard containing spectacularly decorated military gear from around this time fits with this picture of frequent conflict. It does not mean that all the military items were made or used locally, just that someone living in the area or passing through it had gathered them all together. For Kevin Leahy, the hoard appears to be accumulated war loot or trophies gathered from multiple sources during a long military career.

The material also represents the largest hoard of Anglo-Saxon gold ever found. At almost 4 kg the total amount of gold in the hoard is much greater, for example, than what is present in the famous Sutton Hoo ship burial (now in the British Museum), which is thought to be the royal grave of King Raedwald of East Anglia who died *c.* 624 (so also 7th century, like the Staffordshire Hoard). This comparison is imprecise, however, because the ship burial at Sutton Hoo represents the complete grave goods of only one person, and the gold objects in it were accompanied by a great deal of other valuable non-precious metal items. The Staffordshire Hoard is something different: a collection of components of mostly martial items that most likely came from a large

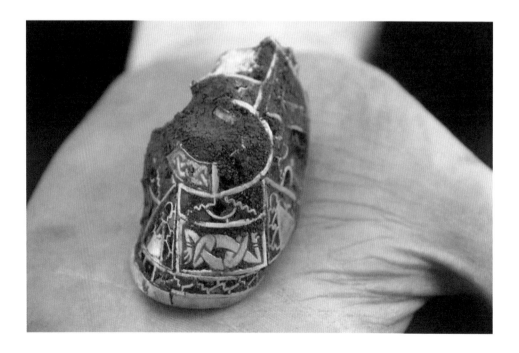

BELOW Gold and garnet object in
the form of a bird, perhaps from
a sword hilt.

BELOW British Museum conservator
Marilyn Hockey and scientist Susan
La Niece studying the Staffordshire
Hoard.

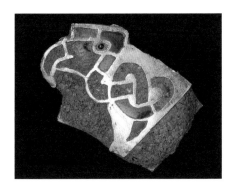

number of individuals. The hoard assemblage
shows archaeologists that the use of gold was
potentially more widespread than is evidenced
in the rest of the archaeological record; as an
example, against the 62 gold sword pommels
in the hoard, there are only 9 others recorded
on the entire PAS database!

Regarding the items with a religious
association, Chris Fern (Cotswold
Archaeology) thinks that they are among the
most important Christian objects to survive
from the early Anglo-Saxon period. It is
interesting that they were found in a location
which in the mid-7th century would have
only recently transitioned from paganism.
Following the mission of St Augustine of
Canterbury from 597 CE, which initially
targeted the Anglo-Saxon kingdom of King
Æthelberht of Kent, Christianity spread to
further Anglo-Saxon kingdoms, along with
competing Celtic missionaries such as Aidan
of Lindisfarne (d. 651) who was 'Apostle to the
Northumbrians'. The hoard was found about
6 km (4 miles) from the city of Lichfield, which
was established as the seat of the diocese by
St Chad (c. 632–72), a student of Aidan's. The
degree to which the people who left the hoard
had been exposed to Christianity is unknown,
but its contents reflect the religious changes
affecting Anglo-Saxon England at this time.

SAVED FOR THE NATION

Kevin and Dianne's report was shared with
the Senior Coroner for South Staffordshire,
Andrew Haigh, who scheduled an inquest
into the find on 24 September 2009. As for
all coroners, the majority of Andrew's work
involved modern-day deaths, so Treasure
matters proved a welcome distraction – even
more so in this case, since he was able to visit
the excavation with Duncan and witness some
of the material coming out of the ground,
and also got to see Kevin and Dianne at
work in the bowels of Birmingham Museum.
Despite the size and complexity of the hoard,
Andrew remembers the inquest being quite
straightforward. Unsurprisingly, the hoard
was officially found to constitute Treasure.

This is when the hoard came to the attention
of the public. Following a press conference
in Birmingham, where some of the artefacts
were first shown to the media, news of its
discovery spread around the world in a frenzy.
In response to the public excitement, a small
selection of the pieces – uncleaned, because
the hoard was still undergoing valuation for
the Treasure process 'in the condition in which

BELOW Terry Herbert, finder of the Staffordshire Hoard, assisting archaeologists investigating the hoard site.

BOTTOM Part of the hoard in situ, photographed during the archaeological excavations.

OPPOSITE Kevin and Dianne Leahy used raffle tickets to catalogue the huge number of items in the hoard.

it was found'– went on display at Birmingham Museum and Art Gallery for a few weeks, and visitors queued around the block for hours to view them. Dan Pett, then the IT adviser for the PAS, built a website for the hoard with hundreds of photos and news updates made available to the public. Prince Charles even came to see the hoard twice, first at the British Museum and later in Stoke-on-Trent.

The Treasure Valuation Committee convened an extraordinary meeting to recommend a value for the hoard to the Secretary of State (a normal meeting of the Committee covers 60 or more discoveries). It concluded that the hoard was worth £3,285,000 – more than £2,000,000 higher than any other previous find of Treasure in Britain at the time. Birmingham Museum and Art Gallery and the Potteries

Museum and Art Gallery in Stoke-on-Trent, with the support of local councillors, agreed to pursue the acquisition of the hoard jointly. The Art Fund launched a major fundraising campaign at the House of Lords, which was supported by a combination of public subscriptions, grants from multiple funding bodies and the sale proceeds from a book on the hoard swiftly written for that purpose by Kevin and Roger.

Although the money required was substantial, the fabulous nature of the hoard and its widespread fame meant that the sums were raised in good time, with a remarkable number of donations from members of the public, and the material was safely acquired by the two Midlands museums. All of the items, including the further 86 objects found in 2012, underwent extensive cleaning, conservation and study. To do justice to the hoard and its story, bespoke galleries were created in Birmingham and Stoke-on-Trent. The hoard remains a hugely popular visitor draw and an important source of local pride and identity.

For academics, the hoard has proven an invaluable source of information about the early medieval period. In March 2010, before the hoard had even been acquired, a symposium was convened at the British Museum which brought together a range of experts who presented more than two dozen papers on various aspects of the hoard and its context. This proved to be the genesis for a long-term research strategy. Project-managed by Jenni Butterworth, the research culminated in a comprehensive monograph on the hoard by Chris Fern, Tania Dickinson and Leslie Webster in 2019 to which much of this chapter is indebted. However, like many of the finds covered in this book, this is only the beginning of the story of the Staffordshire Hoard, and it will continue to be studied for years to come.

550	652	655
AA3Z CE5A	AA3Z CE5A	AA3Z CE5A

656	657	658
AA3Z CE5A	AA3Z CE5A	AA3Z CE5A

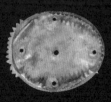

659	820	920
AA3Z CE5A	AA3Z CE5A	AA3Z CE5A

cm

WINFARTHING PENDANTS BURIAL

A 7th-century Anglo-Saxon woman's grave that 'highlights the seismic changes then occurring in society, her cosmopolitan outlook and the far-reaching connections of her family.'

TIM PESTELL, NORWICH CASTLE MUSEUM AND ART GALLERY

NMS-E95041

OBJECT TYPE Hoard (burial assemblage)

MATERIALS Gold (pendants and beads), garnets (pendant), copper alloy (bowl, chatelaine rings), iron (knife, buckle, nails), ceramic (vessel)

DATE 650–80 CE

LOCATION Winfarthing, Norfolk

DISCOVERY METHOD Metal detecting

COLLECTION Norwich Castle Museum and Art Gallery

CONTENTS OF GRAVE

1 composite gold and garnet pendant

2 gold coin pendants

1 gold openwork filigree pendant

copper-alloy bowl

2 gold biconical spacer beads

16 copper-alloy chatelaine rings (one with remains of girdle-hanger)

1 iron buckle, 1 iron knife, 3 iron nails

ceramic biconical vessel

OPPOSITE The pendants and spacer beads from the burial.

BELOW X-ray of the largest pendant.

THE 'DETECTOROLOGIST'

Tom Lucking is one of a rare but growing breed: a keen metal detectorist who was also an archaeology student, based at the University of East Anglia, when he made his discovery of a lifetime. On 21 December 2014, Tom was detecting on a permission at Winfarthing, near Diss, Norfolk, and came across a copper-alloy bowl. He knew it to be of archaeological interest so stopped digging and contacted Norfolk County Council's Finds Identification and Recording Service (I&RS), which includes the Finds Liaison Officers working for the PAS in Norfolk. Andrew Rogerson, then head of the I&RS, realised that the find might well be part of an otherwise undisturbed inhumation burial. He rapidly organised an archaeological excavation since the grave was clearly at risk of being ploughed-out. The excavation was carried out in January 2015 by Andrew, Steven Ashley (Norfolk I&RS) and Helen Geake (Norfolk FLO), with Tom in close attendance with his detector.

The grave was found to be that of an Anglo-Saxon woman and dated to no earlier than 634–56 CE, based on the presence of two coins converted into pendants. Each pendant had been made from a gold *solidus* in the name of the Merovingian king Sigebert III (r. 633–56), struck at what is now Marseille, France. One of the coin pendants was found with its suspension loop detached, revealing a piercing to enable its attachment; it had come apart because the rivet was lost. The other was complete and showed that the coins were duplicates, struck from the same pair of dies. This proved that the two pendants must have been made together and converted into matching jewellery. Intriguingly, the purity of the gold in the fittings is greater than that of the coins, which had been debased with silver. In appearance, therefore, the gold fittings look noticeably brighter.

The woman's grave contained two further pendants. One was made of gold in the form of an openwork 'Maltese cross', decorated with interlace in gold filigree and a gold-beaded wire border. At its centre is a gold boss surrounded by beaded wire. The other pendant was even more impressive, a masterpiece of the Anglo-Saxon craftworker and the stand-out object in

BELOW Objects found in the 2015
excavation demonstrated that this
was a grave of a high-status woman.

the group. It is constructed from a sheet of gold to which are attached a network of cells, each filled with a cut garnet, forming six concentric bands of decoration. Each band has a different design: the most complex comprises delicate interlacing serpents with open jaws and, most remarkably, tiny inlaid eyes made from garnets half a millimetre in diameter! Five bosses are fixed in this field of gold and garnets, one in the centre and the other four evenly spaced around it, surviving in varying degrees of preservation. Two hold the remnants of a white material, thought to be shell; and two more contain the same white material additionally topped with a gold setting inlaid with a garnet. The central boss is most impressive, formed of cut garnets within gold cells, as is the suspension loop.

The sophistication of the piece is apparent even on the back of the pendant where, despite it being hidden from view when worn, the backs of the rivets that attach the decorative bosses are capped with gold settings inlaid with more garnets; two remain in situ, with three now detached.

Two gold biconical spacer beads made from wound gold wire were also found within the grave. In contrast to some found elsewhere, these are made of plain rather than beaded wire. The three smaller pendants and the two spacer beads were probably from the same necklace: perhaps the cross-shaped pendant was worn in the middle of the necklace, with a spacer bead on either side and then the coin pendants on either side of those, creating symmetry in design.

BELOW The copper-alloy bowl (top) and sherds of a Frankish ceramic vessel (bottom).

BELOW The reconstructed Frankish ceramic vessel. Its presence in the grave suggests that the woman or her community had trade contacts with the Continent.

In addition to the copper-alloy bowl originally located by Tom, the grave contained a Frankish biconical ceramic vessel, complete but badly cracked. It had been damaged by the weight of soil pressing down on it over time and was recovered in fragments. The vessel was made of sandy wheel-thrown clay and decorated with horizontal grooves. Among the other grave goods were several copper-alloy rings, seemingly part of a chatelaine used to suspend household items from a belt. Indeed, one of these chatelaine rings was still attached to what seemed to be part of a girdle hanger. Also recovered were ferrous objects, including an iron buckle, part of an iron knife and some nails. Together these objects helped to identify the grave as belonging to a woman.

STATELY SYMBOLS

Tim Pestell, Senior Curator of Archaeology at Norwich Castle Museum and Art Gallery which acquired the Winfarthing assemblage, thinks that even in the first half of the 7th

century – an age of ostentatious burials – the opulence of the gold and garnet pendant stands out, and recalls the similar garnet-inlaid jewellery found at the Sutton Hoo ship burial in Suffolk. In death, the Winfarthing pendant had been placed upon the deceased woman's chest, and that action must have had relevance to those who survived her. This pendant was a signal not only of the woman's wealth, but also that of her family who could afford to bury such valuable jewellery. Important, too, is the fact that three of the woman's cross-shaped pendants highlight her connection with the Christian faith, even while her burial – with grave goods and not in a churchyard – reflects the older pagan traditions of her forbearers. As Tim describes, 'This not only highlights the seismic changes then occurring in society, her cosmopolitan outlook and the far-reaching connections of her family, but it speaks of her aristocratic place in the contemporary hierarchy of East Anglian society.' Only a handful of high-status burials of similar date are known from this eastern Anglo-Saxon kingdom; they include Harford Farm near Norwich, and Boss Hall near Ipswich, Suffolk. These high-status Anglo-Saxon individuals must have known each other in life – indeed, according to Tim, they were possibly related.

THE WATLINGTON HOARD

'I was doing the zig-zag motion over the land when my metal detector went crazy…'

JIM MATHER, DETECTORIST

SUR-4A4231	
OBJECT TYPE Hoard (coins, ingots and jewellery)	
MATERIALS Silver and gold	
DATE *c.* 880 CE	
LOCATION Watlington, Oxfordshire	
DISCOVERY METHOD Metal detecting	
COLLECTION Ashmolean Museum	

CONTENTS OF HOARD
15 silver ingots
3 complete silver armrings and 1 fragment
2 hack-silver neck-ring terminals
1 fragment of hack-gold rod
1 silver hooked tag
203 silver coins

OPPOSITE Ingots, jewellery and a selection of coins from the hoard.

BELOW Among the coins in the hoard were thirteen 'Two Emperors' silver pennies, important evidence for a previously unknown alliance between the Anglo-Saxon kings Ceolwulf II of Mercia and Alfred the Great.

THE WATLINGTON HOARD

James (Jim) Mather was an experienced detectorist, but nothing could have prepared him for discovering the Watlington Hoard, which transformed understanding of King Alfred the Great (r. 871–99 CE). In October 2015, Jim was exploring one of his usual haunts, on cultivated land near Watlington, Oxfordshire. His search that day wasn't going well. He had unearthed only a few corroded coins and some shotgun cartridges and was about to give up and go home. Then, spotting an area of higher ground that he had not detected before – and knowing that such places were where people had often built settlements in the past – he decided to search it. 'I was doing the zig-zag motion over the land when my metal detector went crazy,' Jim recalls. He dug down to retrieve what turned out to be a silver ingot and part of the find of a lifetime.

Realising that the ingot might date to the Viking Age, Jim decided to detect further around the findspot, and found a silver Anglo-Saxon coin. Further searching revealed a group of them. Knowing that he had found a hoard, Jim stopped digging, contacted the farmer who owned the land and sought archaeological help – but it was harder to come by than he had expected. Anni Byard, his local FLO, was about to board a plane for holiday, so Jim then reached out to David Williams, the neighbouring Surrey FLO and an experienced field archaeologist (who has now sadly passed away). Since David was not able to organise an excavation immediately, Jim was told to cover the hoard and wait for him to arrive on site the following Tuesday. Jim buried some crotal (animal) bells at the hoard site to aid in relocating it with a metal detector. That evening he gently cleaned the 88 coins he had extracted and tried to identify them with his books at home. The next day he took them to the Ashmolean Museum in Oxford for safekeeping.

Jim recalls how he then had several sleepless nights worrying about his hoard, pacing up and down the house, and making trips to the findspot to ensure everything was still as he had left it. Finally, the day of the excavation arrived. One of David's first tasks was to order the landowner to acquire 'the best quality clingfilm' for the task of block-lifting the hoard (so that it would stay in one clump for later micro-excavation in lab conditions), which David undertook with his colleague Emma Corke. Jim detected the spoil to ensure that no coins had been missed.

David delivered the packaged hoard to the British Museum to be examined by conservators. The security guards queried his need to bring in a suitcase and thought he was joking when he explained he was delivering a Viking Age hoard. Conservator Pippa Pearce, who received the hoard at the Museum, described it as resembling 'a greasy haggis with bits of treasure sticking out'. These treasures included very thin and delicate Anglo-Saxon silver coins that were more than a thousand years old. The hoard was X-rayed, and then the painstaking work of extracting the fragile coins via micro-excavation could begin.

In total, the Watlington Hoard consisted of 15 silver ingots, 3 complete silver armrings and 1 hack-silver armring fragment, 2 hack-silver terminals of neck rings, 1 fragment of hack-gold rod, 1 silver hooked tag, and 203 coins. The ingots, hack-silver and hack-gold (precious

metal items that have been deliberately cut up or 'hacked' to pieces) reveal a bullion economy, based on lumps of precious metal valued by weight, operating alongside one using coinage. This is typical of the early medieval period and likely identifies this hoard as one assembled by Vikings rather than Anglo-Saxons, who typically used coins at this time. The coins date to the period *c.* 875–79/80, suggesting that the hoard was deposited shortly afterwards.

This was at a time when Anglo-Saxon rule in England faced being wiped out by invading Vikings. Following its conquest of the Anglo-Saxon kingdoms of Northumbria in 866 and East Anglia in 869, the so-called Viking Great Army had turned on Mercia and Wessex. In 877, according to the *Anglo-Saxon Chronicle*, Mercia was divided between King Ceolwulf II of Mercia (r. *c.* 875–79) and the Vikings. The following year, the Vikings attacked Chippenham, Wiltshire, forcing King Alfred of Wessex (later known as Alfred the Great) into exile in the marshes at Athelney in Somerset. But fortunes quickly changed for the Anglo-Saxons when at the Battle of Edington (878) Alfred defeated the Viking army under

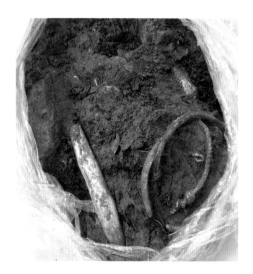
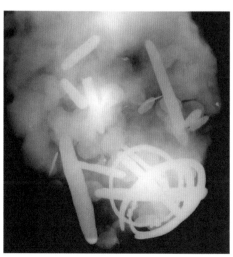

BELOW Finder Jim Mather and
Ashmolean Museum curator Eleanor
Standley examining the hoard.

Guthrum. At this time Ceolwulf was likely still
alive and based near London, while Guthrum
remained in south-west Mercia for a year
before settling in East Anglia. A treaty created
a boundary between the lands of Alfred (in
Wessex and part of southern Mercia) and those
still controlled by Guthrum, but it only held for
a few years. Experts believe that the Watlington
Hoard could have been concealed by Vikings
at some time after the Battle of Edington.

REWRITING HISTORY

The coins include ones minted under the
name of Archbishop Æthelred of Canterbury
(r. 870–88), Ceolwulf and Alfred, of which
the majority are silver pennies of Alfred, and
a substantial minority are Ceolwulf's. Also
present are silver *deniers* of the Carolingian
kings Louis II the Younger (r. 855–75) and
Charles the Bald (r. 875–77). A particular
importance of the hoard is that it includes
thirteen so-called 'Two Emperor' coins, jointly
issued by Alfred and Ceolwulf, showing (on
the reverse) two emperors seated side by side,
with a winged angel above them. This design is
based on a late 4th-century Roman gold *solidus*
that depicted the emperors of the Eastern
and Western Roman Empires with a winged
imperial Victory above them. John Naylor, PAS
National Finds Adviser for Medieval and Later
Coins, who studied the silver pennies in the
hoard, says that the 13 'Two Emperor' coins,
as well as 186 'Cross-and-Lozenge types', both
produced by both kings, roughly quadruple
the overall numbers of these coins known.
The Watlington Hoard therefore makes a
massive contribution to understanding levels
and locations of minting, and the relationship
between Alfred and Ceolwulf.

According to Gareth Williams (then Curator
of Early Medieval Coins at the British
Museum), the high numbers of the Two

Emperor coins (probably minted in London)
along with Cross-and-Lozenge types (minted
in Canterbury, London, Winchester and
somewhere in West Mercia) imply that Alfred
and Ceolwulf were in a closer alliance in the
mid/late 870s than written sources suggest.
The *Anglo-Saxon Chronicle*, commissioned by
Alfred later in his reign, described Ceolwulf
dismissively as 'a foolish king's *thegn*' who
became a puppet of the Vikings. It may be
that Alfred, who understood the importance of
written history as propaganda, had suppressed
the recording of his earlier alliance with
Ceolwulf against the Viking invaders, for his
own political advancement – only Alfred has the
epitaph 'the Great'! For Gareth, since the coins
of Alfred and Ceolwulf cover several years and
were struck by several moneyers, the Watlington
Hoard shows that this alliance was lasting and
well-established, which makes sense given the
Viking threat faced by both Mercia and Wessex.

The Watlington Hoard has also enabled
Jim Mather to rewrite family history. He
recalls that his children hadn't always been
particularly interested in his detecting, but that
certainly changed after making this find!

DRINKSTONE *ÆSTEL* AND OTHERS

Could a group of mysterious Anglo-Saxon gold objects previously identified as manuscript pointers actually be something else?

SF-3ABEB9

OBJECT TYPE *Æstel* (pointer)

MATERIALS Gold, glass

DATE Late 9th century CE

LOCATION Drinkstone, Suffolk

DISCOVERY METHOD Metal detecting

COLLECTION Moyses Hall Museum

LENGTH 31 mm

WIDTH 18 mm

OPPOSITE AND BELOW Beaded gold filigree object with glass cabochon, possibly the terminal of an *æstel*, found by Steve Keeble in 2015.

EARLY ENGLISH LITERACY

King Alfred the Great (r. 871–99) was a promoter of literacy in England, especially within his ancestral kingdom of Wessex. He thought that important books, those 'which are most necessary for all people to know', should be made available in the language 'that we all can understand' – that is, the vernacular, not Latin. To further this goal, Alfred commissioned historical annals (the *Anglo-Saxon Chronicle*) in the language now called Old English, as well as translations of Latin texts such as Pope Gregory I's (r. 590–604) *Pastoral Care*, a treatise on Christian stewardship and leadership. In his preface to this translation, Alfred says that he will send a copy of the book to every bishopric in the kingdom, and with it an *æstel* worth 50 *mancuses*. A *mancus* was a gold coin of about 4.25 g, with a worth equivalent to 30 pieces of silver. Alfred commands that the *æstel* should never be removed from the book, or the book taken from the monastery, except by the bishop or if the book was lent out for copying. The *æstel* was clearly precious, and somehow integral to books distributed by Alfred.

It is not known for sure what an *æstel* was. The Old English word may come from Latin *hastula*, meaning 'little spear', which suggests something pointy. Many scholars have believed *æstels* to be manuscript pointers – devices that would be slid across vellum as an aid to reading – which makes sense in the context of Alfred's gift of them with books. This hypothesis seemed to be confirmed by the discovery of the Alfred Jewel, found during ploughing at North Petherton, Somerset, in 1693, and which has upon it the Old English inscription '+ÆFLRED MEC HEHT GEWYRCAN' (Alfred ordered me to be made). Although this inscription lacks any acknowledgment of Alfred's royal status, the proximity of the find to Athelney, where the king founded a monastery, is hard to ignore.

The Alfred Jewel is a well-crafted example of Anglo-Saxon art. Its filigree gold frame encloses a tear-shaped rock crystal, beneath which is a cloisonné enamel plaque depicting an image of a man (sometimes thought to be Christ or even Alfred himself, but could also be a personification of the sense of Sight) holding two flowering stems. The back plate has an

BELOW The Alfred Jewel, found in
North Petherton, Somerset, in 1693;
now in the Ashmolean Museum.
OPPOSITE TOP The Bowleaze Jewel,
probably found in Knowlton, Dorset.

OPPOSITE CENTRE The Minster Lovell
Jewel, found near Witney, Oxfordshire,
in 1869; now in the Ashmolean
Museum.
OPPOSITE BOTTOM The Warminster
Jewel, found near Cley Hill, Warminster;
now in the Salisbury Museum.

incised vegetal design, possibly the Tree of
Life. Around the edge of the object is the
openwork inscription mentioning Alfred. At
its base is an animal-head motif, with a hollow
socket as its snout. This suggests that the object
was designed to hold a rod, stick or similar –
consistent with it being a pointer – presumably
made of organic materials, now lost. The
Alfred Jewel was donated to Oxford University
in 1718, and is now on permanent display at
the Ashmolean Museum.

NEW FINDS

The Alfred Jewel is not the only find that might
be interpreted as an *æstel*. Also in the collection
of the Ashmolean Museum is the Minster

Lovell Jewel, found near Witney, Oxfordshire,
in 1869. It consists of a filigree gold fitting
topped with an enamel cloisonné setting.
The object's design, described as a 'double
cross' motif, is much simpler than that of the
Alfred Jewel. At its base projects a cylinder
for attaching a (presumed, now lost) pointer.
Purchased by the British Museum in 1993 (so
before the advent of the Treasure Act) was
the Bowleaze Jewel, now thought to be from
Knowlton, Dorset. It is similar in size and form
to the Minster Lovell Jewel but has a central
blue glass cabochon (instead of an enamelled
design) and is decorated with gold filigree and
coarse gold droplets. In 1997 an *æstel*-like object,
now in Salisbury Museum, was found by a

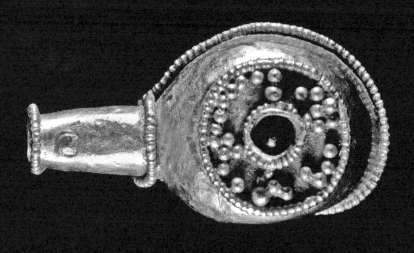

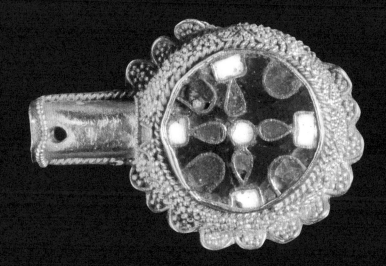

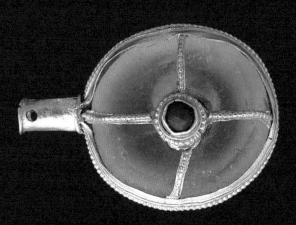

GRETTON

NARC-49D06E
Gretton, Northamptonshire
Gold
c. 850–900 CE
Length: 27 mm
Width: 13 mm (dome) 6 mm (shaft)

YORK

SWYOR-69C958
York
Gold
c. 800–900 CE
Length: 27 mm
Width: 15 mm
Thickness: 6 mm

AUGHTON

SWYOR-C75C64
Aughton, South Yorkshire
Gold
c. 850–900 CE
Length: 31 mm
Width: 13 mm
Thickness: 7 mm

MELTON

LEIC-57BE78
Melton, Leicestershire
Gold and glass
c. 800–900 CE
Length: 29 mm
Width: 11 mm
Thickness: 6 mm

metal detectorist near Cley Hill, Warminster; like the Bowleaze Jewel, it also has a blue glass central cabochon. The object consists of a rock crystal enclosed in a beaded-wire cross-shaped frame, upon which is the mounted cabochon setting. As with the Bowleaze and Minster Lovell Jewels, at its base is a projecting cylinder. Together these objects form a group with some similarities in form and materials, albeit quite different from one another in many respects, and all come from the area that was formerly Anglo-Saxon Wessex.

Through the Treasure Act 1996, the PAS has since recorded at least a further fifteen similar items, of which eight are made of gold. Intriguingly, these have been found across a much wider swathe of England, from North Yorkshire through the Midlands and into East Anglia. In January 2012, John Pawson was metal detecting near York when he found a slightly crumpled gold globular object (SWYOR-69C958). Like the other items, it is decorated with filigree; both beaded and plain wire were used to create its cross-like design. An earlier find from Yorkshire, unearthed in 2005 at Aughton, Rotherham (SWYOR-C75C64), is somewhat different to the others, since it is in the form of an animal's head, although a small beast's head forms the terminal on the Alfred Jewel. The Aughton object is otherwise noticeably plain. The creature's eyes, ears and other facial features are formed with filigree, with one eye retaining a blue stone setting. The hollow that might have held a pointer (or something else) is in this case a cylinder at the back of the animal's head, rather than its snout as on the Alfred Jewel.

Similar to the Aughton find is an animal-head example from Melton, Leicestershire, recovered by Chris Bursnall in 2016 (LEIC-57BE78). When he got the signal from his metal detector, he thought it was 'another ring-pull or bottle top', but on seeing the find he quickly 'realised it was something special'. The animal head is sub-rectangular in shape and described by the PAS recorder as 'horse-like' in appearance. Gold wire has again been used to pick out the animal's features and short segments of gold tube form its nostrils and eyes set with blue cabochons. Small folded gold strips are used for ears. As with the Aughton Jewel, the socket is located at the back of the beast's head.

More akin to the Minster Lovell and the York jewels was an object found near Gretton, Northamptonshire, in 2022 (NARC-49D06E). It has a spherical body with a domed front and flat back, and a projecting cylindrical socket. The upper surface is extensively decorated with beaded wire and granulated gold pellets. The design is cruciform, but much embellished with filigree. At the end of the socket terminal are two filigree rings with central perforations that could perhaps be fixing points for a pointer. But Leslie Webster (formerly Keeper of Prehistory and Europe at the British Museum) has suggested that it could be the terminal of a different object, perhaps attached to a girdle cord as on similar items in the Galloway Hoard, an array of diverse artefacts buried in a vessel during the Viking Age in Scotland.

Perhaps the most stunning *æstel*-like object recorded with the PAS, however, was found in 2015 by Steve Keeble at Drinkstone, Suffolk (SF-3ABEB9). As such, it is one of the most easterly located examples: East Anglia was a separate kingdom at the time of Alfred the Great, under the control of Danish Vikings, and is approximately 140 miles from Winchester. The form of the Drinkstone Jewel is like that of the Gretton example, but its dome is decorated with a lozenge filled with gold pellets, and, at its centre, a tube holding a blue glass cabochon. The rest of the surface

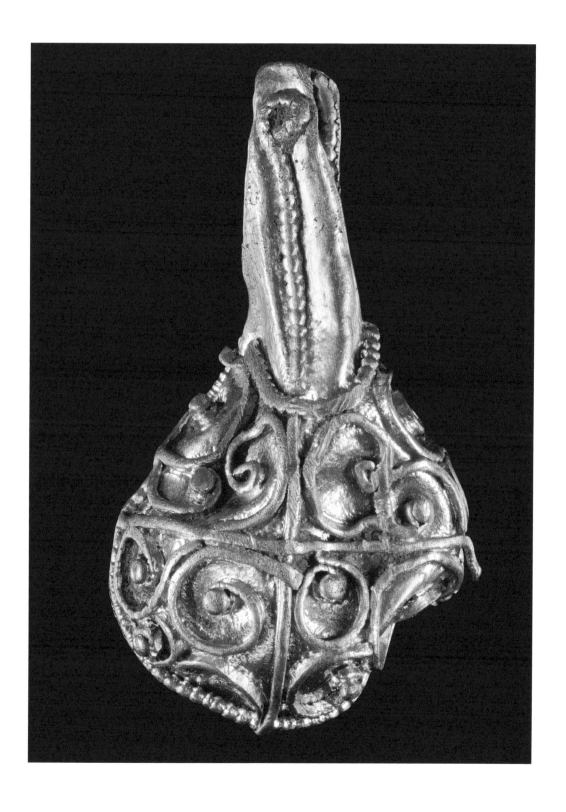

BELOW Andy (Mackenzie Crook) and Lance (Toby Jones) visit the British Museum to see Lance's *æstel* in the BBC comedy series *Detectorists*.

OPPOSITE King Alfred's Preface to the Old English translation of Pope Gregory the Great's *Pastoral Care*.

is embellished with filigree scrolls. It also has fixing holes for attachment to another object.

The PAS has added notably to the corpus of known *æstel*-like finds, but are they all King Alfred's *æstels*? Although the objects are so different, there are aspects in common. Many are gold, incorporate gold wire and most are adorned with a cross motif, suggesting a religious function. They all appear to be late 9th century in date, contemporary with the distribution of Alfred's translations of Gregory's *Pastoral Care*. A complicating factor is that – unlike the pre-PAS examples – many of the new finds have come from well outside the 'Wessex heartlands' of Alfred's kingdom. Also, as Leslie has observed, they vary in quality, which is hard to reconcile with the idea that all were worth 50 *mancuses* as described by Alfred. Their relationship to Alfred's *æstels* is still a riddle, with new finds both adding to and muddling our understanding of these fascinating and beautiful objects.

The mystery surrounding *æstels* has also captured the public imagination. In the 2015 Christmas special episode of the hit BBC television series *Detectorists*, Lance (played by Toby Jones) visits the British Museum where an *æstel* that he had found is on display. Since finding the jewel his detecting luck has run out, which he blames on the 'curse of the gold' and seeks to rebury the object where he found it. Thankfully, his plans change…

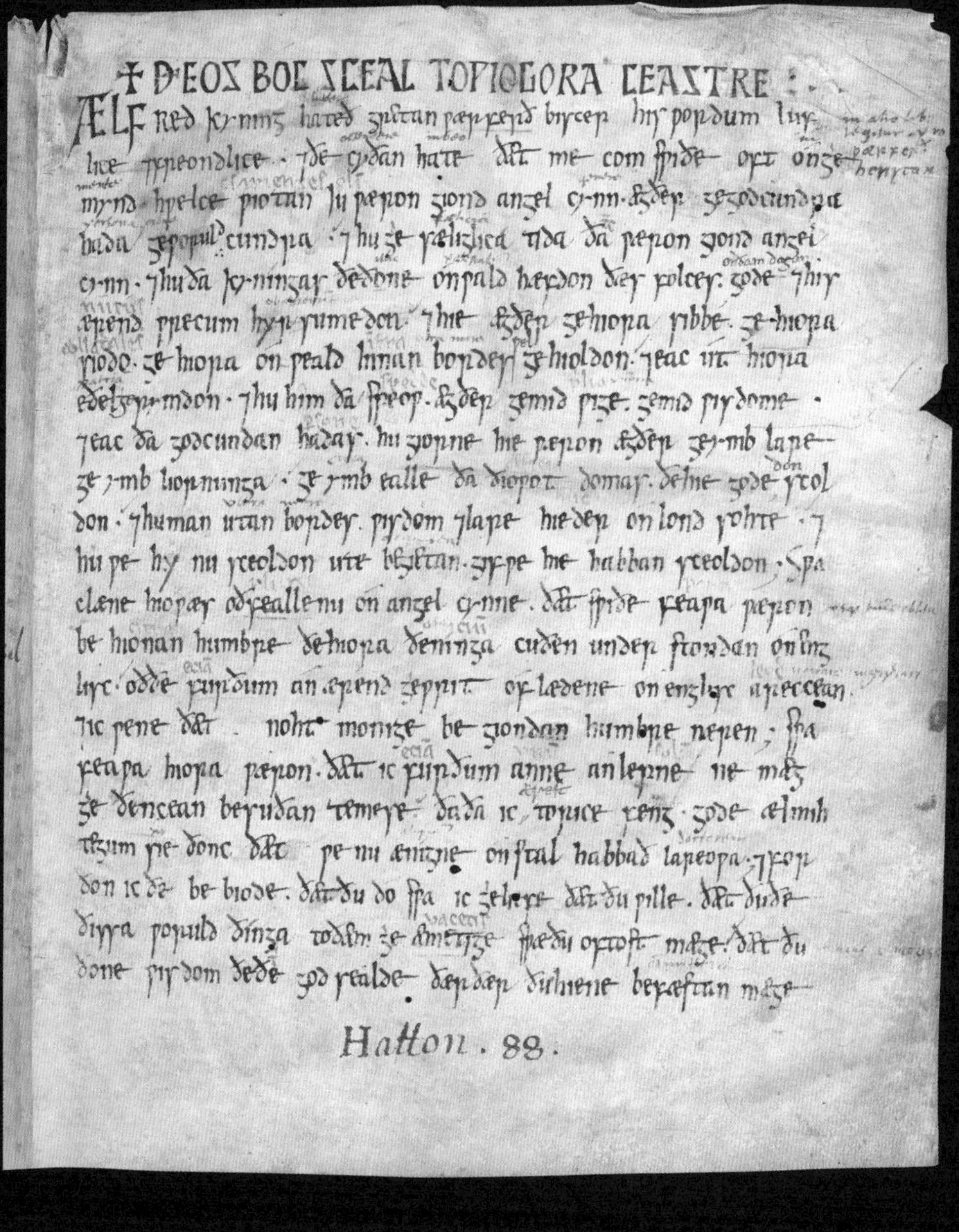
✝ ÐEOS BOC SCEAL TO WIOGORA CEASTRE ::
ÆLFRED kyning hateð gretan wærferð biscep his wordum luf
lice & freondlice & ðe cyðan hate ðæt me com swiðe oft on ge
mynd hwelce wiotan iu wæron giond angel cynn ægðer ge godcundra
hada ge woruldcundra & hu gesæliglica tida ða wæron giond angel
cynn & hu ða kyningas ðe ðone onwald hæfdon ðæs folces gode & his
ærendwrecum hyrsumedon & hie ægðer ge hiora sibbe ge hiora
siodo ge hiora onweald innan bordes gehioldon & eac ut hiora
eðel rymdon & hu him ða speow ægðer ge mid wige ge mid wisdome
& eac ða godcundan hadas hu giorne hie wæron ægðer ge ymb lare
ge ymb liornunga ge ymb ealle ða ðiowotdomas ðe hie gode scol
don & hu man utan bordes wisdom & lare hieder on lond sohte &
hu we hy nu sceoldon ute begietan gif we hie habban sceoldon. Swa
clæne hio wæs oðfeallenu on angel cynne ðæt swiðe feawa wæron
be hionan humbre ðe hiora ðeninga cuðen understondan on eng
lisc oððe furðum an ærendgewrit of lædene on englisc areccean.
& ic wene ðætte noht monige begiondan humbre næren; Swa
feawa hiora wæron ðæt ic furðum anne anlepne ne mæg
geðencean besuðan temese ða ða ic to rice feng. gode ælmih
tegum sie ðonc ðætte we nu ænigne onstal habbað lareowa. & for
ðon ic ðe bebiode ðæt ðu do swa ic geliefe ðæt ðu wille. ðæt ðu ðe
ðissa woruld ðinga to ðæm geæmetige swa ðu oftost mæge. ðæt ðu
ðone wisdom ðe ðe god sealde ðær ðær ðu hiene befæstan mæge
Hatton . 88.

THE VALE OF YORK HOARD

'The links it holds to the Arabic-speaking world are amazing. There is simply nothing else like it in Yorkshire.'
ADAM PARKER, YORKSHIRE MUSEUM

SWYOR-AECB53

OBJECT TYPE Hoard (coins, hack-silver and jewellery in silver-gilt vessel)

MATERIALS Silver and gold

DATE *c.* 927–29 CE

LOCATION Near Harrogate, North Yorkshire

DISCOVERY METHOD Metal detecting

COLLECTION British Museum and Yorkshire Museum

CONTENTS OF HOARD

1 silver-gilt cup

1 gold armring

67 pieces of hack-silver (comprising 5 armrings, and fragments of brooches, ingots and rods)

617 silver coins

OPPOSITE Silver-gilt 9th-century Frankish cup from the hoard.

BELOW The cup prior to conservation, with most of the contents of the hoard still packed inside it.

A GOOD DECISION IN THE FIELD

Father and son David and Andrew Whelan, members of the 'Two Dales' Metal Detecting Club based in Ilkley, West Yorkshire, had detected together over several years, but had yet to unearth anything of note or even record finds with the PAS. That would change on a Saturday in early January 2007 when they were searching a ploughed field near Harrogate, North Yorkshire – in the 'Vale of York' – and received a decent but unremarkable signal. This became stronger as they dug and at a depth of almost half a metre, they uncovered fragments of lead, probably remains of a protective lead sheet that had been wrapped around a vessel that they at first thought was the ballcock from a toilet cistern. Holding it in their hands, the weight of the piece betrayed that it must be filled with something other than dirt, and taking notice of the elaborate decoration on the exterior, they realised it was a container of some sort. Spotting a few stray coins, which they recognised as being of some age, they were overcome by excitement, suspecting that they had found a hoard.

After recovering some more silver fragments that were scattered around the findspot near the vessel, David and Andrew immediately contacted their local Finds Liaison Officer, Amy Downes (South and West Yorkshire) with the news, who collected the find and brought it to the British Museum. Thankfully the finders had made the praiseworthy decision not to remove anything from the cup themselves, thus preserving the position of the artefacts in relation to one another as much as possible. After the pot had been X-rayed (which revealed that it was crammed full of coins and other items) it was micro-excavated by conservator Hayley Bullock over five days.

A COLLECTION FROM ACROSS THE WORLD

Gareth Williams (former Curator of Early Medieval Coinage) and Barry Ager (former Curator of Early Medieval Continental Collections) jointly examined the contents of the hoard. They identified 617 silver coins ranging from the later part of the reign of Alfred the Great (r. 871–99) through to those minted by his grandson Æthelstan (r. 924–39), as well as a gold armring

BELOW Æthelstan coin proclaiming him *Rex Totius Britanniae* ('King of all Britain').

BELOW The gold armring from the hoard: gold is rare in Viking-era hoards. The V-shaped punched decoration is typical of Scandinavian-Irish jewellery from the period.

and 67 pieces of jewellery, hack-silver and silver bullion – as a group, indicative of a Viking Age hoard. It was immediately clear that in addition to the sheer number of items in the hoard and the high quality of many of them, the find was special because it contained artefacts from across Europe and beyond, demonstrating the international connections of the person (or people) who had buried it.

The silver-gilt vessel is the largest and most impressive single artefact in the hoard, as well as being its container. Foliate motifs encircle the upper rim and fill the spaces between six roundels surrounding the belly of the cup. In each roundel is a different animal: two 'big cats' look forward and appear to chase four beasts (deer, stag, antelope and horse) that look backwards. Niello, a black lead and silver paste used to inlay engraved decoration, remains in many places on the exterior of the cup. The vessel was made on the Continent by Frankish craftspeople in the early 9th century, a hundred years prior to the burial of the hoard (Egon Wamers, of Frankfurt University, suggests parallels to the animal scenes in the Stuttgart Psalter, a Carolingian illuminated manuscript of the same date now in the Württemberg State Library). The cup may

have been stolen from a church or other holy site and passed down as a payment or tribute. Its closest parallel is a vessel of remarkable likeness found in 1815 at Halton Moor, Lancashire; indeed, they are so similar that it has been suggested they could have come from the same workshop! Fitting, then, that after these two vessels separately found their way to England, probably as a result of Viking raids in what is now northern France or the Low Countries, they are now on display next to one another at the British Museum.

Barry argues that the form and decorative motifs on the Vale of York cup were ultimately influenced by European connections with the Middle East and Central Asia during the early medieval period. These cultural contacts are complemented by the inclusion in the hoard of fifteen silver Islamic *dirham* coins, from the region that is now Iraq and Afghanistan, likely acquired through trade routes via the Black Sea and Eastern Europe. Two other artefacts in the hoard – a silver 'Permian' ring (actually part of a silver neck ring) and the silver barrel-shaped pendant linked by a chain to a brooch pin (which would have connected to a larger brooch) – have parallels in hoards found in Russia.

The inclusion of the complete gold armring in the hoard is remarkable because, as explained by Barry and Gareth, it is unusual for gold to be present in a silver hoard from the Viking period

BELOW Some important coins from the hoard, left to right: Viking silver penny, minted in York, with the sword of St Peter; Islamic silver *dirham*; and Æthelstan 'building'-type silver penny.

because gold was not widely available at the time. With its V-shaped punched decoration, this gold armring, like the complete silver bracelets, is typical of those found around the Irish Sea and in Scandinavia, perhaps coming from Ireland itself. Other pieces of hack-silver (silver items chopped up into pieces to be traded by weight) have come from jewellery featuring triangular punches with dots, which are also typical of finds from the 'western' part of the Viking world.

Aside from the above-mentioned *dirhams* and four Frankish *deniers*, the coins originate in England. Important among them are a rare 'building' type of Æthelstan's – so called because it features on one side a depiction of a short, peaked, structure thought to be a church – believed to date from after Æthelstan took control of York in 927. Also significant are pennies minted by the Vikings in York, displaying an image of a hammer representing the Norse god Thor, together with the sword of St Peter, the patron saint of York Minster. But the vital piece of evidence in dating the hoard is another coin of Æthelstan's, with the inscription 'REX TO BRIE' – short for REX TOTIUS BRITANNIAE ('King of all Britain'), an accolade he used after meeting other British rulers at Eamont Bridge, Cumbria, in 927. Gareth believes that the

inclusion of the single coin of this type (the latest coin present) indicates that the hoard was buried soon after this coinage was introduced, which could not have been before 927. Therefore, it is suggested the hoard was put in the ground between 927 and 929.

LOOT AND MORE

The hoard was buried during a crucial moment in the formation of the country now known as England. Following the successful resistance by Alfred the Great to Viking invasions (during which at least once Viking ruler, Guthrum of East Anglia, was compelled to convert to Christianity), his children Edward the Elder (r. 899–924) and Æthelflæd, Lady of the Mercians (r. 912–18), consolidated the authority of the house of Wessex. Æthelstan's subsequent defeat of the Vikings at York in 927 saw the unification of England under one rule, albeit temporarily, for the first time since the departure of Roman authority in the 5th century. Recognition of his 'overlordship' later in the year at Eamont Bridge by the kings of what are now Scotland and Wales underlined Æthelstan's power. It would not last beyond his death, however, and in 939 the people of the kingdom of York chose a Viking from Ireland as their leader.

BELOW The hoard as found,
contained within the silver-gilt cup.

OVERLEAF The vessel from the
hoard (right), with the Halton Moor
Cup (left) found in Lancashire in
1851; they are so similar that they
might be from the same workshop.

This period, then, was one of episodic fighting and political change. Since the discovery of the Vale of York Hoard, detectorists have found substantial hoards from the Viking Age (9th to 10th centuries) at Silverdale, Lancashire (LANCUM-65C1B4), Barrow-in-Furness, Cumbria (LANCUM-80A304), Bedale, North Yorkshire (YORYM-CEE620), Watlington, Oxfordshire (SUR-4A4231; see pp. 150–53) and Balmaghie, Dumfries and Galloway (better known as the Galloway Hoard; see p. 160). These hoards show that it was not unusual for Vikings and their contemporaries to gather a mix of coins, bullion and intact jewellery originating from various places, and then to bury them for safekeeping. They also seem to have chosen 'out of the way' places – away from contemporary structures, as demonstrated by further archaeological investigation by York Archaeological Trust at the findspot of the Vale of York Hoard. The people who buried these hoards obviously never retrieved them. Perhaps some were killed in military conflicts of the day – or lost track of exactly where their hoards had been buried.

Unusually for finds of Treasure, the Vale of York Hoard was jointly acquired by two institutions, the British Museum and York

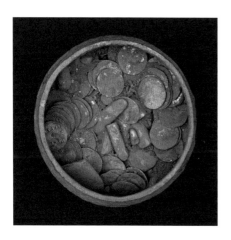

Museums Trust. The objects were expertly cleaned by conservators at the British Museum deploying a variety of techniques, including using porcupine quills to painstakingly scrape away tiny traces of dirt without scratching the delicate metal surface.

Adam Parker, Curator of Archaeology at Yorkshire Museum, explains that the Vale of York Hoard is of central importance because of its size, scope, and excellent preservation. 'Much of the hoard was contained within the vessel, preserving its contents in excellent condition. The huge number of coins from this hoard provided us with valuable new information about the history of England in the early 10th century as well as Yorkshire's wider cultural contacts in the period. The links it holds to the Arabic-speaking world are amazing.…There is simply nothing else like it in Yorkshire.'

The Vale of York Hoard featured in a major exhibition 'Vikings: Life and Legend' at the British Museum in 2014, and in the associated cinema showing of *Vikings Live*. It toured the country as part of the 'Viking: Rediscover the Legend' show, stopping at the Djanogly Gallery, Nottingham, The Atkinson in Southport and Norwich Castle Museum and Art Gallery in 2017. In 2024 the cup was displayed in the British Museum 'Silk Roads' exhibition alongside a similar one from the Galloway Hoard. In addition to being a permanent part of the collection at Yorkshire Museum, the hoard has been on display locally in the region where it was found – in Harrogate Museum, North Yorkshire, and at the Jorvik Viking Centre, York. It has also travelled internationally, visiting the Museum für Vor- und Frühgeschichte in Berlin and the National Museum Denmark in Copenhagen. So, in a manner of speaking, it has resumed its journey across the Viking world that was begun over 1,000 years ago.

BELOW LEFT AND BELOW RIGHT Two pieces of hack-silver (chopped-up silver jewellery used as money) from the hoard.

BOTTOM The complete hoard after conservation.

Medieval

TOTAL FINDS RECORDED ON PAS DATABASE

323,635

MOST COMMON ARTEFACT TYPES ON DATABASE

coin, buckle, vessel, strap fitting, mount

TOP 5 COUNTIES ON DATABASE

Norfolk, Suffolk, Lincolnshire, North Yorkshire, Hampshire

PAS data as of October 2024

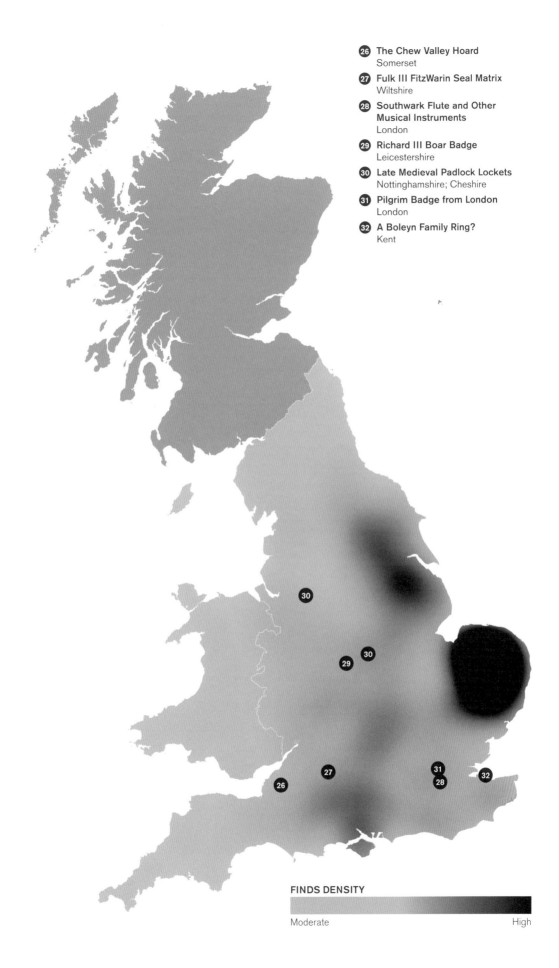

26 The Chew Valley Hoard
Somerset

27 Fulk III FitzWarin Seal Matrix
Wiltshire

28 Southwark Flute and Other
Musical Instruments
London

29 Richard III Boar Badge
Leicestershire

30 Late Medieval Padlock Lockets
Nottinghamshire; Cheshire

31 Pilgrim Badge from London
London

32 A Boleyn Family Ring?
Kent

FINDS DENSITY

Moderate   High

THE CHEW VALLEY HOARD

A hoard of almost 3,000 silver coins that was stashed for safekeeping during the Norman conquest of England

GLO-D815B3

OBJECT TYPE Hoard (coins)

MATERIALS Silver

DATE c. 1066–70 CE

LOCATION Chew Valley, Somerset

DISCOVERY METHOD Metal detecting

COLLECTION Museum of Somerset, Taunton (South West Heritage Trust)

CONTENTS OF HOARD

2,584 silver coins, including 69 cut halves and 3 'mules'

OPPOSITE Silver pennies of Edward the Confessor (top), Harold II (below right) and William I (below left) from the hoard.

OVERLEAF Some of the 2,584 late Anglo-Saxon and Anglo-Norman silver pennies in the hoard, after conservation.

DISPERSED HOARDS

The *Code of Practice for Responsible Metal Detecting in England and Wales* makes it clear that detectorists should stop and get archaeological help when they make a find that has been undisturbed below the level of ploughsoil or discover a concentration of material or something else unusual. In the field, however, it is sometimes hard for detectorists to know when this is the case, especially with a coin hoard that seems to have been disturbed and dispersed by the plough.

The Chew Valley Hoard was discovered in January 2019 by a group of seven detectorists including Adam Staples and Lisa Grace. They immediately contacted the Portable Antiquities Scheme (PAS) to report the discovery and seek advice on what to do. They believed that the hoard was dispersed, and based on that understanding were told by several archaeologists that it would be fine to remove from the ground any coins clearly outside an archaeological context (so in the plough zone) and bag any clumps found together. Unfortunately, an archaeologist could not visit the site that day and the detectorists – worried that the hoard site might be looted by nighthawks – were keen to recover the hoard in its entirety. The nature of their excavation meant that the precise findspot for each of the coins was not recorded, and the recovered coins were bagged more arbitrarily than the archaeologists expected: they were delivered to the British Museum in bags, each one containing 100 coins.

Gareth Williams (former Curator of Early Medieval Coinage at the British Museum) observed that the hoard contained clusters of coins struck from the same dies, which does suggest that the hoard had some internal grouping when deposited in the ground; it may have been made up of multiple batches of coins enclosed in leather or textile bags, now decomposed. A detailed analysis of the exact original layout therefore would have been extremely valuable for the interpretation of the hoard, but this information was lost when the coins were removed from the ground. Even so, the hoard is clearly of national significance, especially for understanding events at the time of the Norman Conquest of England.

as William's first issue (so *c.* 1067–70), but in each case the moneyer was illicitly reusing an earlier die, presumably to avoid the payment owed to the king for the issue of replacement dies. Moneyers who did this were playing a dangerous game since defrauding the king could result in severe sanctions. At this time coinage was heavily regulated, with only current issues permitted to circulate. Older issues (and foreign coins) could be exchanged for new coins, but at a premium that went to the ruler (as a fee might be charged when converting modern foreign currency).

To put the size of the Chew Valley Hoard into context, the entire PAS database contains only *c.* 30 single coin finds of Harold and *c.* 250 of William. The hoard is a significant find, of great importance for understanding currency circulation at the time of the Norman Conquest. Given that the coins are of Harold II, and William I's first issue, the hoard was probably deposited no later than 1070, or maybe in 1068 since the dating of the first issue of William I is not completely understood.

England was not entirely conquered when William's army defeated Harold at Hastings and killed him. Even after the formal submission of the English aristocracy at Berkhamsted and then London in late 1066, rebellion was common. This was especially the case in the North, notably in Yorkshire which received the wrath of William's anger, but also in East Anglia. More local to the findspot of the Chew Valley Hoard, Exeter was the site of a major insurgency against William's rule in 1068. Later that year, sons of Harold Godwinson – named in later sources as Godwine, Edmund and Magnus – arrived from exile in Ireland with a naval force and attempted to take Bristol. The attack failed, though they plundered Somerset.

1066 AND ALL THAT

The hoard contained 2,584 late Anglo-Saxon and Anglo-Norman silver pennies, including 69 cut halves, and some that are damaged and fragmentary. They weigh 3367 g in total – a large amount of high-quality silver. Besides one coin depicting Edward the Confessor (r. 1042–66), all the others are of Harold II (Godwinson) (r. 1066) and his successor William I (the Conqueror) (r. 1066–87), who fought each other for control of the English crown at the Battle of Hastings (14 October 1066). 1,238 were of Harold's 'PAX' (peace) type, and 1,343 were first issues of William (minted 1066–87) known as the Profile/Cross Fleury type.

Three 'mules' were discovered among the coins. Mules are coins with non-standard combinations of obverse and reverse designs. One used the Pyramids type of Edward with the Profile/Cross Fleury type of William, and another two combined the PAX type of Harold with the Profile/Cross Fleury type of William. Gareth thinks that these mules would have been struck around the same time

The following year they ravaged Devon. Both incursions might be seen as piracy, but a serious attempt to gain a foothold in their father's kingdom cannot be discounted.

It is not known who might have buried the Chew Valley Hoard, or even whether they were English or Norman, but it was likely buried for safekeeping during this turbulent period in William's early reign. Gareth has estimated the value of the hoard to be worth more than 500 sheep, or the annual income of a medium-sized estate. It would have represented a huge financial loss to the people who buried it and were unable to return for it – though perhaps they had been killed in one of the rebellions against William.

SAVING THE HOARD

When the Chew Valley Hoard was first announced to the press it was very much hoped it could stay together. If that was not possible, various museums also expressed interest in acquiring individual coins that were particularly rare or had a local connection.

The obstacle for museums in acquiring the entire hoard is its value (recommended by the Treasure Valuation Committee): an incredible £4,300,000. The task of raising such a large amount of money – the largest Treasure reward ever – is enormous.

In June 2024, the South West Heritage Trust (SWHT) acquired the hoard on behalf of the nation. It will be on permanent display at the Museum of Somerset, Taunton. The acquisition and display were made possible by a £4,420,527 grant from the National Lottery Heritage Fund and a £150,000 grant from the Art Fund, alongside smaller but vital grants from the Friends of the Museum of Somerset, the Somerset Archaeological and Natural History Society and SWHT. Amal Khreisheh, Curator of Archaeology at SWHT, says that her institution 'stepped forward to prevent the Hoard from being dispersed and lost to scholarship', believing it essential that the whole hoard was retained together, in public ownership, so that it can continue to be studied by researchers and enjoyed by the public.

FULK III FITZWARIN
SEAL MATRIX

The personal seal of a powerful Marcher lord from Shropshire who rebelled against the king – and lived to a ripe old age!

BERK-FDCFD2	
OBJECT TYPE	Seal matrix
MATERIALS	Copper alloy
DATE	Late 12th–early 13th century
LOCATION	Little Bedwyn, Wiltshire
DISCOVERY METHOD	Metal detecting
HEIGHT	13 mm
THICKNESS	7 mm
DIAMETER	54 mm

OPPOSITE Part of a two-part seal matrix for Fulk III FitzWarin, it would have been used to create a double-sided wax seal to attach to official documents.

BELOW A modern impression of the seal matrix showing FitzWarin on horseback; his coat of arms is visible on the shield.

SEAL MATRICES

Medieval seal matrices are relatively common metal-detector finds and almost 7,000 have been recorded with the Portable Antiquities Scheme (PAS). These items functioned a bit like a signature or PIN does today. A matrix (stamp) was used to create a personal seal, usually in wax, which the owner applied to a vellum document to authenticate or 'sign' it. They were used by a wide variety of people in the Middle Ages and the matrices that have been found and recorded are of varying quality. Most are copper alloy (3,800 matrices on the PAS database) or lead (2,800), but occasionally they can be made of precious metal. Many are personal seals, although some were so-called 'off-the-shelf' varieties that do not name individuals but instead have a standard design (such as a fleur-de-lis) and common Latin phrases (such as SIGILLVM SECRETI, 'secret seal'). Personal seals are interesting to archaeologists and historians because there is an opportunity to link them to someone who once lived, even if all we know is that they were called John or Joan!

FULK FITZWARIN

In 2014 an especially interesting personal seal matrix, inscribed with the legend 'SIGILLVM F[VLCONIS FIL]II WARINI' ('Seal of Fulk FitzWarin'), was found at Little Bedwyn, Wiltshire, and recorded with Anni Byard, then Berkshire and Oxfordshire Finds Liaison Officer (FLO). It was larger than most, with a diameter of about 54 mm, finely detailed and in extremely good condition. Its centre bears the image of a helmeted knight on horseback, charging towards the right (in the impression) with a shield in his left hand and sword raised behind his body. The image is so detailed that the knight's mail, the folds in his surcoat, the slit and grill in his helmet, and his swordbelt strap and shield are all clearly visible. On the shield is half of the blazon of FitzWarin's arms, which in heraldic language would be described as *quarterly per fess indented argent and gules* (the shield is quartered, and each quarter is silver or red, and a zig-zag line divides the upper and lower parts). The horse wears a high saddle and its mane has been plaited. The bridle and reins are clearly

BELOW Whittington Castle, Shropshire, seat of the FitzWarin family; its seizure by King John led to Fulk III's rebellion.

visible and the strap across the horse's chest is decorated with dangling harness pendants in the shape of crosses; these objects themselves are also relatively common detector finds. The reverse of the matrix is plain and undecorated.

The object has a four-sided knop projecting from the top with a 'pin' in its centre, which shows that it was part of a two-part seal matrix. As Adrian Ailes of the National Archives describes in the PAS record, 'The projecting lug at the top would slot into a hole projecting from the edge of the reverse matrix. This ensured that the two matrices (obverse and reverse) when brought together would be aligned and that pressure could be put on to the soft wax cake in between to ensure a good seal impression.' Most of the matrices recorded with the PAS are constructed more simply, for a one-sided design to be stamped into hot wax. The FitzWarin seal matrix would have been used to make a hanging double-sided seal, which is more common for high-status seals.

MYTHS AND LEGENDS

Through the work of Adrian, and Clive Cheesman (Richmond Herald) at the College of Arms, this seal has been identified as once belonging to Fulk III FitzWarin. The first Fulk of this family (b. 1115) was a powerful Marcher lord seated at Whittington Castle, Shropshire, on the English-Welsh border, and also at Alveston in Gloucestershire. Fulk III (b. *c.* 1160) was an equally powerful man, later made famous by the Anglo-Norman romance *Fouke le Fitz Waryn*, which mixes fact with legend, but recounts a story of how Fulk III rebelled against King John to regain his patrimony, which Anni explored further in her PAS record. In 1165, Henry II had granted Whittington to Roger de Powys and later gave him money to repair the castle. Fulk III's father, Fulk II, successfully claimed restitution for the seizure of Whittington, but never paid the fee of 40 marks for legal possession. Upon Fulk II's death, Fulk III renewed this claim and in 1197 offered £100

BELOW King John (shown hunting in a 14th-century manuscript of the Statutes of England) suppressed Fulk III's rebellion, but later reconciled with him.

to settle it, but in 1200 King John successively granted it first to Roger de Powys's son Maurice and then, upon Maurice's death shortly afterwards, to Maurice's son Werennoc.

By April 1201, this had led Fulk III to rebel against the king. According to *Fouke le Fitz Waryn*, he was joined by his brothers, cousins and other family members, tenants and allies in the English and Welsh Marches. King John reacted by asking Hubert de Burgh to suppress the rebellion, assigning him a hundred knights for the task. The following year, Fulk took refuge in Stanley Abbey, near Studley, Wiltshire, where he was besieged by the king's forces. Significantly, Stanley Abbey is only 30 km (20 miles) to the east of the findspot of Fulk's seal matrix, so perhaps it was broken and lost or deposited around this time.

Fulk III eventually managed to escape from Stanley Abbey with the help of the Archbishop of Canterbury, Hubert Walter, before joining forces with King Philip II of France. In November 1203, Fulk made peace with the king. A somewhat surprising twist in the story of Fulk III FitzWarin is that, even with all this drama, he (apparently) lived to an incredible age for a medieval person and was almost 100 years old when he died!

SOUTHWARK FLUTE AND OTHER MUSICAL INSTRUMENTS

The remains of a rare bone flute and medieval stringed instruments that were miraculously preserved for centuries in the mud of the River Thames

LON-58D1C9	
OBJECT TYPE	Musical instrument
MATERIALS	Bone, cork
DATE	11th–13th century CE
LOCATION	Southwark, London
DISCOVERY METHOD	Mudlarking
COLLECTION	London Museum

LENGTH	154 mm
WIDTH	25 mm
DIAMETER	9 mm

RIVER FINDS

The River Thames is not only a waterway enabling the transportation of goods in and out of London, but also a dump! The mudlarks who search its foreshore at low tide find all manner of items that were thrown away, deposited or lost in the past, as well as modern credit cards, mobile phones and cigarette lighters. All contribute to the pollution of the river, but also enrich its archaeology. The oxygen-free conditions of the river mud protect metal finds from oxidising, but significantly ensure the survival of organic materials, including numerous small bone components of medieval stringed musical instruments, which do not usually survive well buried in soil on dry land. Indeed, with such good preservation, it can sometimes be a challenge to tell whether a mudlarking find is centuries old or modern, given that the forms of some items have not changed much over time, highlighting the importance of showing finds to FLOs working for the PAS. This is particularly the case if items are simply made or unusual, such as the bone flute from Southwark.

OPPOSITE AND BELOW The flute, found by a mudlark on the River Thames foreshore at Southwark, is made from a sheep or goat tibia.

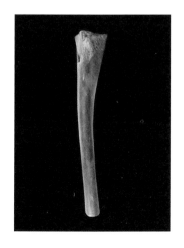

FLUTE OR WHISTLE?

Alan Murphy was a veteran London mudlark well known to Ben Paites (then the Finds Liaison Assistant based at the London Museum) when he found the bone flute at Southwark in 2014. Unsure of its date, and observing that it was a modified piece of bone, Alan took it along to Ben to get more information and report the find to the PAS, as is now required of everyone holding a permit to search the River Thames foreshore. The object was shown to Hazel Forsyth (Senior Curator at the London Museum), an expert in foreshore finds. She confirmed that the flute is made from a tibia, probably sheep or goat, and dates to the medieval period, approximately 11th–13th century. As such, it is both an intriguing find, as well as a remarkable survival.

The object is cylindrical, flaring at one end. The tissue inside the bone has been removed to make it hollow and function as a wind instrument. A cork block is wedged inside the flared end; it is probably a fipple, forming the blowhole to regulate the amount

BELOW Bone tuning pegs for medieval stringed instruments, found by Thames mudlarks, left to right: LON-BFE4E8, LON-510B6C, PUBLIC-D99BF1.

of breath that passes through the flute. The square perforation on the shin side of the bone, forming a finger-hole, helped to identify the find as medieval. Parallels include a flute made from goose ulna found on the waterfront area adjacent to the site of the medieval London Bridge and probably dating from the 11th century. Other similar examples, all made from goose bones and with no tone holes, have been found at King's Lynn, Norfolk, and Rayleigh Castle in Essex.

It was the cork fipple that interested Hazel most. Fipples are rarely found in place, so its survival in this instance was exciting. In Continental instruments, this element tends to be made of beeswax, wood or clay. Historical records show that cork was imported to medieval England and would therefore have been available as a material. Helen Leaf, who studied English medieval bone flutes for her PhD at University College London, thinks that

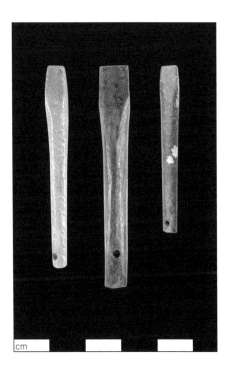

the presence of cork in this piece may suggest an Iberian or Mediterranean origin, however. The problem for Hazel and her conservation colleagues was that the substance of the fipple was hard to make out for sure (even under a microscope) and determining whether the apparent slot in it (necessary for it to work as an instrument) was created on purpose, or just a product of decay. Furthermore, Hazel reckons that the object is technically a whistle as it has no thumb or tone holes. Even so, she suggested it would be possible to create a double octave (sixteen notes) with constant breath, over-breathing and under-breathing, and to alter the timbre with pressure over the open end.

It is not known who lost the find, but given that it might have been made abroad, Hazel speculates that it could have been dropped overboard in the Thames by a sailor or a traveller from overseas. Certainly, it has no obvious damage, so it is likely to have been lost accidentally rather than cast into the river as rubbish, or otherwise on purpose.

STRINGED INTRUMENTS

Bone tuning pegs from medieval stringed instruments – such as harps, lyres or fiddles – are occasional Thames mudlarking finds, with at least ten examples from London recorded with the PAS (e.g., LON-BFE4E8, LON-510B6C, PUBLIC-D99BF1), but they are rare elsewhere. Although medieval London had many palaces, monastic residences and merchant houses that would have employed or hosted musicians, the relatively high number of bone tuning pegs from the Thames is best explained by the favourable conditions of the river mud for their preservation – in the soil of arable farmland, the source of most finds recorded with the PAS, these tiny bone items (average length 50–60 mm) would have rotted away.

BELOW Musicians playing stringed instruments in an illustration from an early 13th-century psalter.

OVERLEAF The Thames foreshore at Southwark, with the City of London visible across the river.

The tuning pegs found in London mostly date from the 13th to 15th centuries. They have a distinctive shape that makes them easy to identify: round in cross-section at one end, with a hole to hold the string (which would have been made from animal gut or thin wire); and square at the other end, to be gripped with a wrench to turn the peg during tuning. Most of the pegs found in the Thames appear to be intact, without obvious signs of breakage. They might have been replaced individually when they became worn out by the pressure of the wrench and strings. Others might have been discarded with a complete instrument if it was broken beyond repair or had gone out of fashion. Perhaps these bone pegs also had a (now unknown) alternative use. Whatever the reasons for their loss, bone musical instruments are interesting objects, providing insight into the medieval people who frequented London's streets and waterways. They are also easy to miss among the large amounts of animal remains on the Thames foreshore, so a good spot for the mudlarks who find them.

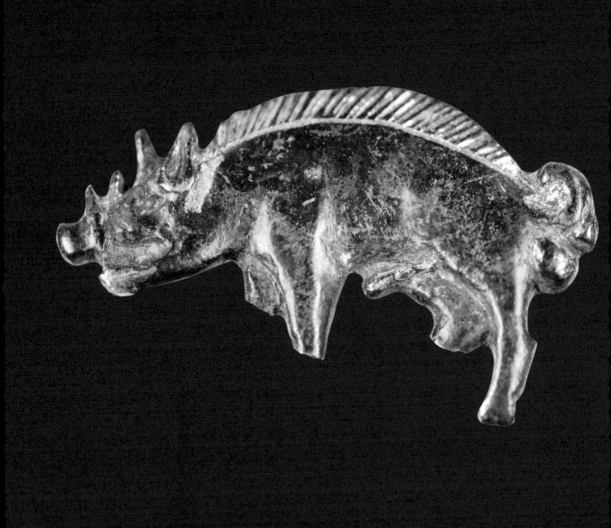

RICHARD III
BOAR BADGE

A silver-gilt livery badge that was probably worn at the Battle of Bosworth in 1485 by a knight 'who rode with the king in his last desperate cavalry charge'

GLENN FOARD, UNIVERSITY OF HUDDERSFIELD AND THE BATTLEFIELD TRUST

LEIC-A6C834

OBJECT TYPE Livery badge

MATERIALS Silver gilt

DATE 1470–85 CE

LOCATION Bosworth, Leicestershire

DISCOVERY METHOD Metal detecting

COLLECTION Bosworth Battlefield Centre

LENGTH 28 mm

WIDTH 15 mm

THICKNESS 2 mm

OPPOSITE This silver-gilt boar badge was found on the site of the Battle of Bosworth where Richard III was killed in 1485.

WHITE BOARS

The emblem of King Richard III (r. 1483–85) is the white boar. It is not known for sure why Richard took the boar as his symbol, but tradition says that he chose it because the word 'boar' plays on the Roman name for York (*Eboracum*), abbreviated as Ebor: before Richard was made Duke of Gloucester (in 1461) he was known as 'Richard of York'. Richard is known to have distributed large numbers of boar badges at his coronation on 6 July 1483, and at the installation of his son, Edward of Middleham, as Prince of Wales at York Minster on 8 September in the same year. The boar might also have been appropriated by Richard III because it was an ancient symbol of royal blood. It was clearly not a lucky charm, for Richard's bloodline was soon extinguished – Edward died of a sudden illness on 9 April 1484, and Richard himself was killed at the Battle of Bosworth on 22 August 1485. William Shakespeare famously gave Richard the lines 'my kingdom for a horse', but the Yorkist king is also described (in the same play) as an 'elvish-marked, abortive, rooting hog', words undoubtedly inspired by his emblem, the white boar.

Richard's death in battle is well remembered – not least because of the mnemonic for the order of the colours of the rainbow: 'Richard Of York Gave Battle In Vain'. In 2009 a remarkable discovery was made at Bosworth: a silver boar badge (LEIC-A6C834), recovered by an amateur detectorist who was assisting archaeologists with a survey that had been undertaken to establish the exact location of the battlefield. Such badges, known as livery badges, were worn by the retinue and followers of high-status individuals or families. For Glenn Foard, of the University of Huddersfield and the Battlefield Trust, who led the archaeological works at Bosworth, the badge was not only 'an amazing find', but one that helped to identify the spot where Richard III was killed. Because the badge is silver gilt, rather than the base metal used for lower-status livery badges, Glenn believes that it was almost certainly worn by a knight in Richard's retinue 'who rode with the king in his last desperate cavalry charge'. It was discovered near the site of

BELOW Silver-gilt boar badge found in Stillingfleet, North Yorkshire, YORYM-1716A4.

BOTTOM Silver-gilt livery badge or mount with a five-petalled flower surrounded by antlers, found in Colyton, Devon, DEV-01C907.

BELOW Richard III, who used a white boar as his emblem, was one of England's most notable kings, not least because of his untimely death in battle.

a medieval marsh as cited in historical tradition, which added credence to the view that this is where Richard was slain, and is now housed in the Bosworth Battlefield Centre.

Other boar badges have been found through metal detecting. One of the best-preserved is a silver-gilt example found at Stillingfleet, North Yorkshire (YORYM-1716A4), a year after the Bosworth boar. On the Stillingfleet badge the head and facial features of the boar are clear, along with its curly tail and obvious genitalia. Stippling on its body represents fur and incised lines on its back suggest bristles standing on end. A circular loop on the back of the badge would have been sewn through to attach it to clothing. Natalie Buy (née McCaul, then Assistant Curator of Archaeology at the Yorkshire Museum) led the successful appeal to raise money for its acquisition, arguing that 'its connection to Richard III...makes the boar badge something very important to Yorkshire'.

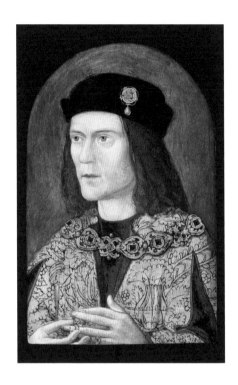

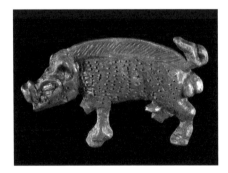

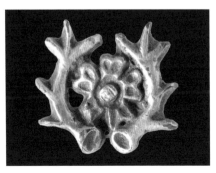

LIVERY BADGES

Precious-metal livery badges are not common, but a number have been recorded with the PAS under the Treasure Act in recent years. A particularly nice example in the form of a gilded silver stag's head was found in 2011 at Beal, North Yorkshire (SWYOR-625C53), by detectorist Brent Scriven. The stag's head is shown in profile, with its antlers pointing upwards, and somewhat comically sticks out its tongue. Stags and deer were popular aristocratic symbols in the Middle Ages, reflecting the fondness of the elite for hunting, so it has not been possible to link the Beal Stag Head Badge to a particular individual. By 1386, Richard II (r. 1377–99) was known to have adopted the emblem of a 'hart lodged' (that is, a male red deer lying down), perhaps because his mother, Joan of Kent, used a white hind (female deer) as her emblem; or perhaps even a pun on his own

BELOW Stag's-head livery badge
found in Beal, North Yorkshire,
SWYOR-625C53.

BELOW Silver-gilt livery badge with
a bird of prey, found in Branston,
Lincolnshire, LIN-497856.

name, as 'Richart'. But the hart emblem was also used by other aristocrats, including William Ferrers (1372–1445) and Richard II's half-brother Thomas Holland (1350–97). A small silver-gilt badge (or mount; the attachment does not survive) with a five-petalled flower surrounded by antlers was found in 2017 by a detectorist at Colyton, Devon (DEV-01C907). The antlers could signify an association with Richard II or his supporters, but if the ungilded silver flower was meant to represent the white rose of York, a 15th-century date is more probable for the badge, perhaps worn by someone with Yorkist allegiance during the Wars of the Roses.

Richard II also used the emblem of a white falcon. Prized for their hunting skills, birds of prey were particularly popular choices for badges among the aristocracy: Henry IV (r. 1399–1413) took as his emblem a crowned (or displayed) eagle and Anne Boleyn (d. 1536) and her daughter Elizabeth I (r. 1558–1603) used a crowned falcon. Birds were also common on secular badges worn by the

wider population as fashion accessories or expressions of allegiance: lead-alloy badges of hawks and popinjay have been found in excavations in London and are represented in metal-detecting finds from other locations recorded with the PAS – for instance, a silver-gilt livery badge of an eagle or hawk found by a detectorist at Branston, Lincolnshire (LIN-497856). The bird is standing attentively with its wings folded in; incised crescents and narrow vertical lines have been used to mark out the bird's beak, eye, wings and feathering. Sadly, the badge is broken, so parts of the bird's legs and tail are missing, as is the attachment. However, casting marks on the reverse of the object suggest that it was moulded in a cuttlefish bone, useful for creating a mould as the bone is easy to carve.

All four livery badges have since been acquired through the Treasure process. The Stillingfleet boar and the Beal stag's head are now in the Yorkshire Museum. The Colyton antler-and-flower and the Branston bird of prey are in the British Museum.

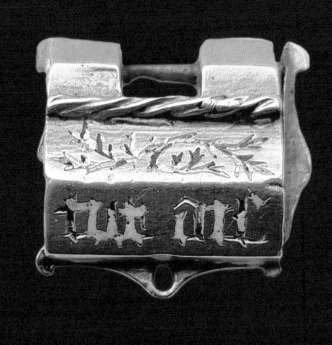

LATE MEDIEVAL PADLOCK LOCKETS

'As is our usual custom when we find any gold items, I then burst into a rendition of Spandau Ballet's "Gold".'

IAN MORRISON, DETECTORIST

DENO-E69756, LANCUM-8B79D3	
OBJECT TYPE	Locket
MATERIALS	Gold
DATE	c. 1400–1550 CE
LOCATION	Rolleston, Nottinghamshire; Adlington, Cheshire
DISCOVERY METHOD	Metal detecting
COLLECTION	British Museum (DENO-E69756)

DENO-E69756	
LENGTH	13 mm
WIDTH	13 mm
THICKNESS	3 mm

LANCUM-8B79D3	
LENGTH	13 mm
WIDTH	13 mm
THICKNESS	7 mm

OPPOSITE Two gold padlock lockets: LANCUM-8B79D3, found in Adlington, Cheshire (above); DENO-E69756, found in Rolleston, Nottinghamshire (below).

BELOW Reverse of both lockets.

LOVE LOCKS

Prior to the Industrial Revolution, when machine manufacturing made possible the production of items of consistent uniformity and exact similarity, each handmade object was unique. This was especially the case for medieval gold jewellery, but some types share broad similarities in form and decoration. New discoveries by the public that are recorded with the PAS can broaden the range of known jewellery types. Without two recent finds reported by metal detectorists, the late medieval vogue for padlock-shaped lockets worn as love tokens would have remained largely unknown.

WITHOUT REGRET

Darren Hoyle discovered a curious tiny gold padlock while detecting on a permission in the Nottinghamshire parish of Rolleston (DENO-E69756) in 2008. It is made up of two components: an outer casing and a horizontal bar that would have been disengaged by means of a U-shaped key fitting into a slot in the bottom of the outer case. The lock is decorated on both sides with engraved rosettes and a banner with a short inscription in gothic 'black-letter' script, reading *cauns* (or *sauns*) / *repentir* ('without regret'), suggesting that the 'padlock' was a love token. Darren recognised that it was something he should show to an archaeologist and brought it to Anja Rohde (then FLO for Nottinghamshire and Derbyshire) for advice. Anja delivered it to Beverley Nenk (Curator of Later Medieval Collections at the British Museum), who was able to confirm that, remarkably, a very similar item (with no other known parallels) had been found more than 40 years previously in a large hoard of gold coins and jewellery from the Fishpool area of Ravenshead, Nottinghamshire, and which was on display at the British Museum. The relative closeness of the findspots of the two padlocks added to the interest.

The padlock from the Fishpool Hoard is actually a gold locket, suspended at the neck and probably originally fastening together two ends of a chain. At just over 20 mm across, it is slightly larger than the Rolleston locket, and more complete as

BELOW The Adlington locket freshly emerged from the soil, held by finder Ian Morrison and about to be serenaded with his rendition of Spandau Ballet's anthem 'Gold'.

it retains the long U-shaped key to 'unlock' the unit, as well as three loops on the base of the locket from which pearls might have hung. Like the Rolleston locket, the Fishpool example also has a black-letter inscription in French, in this case bearing traces of white enamel and reading on one side *de tout* and on the other *mon cuer* ('with all my heart').

The Fishpool Hoard, found by workmen using a mechanical digger in 1966, is dated by its 1,237 gold English and Continental coins to 1464 – just before or after the distant Battle of Hexham (Northumberland) fought during the Wars of the Roses. It is the largest hoard of medieval gold coins ever found in Britain. The value of the coins alone represented a massive sum of money at the time and would have belonged to someone of great influence. In addition to the padlock, the hoard contained four gold finger-rings, which John Cherry (former Keeper of the Department of Medieval and Later Antiquities at the British Museum) accepted as likely English in origin, and other items of jewellery whose place of manufacture is less certain, such as an inscribed and enamelled gold

heart-brooch. John points out that during the mid-15th century, there were close connections between English and Burgundian-French nobility (who at the time also controlled the nearby Low Countries); indeed, among the coins in the Fishpool Hoard are more than 200 that were struck for the Dukes of Burgundy, predominantly Philip the Good (r. 1419–67). These connections affected the style and manufacture of jewellery. A high percentage of the craftsmen registered with the Goldsmiths' Company that regulated the making of items in gold and silver in England were 'aliens' from the Continent. This means that it can be difficult to tell whether individual jewellery items from this period were made in England by 'native' craftspeople, made in England by immigrant goldsmiths, or made abroad.

The Rolleston locket does not help in identifying the origin of the Fishpool locket, since it was not found in an archaeological context or with any other material. Its findspot is a remarkable coincidence, however, since Rolleston is about 16 km (10 miles) east of where the Fishpool Hoard was unearthed. Despite their close findspots and clear resemblance, John doesn't believe that there is enough evidence to show that the two lockets were connected in either manufacture or ownership; but their discovery has made specialists aware of a previously unknown very specific type of jewellery that seems to have been fashionable during the later medieval period. The Rolleston locket was eventually acquired by the British Museum and serves to complement the original padlock.

ALWAYS JOYFUL

A third gold padlock locket was discovered in 2022 by Ian Morrison near Adlington, Cheshire (LANCUM-8B79D3). Ian was a detectorist with about fifteen years of experience when he

BELOW A wealthy couple buying wedding jewellery from a goldsmith in 15th-century Bruges. Petrus Christus, *A Goldsmith in His Shop*, 1449 (detail).

BELOW Memorial alabaster of Elizabeth Cockayne (d. 1418) with a pendant resembling a padlock locket, from Polesworth Abbey, Warwickshire.

attended a detecting rally with a good friend. He spotted a piece of land near a brook that looked 'interesting' but as others were already searching there he and his friend bided their time and had lunch until the area was clear. After only a few minutes Ian found an artefact that they recognised immediately as gold. He said, 'As is our usual custom when we find any gold items, I then burst into a rendition of Spandau Ballet's "Gold", but maybe started a bar too early because by the time I got to the word "gold" people had noticed I was singing and had started heading over!' Ian thought it might perhaps be a Victorian charm-pendant, until he posted photographs of it online and an experienced detectorist, Julian Evan-Hart, pointed out its likely medieval date.

The Adlington locket does not resemble the Rolleston or Fishpool lockets as closely as they do each other, but it is certainly from the same 'oeuvre'. At just over 13 mm across it

is smaller than the other two, though it lacks the hoops which the other two lockets have retained at both ends of the gold bar. Instead of being rectangular in profile, it is hexagonal and bulges out at the base. It has two panels on each face, the upper panels engraved with a floral motif and the lower panels bearing a black-letter inscription, *tut dic / en ioie* ('always joyful', according to historian Malcolm Jones). As with the Fishpool locket, some of the original white enamelling in the letters is retained. It is possible that the lettering on the Rolleston locket may also have contained enamel, though no trace of any remains.

John points to several alabaster effigies in English churches which seem to have been depicted wearing similar padlock-shaped lockets, although they are difficult to make out. The Adlington find shows that these items of jewellery, which prior to 1966 had not been known about in any detail, were potentially more common than previously thought, and helps provide more context for the earlier finds. In doing so it illustrates the ongoing contribution to knowledge that new finds from members of the public continue to make.

LANCUM-8B79D3

a. Black-letter inscription, without
enamel: *tut dic / en ioie* ('always
joyful')
b. Engraved with a floral motif
c. Horizontal locking bar (without
attachment loops)
d. Hexagonal rather than rectangular
in profile

FISHPOOL HOARD LOCKET

a. Horizontal locking bar (shown
disengaged) with chain
b. U-shaped locking bar (missing from
the other two)
c. White enamel inscription: *de tout
mon cuer* ('with all my heart')
d. Three loops that may once have
suspended pearls

DENO-E69756

a. Inscription in gothic black-letter
script: *cauns* (or *sauns*) / *repentir*
('without regret')
b. Loops for chain attachment
c. Horizontal locking bar (engaged)
d. Engraved rosettes
e. Slot for insertion of missing
U-shaped key

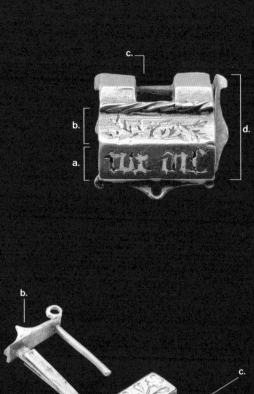

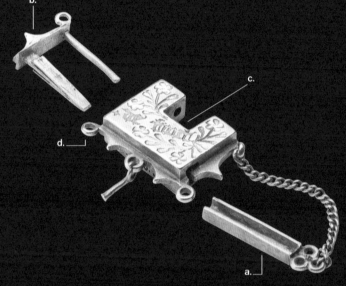

cm

PILGRIM BADGE FROM LONDON

Found by a Thames mudlark, this fragile, intricate pilgrim souvenir was thought to be one of many commememorating the assassination of St Thomas Becket that shocked Christendom – but was it?

PUBLIC-364487	
OBJECT TYPE	Pilgrim badge
MATERIALS	Lead alloy
DATE	1381–1500 CE
LOCATION	London
DISCOVERY METHOD	Mudlarking
LENGTH	73 mm
WIDTH	35 mm
THICKNESS	1 mm

OPPOSITE The pilgrim badge found by Corneliu Thira on the Thames foreshore shows the martyrdom of an archbishop by a knight inside a church or cathedral.

BELOW Back of the badge, with pin for attachment to clothing visible.

A SAINTLY MARTYR

The murder of Archbishop Thomas Becket in Canterbury Cathedral on 29 December 1170 shocked Christendom and made him an instant martyr, more famous in death than he had been in life. Thomas had achieved high office – first Lord Chancellor (1155–62), then Archbishop of Canterbury (1162–70) – thanks to his friendship with King Henry II (r. 1154–89). As chancellor, Becket effectively enforced traditional sources of royal income and enjoyed the finer things in life, including the latest fashions, feasting and hunting. When the See of Canterbury became vacant, Henry pushed for his friend to become archbishop, believing it would give him more power over the Church in England. However, once promoted, Becket sided with the interests of the Church over those of the King, causing a great rift between them. Things came to a head in November 1070 when Becket excommunicated three bishops (of Salisbury, London and York) for crowning Henry II's eldest son, another Henry, as his heir apparent. This enraged the king, who (according to tradition) uttered the words 'Will no one rid me of this turbulent priest?', leading to four of his followers travelling to Canterbury to assassinate the meddlesome archbishop.

The murder was shocking and gory – Thomas was hacked to death by the four knights while he stood before an altar in Canterbury Cathedral. Quick-thinking monks collected blood from the body of the deceased archbishop at the scene. When added to water, the blood was credited with wonder-working powers to protect and heal. Pilgrims travelled to Canterbury to take this water, which they collected in *ampullae* (leaden vessels to hold holy liquids). A cult had been born. On 21 February 1173, Becket was canonised by Pope Alexander III, and the following year Henry II did public penance at Becket's tomb. Eventually the holy liquid tinged with Becket's blood – known as Canterbury Water – ran dry, but pilgrims were still able to take advantage of the protective powers of St Thomas Becket by buying an array of pilgrim souvenirs, including bells and badges, that when touched to Thomas's shrine had the same efficacious properties.

BELOW Murder of Simon Sudbury at the Tower of London in Froissart's *Chroniques de France et d'Angleterre*, 1460–80. This illustration was modelled on ones of Becket's murder, so has multiple knights present.

BELOW Badge maker Colin Torode (Lionheart Replicas) demonstrating how pilgrim badges (here, his own replica badges) were sometimes worn pinned or sewn on hats.

ST THOMAS BADGES

The near-complete survival of this lead-alloy pilgrim badge in the River Thames is remarkable, especially given its large size and complex design, which makes it relatively fragile. It was discovered by Corneliu Thira while mudlarking in January 2016. As a 'self-recorder', a finder trained to log his own finds, he recorded it directly onto the PAS database for his local FLO to approve: the PAS is keen to encourage more self-recording as it enables finders to get more closely involved in the process and ensures that more finds can be recorded on the database.

The badge appears to show the murder of Becket, but he is attacked only by one knight (rather than the usual four), raising the possibility that this might be a badge commemorating a different martyr. In 1381, another archbishop of Canterbury, Simon Sudbury, was murdered during the Peasants' Revolt. Like Becket, he was also Lord Chancellor of England. Sudbury was leading Mass at St John's Chapel in the Tower

of London when he was interrupted by an angry mob and dragged to Tower Hill, where he was beheaded; it is said that he was so unpopular with the people that the guards at the Tower didn't even bother trying to stop his abduction! Sudbury's disarticulated head was first fixed to a spike on London Bridge before being housed at St Gregory's Church in Sudbury, Suffolk, where it remains to this day. Sudbury's body was buried at Canterbury, with a cannonball replacing his head. On Corneliu's badge, the murder is depicted within an architectural frame mounted by a cross, suggesting that the events are taking place in a church, which works for both Becket and Sudbury.

Over 400 lead-alloy medieval pilgrim badges have been found across the country and recorded with the PAS, and more than 150 of these are from London. The London survivals are mostly thanks to the anaerobic conditions of the foreshore mud, which also explains their completeness. Pilgrim souvenirs of St Thomas Becket are relatively common; he was an especially popular saint and London was the start of the main pilgrimage route to his shrine at Canterbury. Badges from London recorded with the PAS include those of the 'bust reliquary' housed at Canterbury Cathedral

BELOW Half of a two-part stone casting mould, similar to those used for medieval badges. This one (LON-E0BD25) is from London and was used to make lead tokens with the arms of a carpenter's guild.

BOTTOM Thomas Becket badge found in Wragby, Lincolnshire, LIN-D80A35.

that contained part of St Thomas Becket's head – a slice lopped off by the knights during the attack. In most examples recorded with the PAS the head reliquary is shown alone, but a badge found upriver in Wandsworth by Lukasz Orlinski presents the reliquary within an openwork square frame (LON-205673). Another lead-alloy badge from London associated with St Thomas is of an episcopal glove (SUR-E42C11); it was discovered by a detectorist at Greenwich and would have been part of a conjoined pair. Other relics of St Thomas Becket include a miniature sword that can be unsheathed from its scabbard, mimicking the murder weapon.

The importance of St Thomas Becket's cult outside Canterbury (and beyond London) is attested by finds from elsewhere. A copper-alloy badge of St Thomas's bust reliquary (NMGW-DB8D66), in the form of a forward-facing mitred head, was found as far west as Swansea by a detectorist; in this badge the upper parts of Becket's garments are also depicted, showing him to wear an amice, a type of liturgical vestment, decorated with raised lines and pellets: tradition has it that while Becket wore this fine ecclesiastical garb of an archbishop, beneath it he wore an uncomfortable hairshirt as a sign of penance. Another St Thomas bust reliquary badge, found by a detectorist in Wragby, Lincolnshire (LIN-D80A35), is of similar design but much more ornate than the Welsh find. This badge was found in three parts: the bust reliquary is largely complete, but the frame is fragmentary, and the other piece is a representation of an angel. Its detailed and intricate design shows the skill of the badge-maker, who would have created the souvenir by carving a reverse image in a fine-grained stone (limestone from Solnhofen, Bavaria, was especially sought after for this purpose) to make a casting

mould, usually in two halves (front and back). The molten lead alloy was poured in, allowed to cool very briefly, and then the mould could be opened to release a shiny, silver-looking pewter badge. This process would have amazed people who saw them made, adding to the wonderous nature of the badges. Since they could be mass-produced so quickly, pilgrim badges were affordable to a wide range of people, and popular because of the wonder-working powers associated with them, but also as travel souvenirs.

A BOLEYN
FAMILY RING?

'I'll probably never find anything as important again, but there's always hope!'

ASH SOLLY, DETECTORIST

KENT-D29B09	
OBJECT TYPE	Finger-ring
MATERIALS	Gold
DATE	15th or early 16th century CE
LOCATION	Eastchurch, Kent
DISCOVERY METHOD	Metal detecting
COLLECTION	Historic Royal Palaces

DIAMETER	33 mm (max)
WIDTH	28 mm (max)

OPPOSITE The gold bull's-head ring found by Ash Solly.

BELOW The shoulders of the ring have images of female saints; the band is decorated with a twisted-wreath pattern.

A RING FROM SHURLAND HALL

Anne Boleyn (c. 1501–36) – the second wife of Henry VIII (r. 1509–47) and the mother of the future Elizabeth I (r. 1558–1603) – was convicted of high treason and executed after only three years of marriage. The circumstances of her ascension to the throne (Henry's annulment of his first marriage and the resultant schism with the Roman Catholic Church), the influence she had over the king and her tragic fate make for a compelling story that resonates to the present day. Historical artefacts that may have a connection with her, however remote, are always of special interest to the public.

In August 2019, Ash Solly was detecting with his fellow members of the Medway History Finders Club in Eastchurch, Kent, on the Isle of Sheppey. In a ploughed field, in the vicinity of the substantial remains of Shurland Hall, he uncovered a very large gold seal (or signet) ring, which he took to his local FLO, Jo Ahmet, for recording. On each shoulder of the ring is an engraved panel depicting a female saint. The central circular bezel (supported by rays of white enamel) is adorned with a bull's head, and the band of the ring has the shape of a twisted wreath. In short, it is an impressive piece of jewellery that would have belonged to an important person.

Built during the early 16th century, Shurland Hall was the residence of Sir Thomas Cheyne (or Cheyney) (c. 1485–1558), a knight who served as a diplomat and Lord Warden in Henry VIII's court. In October 1534 he hosted Henry and Anne who were on their way to France and would have been accompanied by a large retinue of several hundred people, no doubt imposing a massive financial obligation on Sir Thomas. It is tempting to see the bull's head on this ring as a play on Anne Boleyn's surname. Anne normally used a white falcon as her heraldic badge, but her father's coat of arms featured bulls. The bull's head was a common device in heraldry, so not enough to associate the ring with Anne or her family on its own. But for other reasons, as will be seen, the possibility of this association remains.

BELOW Iconographic ring with
St George and St Catherine,
found in Beverley, East Yorkshire,
YORYM-FCA9E5.

BELOW Iconographic ring with
St Christopher and probably
St John the Baptist, and a windmill
seal bezel, found in St Martin's,
Shropshire, WREX-5078E9.

ICONOGRAPHIC RINGS

The veneration of saints under Roman
Catholicism (until its suppression in England
by Henry VIII and his successors) found a new
form of expression in the 14th century with
the wearing of so-called iconographic rings.
Rings of this type carry small images of holy
individuals and are thought to have been worn
for protection against particular calamities
or for divine aid in certain undertakings –
St Christopher, for instance, is the patron
saint of travellers.

More than 250 iconographic rings have
been recorded with the PAS. Most are made
of silver, some also gilded, but a substantial
number (more than 70) are gold, like the
Eastchurch ring. The representations of the
holy figures or religious scenes are usually
on the bezel of the ring. An example with a
female saint, thought to be Mary Magdalene
or Saint Barbara, was found in Roxwell,
Essex, in 2017 by Rob Abbott (ESS-7CA61A).
The bezel is sometimes divided into two or
more panels with multiple figures and scenes.
A ring showing St George and St Catherine
found in the Beverley area of East Yorkshire
(YORYM-FCA9E5) by Adam Day in 2016 has a
bezel divided into two panels by a sharp ridge,

another common form for iconographic
rings. An exceptional finger-ring (PAS-D077FE),
with five panels spaced equidistantly around
the band, each showing a scene from the New
Testament, has retained some of the black
enamelling that fills in the background to
the imagery. This was found in 2002 by Alan
Croker in Sleaford, Lincolnshire, and is now
in the collection of the British Museum. Some
'iconographic' rings have floral or geometric
designs on the bezel instead of actual religious
figures or scenes, showing that there was a
broader fashion for this style of ring.

Seal or signet rings remained popular
for much longer than iconographic rings –
indeed, they are still made and worn today.
As a group, they have bezels engraved with
a heraldic element, the initials of the owner
or some combination of the two, and were
usually designed to be pressed into wax
to seal documents as a form of signature.
When lettering is present on the bezel it
is usually reversed so that the letters are
rendered correctly as an impression in the
wax. The majority of the nearly 50 gold
versions currently recorded on the PAS
database are dated to the post-medieval
period.

It is uncommon, though not unique, for
a ring to have both signet and iconographic

BELOW Iconographic images of
St Catherine (left) and the Virgin
and Child (right) on the bull's-head
ring found near Shurland Hall.

elements, as is the case with the Eastchurch
ring. A ring in the collection of the Victoria
and Albert Museum, for instance, has the
device of an eagle on the bezel, the Virgin
and Christ Child on one shoulder and
St John the Evangelist on the other. A gold
iconographic ring with a seal bezel, found
in St Martin's, Shropshire, in 2017 by Bartosz
Kucharski (WREX-5078E9), has images of
St Christopher and the Christ Child on
one shoulder and a bearded saint, thought
to be St John the Baptist, on the other; the
central seal, somewhat intriguingly, is of
a windmill.

The iconographic representations on the
ring found by Ash are clear and well-executed.
On one side of the bezel is the crowned
Virgin and Christ Child, and on the other
a crowned St Catherine of Alexandria, who
is recognisable by the attribute above her
right shoulder, the wheel on which she was
tortured. The engraving of the bull on the
bezel, the seal, is a front-on view of the animal
surrounded by a double-lined circular border.
The ears of the bull extend horizontally on
either side. Between the horns, in gothic
'black-letter' script, is a tiny character which
provides another clue to the potential owner
of this ring.

POTENTIAL BOLEYN CONNECTIONS
Anne Boleyn's father, Thomas Boleyn (*c.* 1477–
1539), was well-connected to the royal court
of Henry VIII and it was his position that
first brought Anne and her older sister Mary
(*c.* 1499–1543), who was later mistress to the
king, into Henry's orbit. Thomas was knighted
in 1509 and had diplomatic roles before being
created 1st Viscount Rochford in 1525 and the
Earl of Ormond and Earl of Wiltshire in 1529.
He had the arms *argent a chevron gules between
three bulls' heads afronty sable* (three black bulls'
heads arranged either side of a red chevron,
on a white background). As suggested above,
the bull on the ring from Eastchurch could be
a play on the Boleyn family name – indeed, on

BELOW Late 16th-century English painting of Anne Boleyn, thought to have been copied from a portrait made during her lifetime.

BELOW Between the bull's horns on the ring is a tiny gothic letter, possibly an 'r' for Anne Boleyn's brother, Viscount Rochford.

the monumental brass marking Thomas's tomb in the church at Hever, Kent, his surname is spelled 'BVLLEN' (Bullen). But it is his lesser title of Viscount Rochford that is most interesting in this context. The gothic letter between the bull's horns on the ring is so small that it is difficult to make out with the naked eye, but Rachel King (Curator of European Renaissance and Waddesdon Bequest at the British Museum) took an impression of it, and under magnification, it appears most likely to be a letter 'r'.

Was this a way to indicate that the ring belonged to the Viscount Rochford? If so, it may be a reference to Anne's brother, George (c. 1504–36), who was known by that courtesy title when his father Thomas was elevated to his earldoms in 1529. Anne's conviction for treason included an accusation that she had committed incest with George, for which he, like her, was executed in 1536.

Alternatively, if the letter is a 't' (another possible reading) it may refer to the owner of Shurland Hall, Thomas Cheyne, who was himself a distant Boleyn relation.

Although the association with the Boleyn family remains tantalisingly speculative, it is clear that the ring was owned by someone of wealth and significance in the Tudor period. The British Museum initially intended to acquire the ring, but ultimately it entered the collection of Historic Royal Palaces in 2022. Fittingly, the ring was put on display at Hampton Court Palace (see p. 272) – where the 'HA' monogram of Henry and Anne in the carved wooden panelling at the back of the Chapel Royal has outlived them both.

Ash is proud of the small but vital part he played in the life of the ring. 'It was the first bit of gold I'd ever found,' he said. 'I'll probably never find anything as important again, but there's always hope!'

BELOW Monumental brass
memorialising Thomas Boleyn (with
surname spelled 'Bullen') on his
tomb at St Peter's Church, Hever.

HERE·LIETH·S·THOMAS·BVLLEN
KNIGHT·OF·THE·ORDER·OF·THE·GARTER
ERLE·OF·WILSCHER·AND·ERLE·OF·ORM
VNDE·WICHE·DECESSED·THE·12
DAI·OF·MARCHE·IN·THE·IERE
OF·OVR·LORDE·1538

Post-Medieval and Modern

TOTAL FINDS RECORDED ON PAS DATABASE*

Post-Medieval: 287,803

Modern: 10,211

MOST COMMON ARTEFACT TYPES ON DATABASE

Post-Medieval: coin, buckle, token, jetton, mount

Modern: button, coin, seal, token, toy

TOP 5 COUNTIES ON PAS DATABASE

Post-Medieval: Norfolk, Lincolnshire, Suffolk, North Yorkshire, Hampshire

Modern: Lincolnshire, North Lincolnshire, Surrey, North Yorkshire, Northamptonshire

PAS data as of October 2024

*The Portable Antiquities Scheme is highly selective in recording objects that are less than 300 years old, so the number of records on the database from this time period is relatively small and does not reflect the total number of objects that have been found and reported.

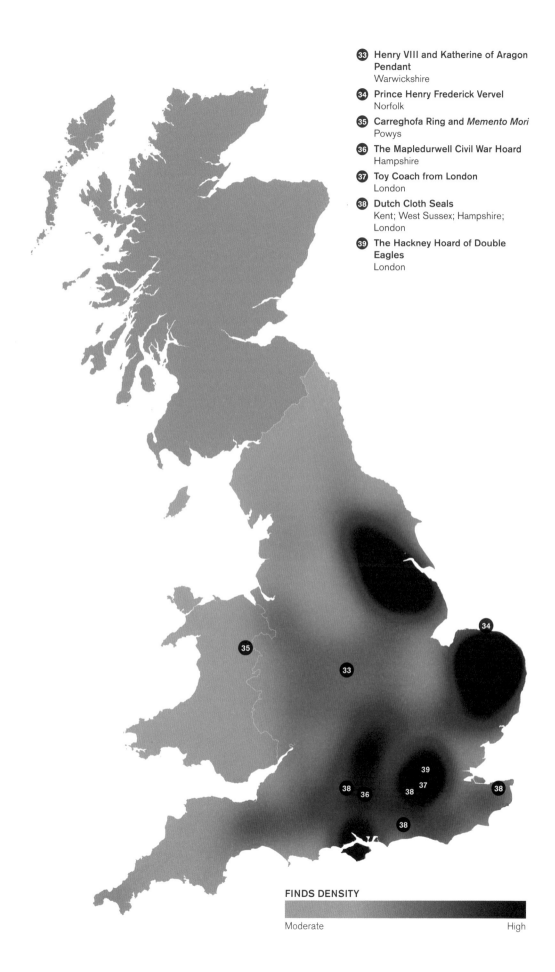

33 **Henry VIII and Katherine of Aragon Pendant**
Warwickshire

34 **Prince Henry Frederick Vervel**
Norfolk

35 **Carreghofa Ring and *Memento Mori***
Powys

36 **The Mapledurwell Civil War Hoard**
Hampshire

37 **Toy Coach from London**
London

38 **Dutch Cloth Seals**
Kent; West Sussex; Hampshire; London

39 **The Hackney Hoard of Double Eagles**
London

FINDS DENSITY

Moderate   High

HENRY VIII AND KATHERINE OF ARAGON PENDANT

'It is important physical evidence of the now-lost great luxury at the young king's court.'
RACHEL KING, BRITISH MUSEUM

WMID-A51F34	
OBJECT TYPE	Necklace
MATERIALS	Gold and enamel
DATE	Tudor, 1509–33
LOCATION	North Warwickshire
DISCOVERY METHOD	Metal detecting

LENGTH	434 mm
HEIGHT	59 mm
WIDTH	56 mm

OPPOSITE The complete pendant: gold linked chain; suspension clasp adorned with an enamelled gold hand; gold heart-shaped pendant with enamelled intertwined rose and pomegranate branches on the front.

BELOW The reverse of the pendant, with Henry and Katherine's initials and the motto 'TOVS IORS'.

ROOKIE FIND

Charlie Clarke was a relative newcomer to metal detecting when he made the discovery of a lifetime. A café owner from Birmingham, he had been detecting for only six months when he unearthed an enamelled gold pendant necklace bearing the initials 'H' and 'K' from the site of a dried-up pond in north Warwickshire. Recognising the pendant's significance, Charlie says he 'shrieked like a schoolgirl' when he first set eyes on it. Charlie immediately contacted his local Finds Liaison Officer (FLO), Teresa Gilmore, who quickly arranged to collect the pendant and bring it to Birmingham Museum and Art Gallery for safekeeping. As Teresa recalls, 'I had a mental checklist on my way down to meet with Charlie. If the item was Tudor as he described, then it needed to be gold and with enamel on it, like the Cheapside Hoard. Which it had.' Closer inspection by Teresa confirmed that this was no ordinary Tudor find. 'I noticed the initials H and K – especially the H, in lower case and a Lombardic script. And then the royal symbols – Tudor rose and pomegranate. All those factors combined made it quite important and not just a piece of Tudor goldwork.' Stunned by the pendant's large size and relatively good state of preservation, Teresa knew that there would be intense interest in its discovery. She contacted the subject specialist at the British Museum and colleagues at Historic England, who subsequently undertook an excavation of the findspot. Charlie was thrilled that archaeologists were so interested in his discovery.

The pendant was photographed by Teresa's colleagues in Birmingham before being transported to the British Museum just before the start of the COVID-19 pandemic. The timing could not have been worse. Subsequent national lockdowns and furloughing of staff, followed by the long, cautious road back to in-person work as the pandemic receded, meant that further investigation of the artefact took several years. Eventually, however, the pendant was scrutinised by British Museum scientists and conservators in one of the widest collaborative assessments of any Treasure find since the Staffordshire Hoard. Rachel King, Curator of European Renaissance and

BELOW Katherine of Aragon, the first wife of Henry VIII.

BELOW A combined rose and pomegranate silver-gilt badge found in North Devon, DEV-1C5D34.

Waddesdon Bequest at the British Museum, invited relevant period and materials experts to view the pendant and contribute their thoughts about its manufacture, purpose and ownership, to undertand the find properly and so that the report for the coroner would be as well-informed as possible.

ROYAL JEWEL?

The jewel that Charlie discovered is believed to be associated with Henry VIII (r. 1509–47) and his first wife Katherine of Aragon (1485–1536). Although their marriage – from 1509 until it was annulled in 1533 – is famous for its acrimonious ending, it was the longest of Henry's six marriages by some margin. The pendant is actually a suite of three objects: a gold chain of 75 links, a suspension clasp in the form of an enamelled gold hand, and a gold heart-shaped pendant with enamelled decoration on both the front and back.

The heart-shaped pendant is itself made up of four detachable parts: a convex-domed front, a concave-dished back, and two pins that secure the back in place. The front features the intertwined branches of a bush. The left half of the bush bears a Tudor rose with red and white enamelled petals, the symbol of Henry's dynasty, and the right half a pomegranate, representing the heraldic arms of Katherine and the Spanish kings of Aragon. Combined rose and pomegranate motifs were worn by loyal subjects on badges (see, for instance, the silver-gilt badge DEV-1C5D34, found by a detectorist in north Devon and now in South Molton Museum) to show their allegiance to Henry VIII and Katherine during their marriage, and also during Katherine's brief previous marriage to Henry's older brother Arthur. Across the bottom of this design, just above the root of the bush, is a banner with red-enamelled text reading 'TOVS IORS', possibly a pun on the French word *toujours* ('always'), with spacing that makes it sound like '*tous* (all) yours' when read aloud. The back has the red-enamelled Lombardic letters 'H' and 'K' (Henry and Katherine) connected by a white-enamelled ribbon; below them, as on the front of the pendant,

BELOW Intertwined rose and pomegranate bush illustrating a collection of poems by Sir Thomas More on the coronation of Henry VIII and Katherine of Aragon.

BELOW Front of the pendant, with intertwined rose and pomegranate bush in enamel.

is a banner with the motto 'TOVS IORS', this time in black enamel.

The chain is impressive in size (it weighs 267 g) and each link has four others attached to it. The clasp, in the form of a clenched hand coloured with red, purplish-pink and black-speckled white enamel, is secured to one end of the chain by a separate pin. Above the hand is a cloud shape. The overall appearance is of a hand coming down from the heavens, a common 16th-century emblem representing the divine hand of God, and which occasionally also symbolised romantic love when combined with a heart. Several historical documents from the 1510s and early 1520s describe a similar hand motif paired with Henry and Katherine's initials on royal horse trappings at public events.

British Museum scientists analysed the metal and enamels in various places of the jewel and found them to be consistent with materials from the early 16th century. This reinforces the possibility that the piece was constructed during the period of Henry and Katherine's long but unhappy marriage.

IMPORTANCE

The pendant is one of the finest and most important post-medieval finds discovered by a detectorist and reported under the Treasure Act. Surviving examples of early Tudor jewellery in public collections are quite rare; indeed, it was the absence of direct parallels for close comparison that made it necessary for specialists to scrutinise this find so closely. According to Rachel, 'If this artefact, either all or in part, really does date from the first decade of Henry VIII's reign, it is important physical evidence of the now-lost great luxury at the young king's court.' She explains that previously it had only been possible to read about the jewels to which the wealthy then had access, but now, 'Thanks to Charlie's find, we can actually hold this history in our hands for the very first time.'

Despite its monogram and decoration associated with Henry and Katherine, the pendant was probably not made as a gift from one to the other. It does not feature in the known inventories of royal jewels from the early 16th century. Although the pendant

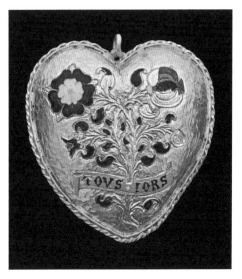

BELOW Henry VIII jousting in front of Katherine in the Westminster Tournament Roll, 1511. Henry's lance shatters as it hits his opponent; Katherine is enthroned to the left of her ladies-in-waiting. The pendant may have been worn or gifted to a participant at a similar event.

and chain appear large and impressive to 21st-century eyes, by 16th-century standards neither is outstanding in this respect and the workmanship is hurried in places, particularly in the hinges and the clasp, lacking the finesse one might expect of a royal recipient. But the items obviously belonged to someone of high standing; sumptuary laws from the early 16th century (such as the Reformation in Excess of Apparel Act of 1533) indicate that a chain of the weight and purity here would not have been suitable to be worn by anyone of lesser rank than the son of a baron, although these laws were not always adhered to.

Though unlikely to be Henry or Katherine's own, this jewel probably has some relationship to life at court. Its imagery echoes an archival account of the embroidered decoration on the caparisons (cape-like textile coverings) that were worn by Henry's horses during jousts celebrating the Treaty of Universal Peace at Greenwich in October 1518; these decorations featured a hand clutching a pomegranate and rose emerging from clouds, surrounded by interlaced letters 'H' and 'K'. It is possible that this pendant was created to be worn by a high-ranking guest as a one-off at such an event, or as a gift or prize for a participant.

POST-MEDIEVAL AND MODERN

At the time of writing, it is not yet certain whether the pendant will end up in a public collection. The British Museum has expressed an interest in acquiring it for the national collection, but this would rely on the success of fundraising. If it does find a home there, it is sure to impress visitors, taking them back to a time in England's history that has left an indelible mark on the national consciousness.

PRINCE HENRY FREDERICK VERVEL

Worn by hunting falcons, these tiny metal objects have huge archaeological significance and can trace the birds' often very famous owners

---

NMS-82AD63

OBJECT TYPE Vervel (hawking ring)

MATERIALS Silver

DATE c. 1600–12 CE

LOCATION Cley next the Sea, Norfolk

DISCOVERY METHOD Metal detecting

COLLECTION Norwich Castle Museun and Art Gallery

WIDTH 8 mm

DIAMETER 11 mm

OPPOSITE AND BELOW Silver vervel found at Cley next the Sea, Norfolk, NMS-82AD63. It has the heraldic badge of the Prince of Wales: a coronet and three ostrich feathers, with the motto 'ICH DIEN' ('I serve'). The band reads 'Henrye Prince'.

HAWKING AND HUNTING

The eldest son of King James I (r. 1603–25), Prince Henry Frederick (1594–1612) was James's heir apparent and a figure of hope for many. Even in his teenage years, Henry was seen as a staunch supporter of Protestantism, and his athleticism, handsome looks and cultured attitude seemed to make him the ideal prince. As such, there was great anticipation of his future accession to the throne. The course of British history might have been significantly different had Henry not succumbed to typhoid fever at the age of eighteen. His death was a heavy blow to his father and triggered a national outpouring of grief. It also meant that the throne eventually passed to Henry's younger brother Charles, who would reign from 1625 until his dispute with Parliament (and supposed sympathy for Catholics) led to the bloody English Civil War, the creation of the Commonwealth and Charles I's own death by execution in 1649.

During Henry's life, the sport of hunting with birds of prey (hawking or falconry) was a popular pursuit for members of the nobility and upper classes, as it had been for many centuries. Hunting birds were captured and sold, or raised from chicks, and trained to fly from their handlers' gloved fists in pursuit of quarry – and, hopefully, to return when called, although that could be unpredictable because these birds remained wild animals. Such was the investment in these birds, in both time and money as well as their owners' personal affection, that it was important to be able to recover them if they became lost. To this end, a small metal hawking ring called a vervel, usually silver and identifying the animal's owner, was affixed to the leather jesses tied to the bird's ankles. A ring-shaped vervel found in Taunton, Somerset (SOM-D02D71), by Doug Turner in 2013 makes the point clearly – it features the message 'RETORNE TOO HVGH PORTMAN'.

These small objects (most vervels weigh only 1–2 g) are a unique archaeological resource because of the possibility of tracing their owners in the historical record. A recent classification of vervels has identified three main types: washer-shaped, ring-shaped and some with heraldic shields.

BELOW Ring-shaped vervel with the message 'RETORNE TOO HVGH PORTMAN', found in Taunton, Somerset, SOM-D02D71.

The Portable Antiquities Scheme (PAS) database now has more than 100 inscribed late medieval and post-medieval vervels, all found by metal detectorists, accompanied by important information about where they were discovered. Vervels not only identify the birds' owners, and sometimes even their place of residence, but also provide information on where the owners were hunting, and with whom.

ROYAL VERVELS

One of these tiny artefacts, belonging to Prince Henry Frederick, was found by Jason Jackson and Alan Daynes in 2012 while metal detecting at Cley next the Sea in north Norfolk. This vervel, which must have come from a bird owned by the prince, consists of a shield-shaped plate just 10 mm long, attached to a ring. On the front of the plate is engraved the familiar heraldic badge of the Prince of Wales: three ostrich feathers arising out of a coronet, below which is a banner with the motto 'ICH DIEN' ('I serve'). Inscribed on the outside of the ring are the words 'Henrye Prince'. Henry was invested as Prince of Wales in 1610, so only had that formal title for two years before he died, though he was known to use the badge earlier in other contexts.

This gives a fairly tight timeframe of the first twelve years of the 17th century for when the vervel was most likely constructed, used on one of Henry's birds, and lost. Unfortunately, there are no historical records of a visit by Henry to north Norfolk, but two other vervels from the same period have been found within a few miles – seemingly unrelated in terms of their owners but nonetheless they are indicative of falconry taking place in the area. Even though the reason for the presence of Henry's vervel in Cley next the Sea remains mysterious, it is fascinating to have recovered an item associated with someone of such historical fame who was only alive for a short time.

ARISTOCRATIC HUNTERS

Vervels that have been linked to recorded individuals are often found near their places of residence; indeed, some vervels also name the location where the owner lived. Others are found in the grounds of another estate, presumably because the owner named on the vervel had brought hunting birds with them on a visit. However, given that a vervel could have been lost at any point after being affixed to a bird, or remained attached after the creature died, some vervels ended up a distance from

BELOW *Henry, Prince of Wales with Robert Devereux, 3rd Earl of Essex in the Hunting Field*, Robert Peake the Elder, c. 1605 (detail).

BELOW Memorial brass showing a hunting hawk with jesses and bells, on the tomb of Sir William Calthorpe (d. 1420), All Saints Church, Burham Norton, Norfolk.

where the bird was released, as is evident from the PAS dataset. It is possible that this was the case with the Prince Henry Frederick vervel.

Most of the individual named bird owners who can be traced from vervels would have been from the landed gentry, with titles such as 'Sir' or 'Baronet' sometimes also recorded on the objects. Several on the PAS database are from high-ranking members of the nobility,

such as the vervel found by Philip Bowes (KENT-91B046) in Eastchurch, Kent, in 2020. Featuring the crest of several members of the Herbert family and inscribed 'E: of Montgomery', it was found on land once belonging to Shurland House and owned by Philip Herbert who was, like King James I, a keen hawker, and created by him Earl of Montgomery in 1605.

The Prince Henry Frederick Vervel is not the only one affiliated with royalty that has been found by detectorists. Shield-shaped royal vervels have been recovered, including one of James I found by Kevin Paine in Angemering, West Sussex (SUSS-D17951), and another, of Charles I or Charles II, found in Thwaite, Suffolk (PAS-EA634F). A rare gold washer-shaped vervel in the collection of the British Museum (1855,1201.217), mentioned in the *Gentleman's Magazine* in 1795 and supposedly found in Biggleswade, Bedfordshire, is inscribed *sum.regis.anglie* on one side and *St.comitis*herefordie* ('I belong to the King of England and Duke of Hereford'),

BELOW Illustration of a medieval king hawking, in a French manuscript *c.* 1300–40.

seemingly referring to Henry IV (r. 1399–1413). Additionally, there is the enigmatic washer-shaped vervel found in Eaton Bray, Bedfordshire (WMID-1738A6), by Ian Wild in 2009, bearing the message 'Prince Edward' which, together with the style of lettering, points to a 15th-century date. The find location was on what would have been the route taken by the future Richard III (r. 1483–85) and his men while escorting the twelve-year-old Edward V (r. 1483) back to London in the spring of 1483 after receiving news of the death of his father, Edward IV. It seemed that this was the vervel of the younger Edward, one of the two child 'Princes in the Tower' who only a few months later disappeared from the Tower

of London, presumed murdered, shortly after the coronation of their uncle as Richard III. It is not clear what opportunity Prince Edward would have had for hawking on his journey back to London, or how his hawk was lost (or at least lost its vervel), but it is illustrative of the importance of these animals to the aristocracy and symbolic of this young man's lonely plight on the threshold of being king.

The Prince Henry Frederick Vervel was acquired by Norwich Castle Museum and Art Gallery where it is now in safekeeping, along with several other vervels found in the county. It is a reminder not just of England's 'Lost Prince', but also how what is now a niche sport was once practised by so many in elite society.

BELOW Prince Edward vervel found in Eaton Bray, Bedfordshire, WMID-1738A6.

BOTTOM King Charles I or II vervel found in Thwaite, Suffolk, PAS-EA634F.

CARREGHOFA RING AND *MEMENTO MORI*

Arresting skull and skeleton jewellery from a time when life was uncertain but death was not

WREX-90A174	
OBJECT TYPE Finger-ring	
MATERIALS Gold, enamel	
DATE 1550–1650 CE	
LOCATION Carreghofa, Powys	
DISCOVERY METHOD Metal detecting	
COLLECTION Amgueddfa Cymru – Museum Wales	
DIAMETER 21 mm	
THICKNESS <1 mm	

REMEMBER THAT YOU WILL DIE

The visage is grim: a bleached human skull in white enamel with details such as cranial sutures and eye sockets picked out in black enamel. Applied to the flat quatrefoil bezel of a gold finger-ring, the design is surrounded by the engraved legend 'Memento Mori' (translating roughly as 'Remember that you will die'), which would have also been filled with enamel. This piece of jewellery, found by long-time detectorist David Balfour in 2019 in Carreghofa, Powys, is one of the most striking examples of an aesthetic and cultural trend that peaked around 1500 and lasted several centuries.

David was taking part in a metal-detecting rally when he found the ring, which he initially took to be a child's pirate-themed toy! When he showed it to the dig organiser and landowner, they realised it was made of gold and much older. After a moment of panic at home when the ring, which had been wrapped in tissue paper for protection, was mistaken for rubbish and thrown in the bin, David retrieved it and deposited it safely with Susie White, FLO for North Wales, who recorded it with the PAS and reported it to the coroner as potential Treasure.

Mark Redknap (previously Head of Collections and Research, Amgueddfa Cymru – Museum Wales), who studied the ring, notes in his PAS report that 'it reflects the high mortality during the 16th and 17th centuries, the motif and inscription acknowledging the brevity and vanities of life.' There was an awareness that life on this earth was transient and that worldly trappings mattered for nothing after death. For some this meant that they should make the most of the time available to them in earthly life; for others, that they should focus on preparing themselves spiritually for death.

FINDS OF *MEMENTO MORI*

OPPOSITE Three 16th/17th-century *memento mori* rings, top to bottom: Carreghofa, Powys, WREX-90A174; Felixstowe, Suffolk, SF-9977A7; parish of Horton Kirby and South Darenth, Kent, KENT-9117D7.

The Carreghofa Ring is a known type of *memento mori* ring, with very similar examples in museum collections (including British Museum, AF.1520). Others have been recorded with the PAS, such as a ring found in 2019 in Shabbington, Buckinghamshire,

BELOW *Memento mori* ring found in Shabbington, Buckinghamshire, GLO-927C54; its design is similar to that of the Carreghofa Ring.

BELOW *Memento mori* ring commemorating the death of Mary Normandy in 1727, found in Hatherton, Cheshire, LVPL-6178C6.

by David Bulley (GLO-927C54) and another from Arreton, Isle of Wight, found in 2013 (IOW-9E6B77). The forms of these rings and the style of writing on the Carreghofa Ring in particular allow it to be dated roughly to 1550–1650.

Other rings with variations on the *memento mori* theme have been found by metal detectorists in recent years. A ring detected in 2018 on the beach in Felixstowe, Suffolk, (SF-9977A7) is of similar form to the Carregofa example but with the inscription 'RESPICE FINEM' ('Think [of] the end') moulded in raised letters around the central skull in four panels. In 2022 an example with an elongated six-sided bezel and the inscription 'MEMNTO MORI' was found in the parish of Horton Kirby and South Darenth, Kent, by Geoff Burr (KENT-9117D7). This ring is not adorned with a skull like the others described above, but bears the motif of a reclining skeleton. More commonly found and reported to the PAS are *memento mori* rings consisting of a simple gold band with a skull or skeleton (sometimes enamelled) on the exterior.

A ring from Hatherton, Cheshire, found in 2008 (LVPL-6178C6), has an entire skeleton encircling the band lengthwise, with a book reading 'MEMENTO MORI' above its head. Inside the band is an inscription commemorating the death of a woman named Mary Normandy who died on 9 January 1727. Finger-rings of this type, known as mourning rings, were intended to commemorate a specific individual. They carry an inscription that identifies the person and often gives their date of death and how old they were when they died. A ring found in Grittleton, Wiltshire (WILT-BDB52C), by Terry Kearton in 2023 has an evocative depiction of a skeleton on its outer surface and the message 'Ri:Bull ob', 4 Feb 1709/$_{10}$ Æta 37', ('Richard Bull, died 4 Feb 1709/10, aged 37') on the interior. The PAS database lists more than 250 rings of this type. In the later 18th century the message could be on the outer surface of the ring, without a skull, as seen on one found in 2024 by Sanna Simone in Sutcombe, Devon (CORN-12FB4B), which bears the message 'PENELOPE CLEVLAND OB:3.DEC:1746 Æ 26' against a black enamel background. Mourning rings were often paid for with money set aside by the deceased for their production and distribution among the person's acquaintances. This practice continued well into the 19th century: for instance, Jeremy

BELOW Two *memento mori* bone rosary beads found on the River Thames foreshore in London, *c.* 1450–1550: LON-78B66F (top); LON-806576 (bottom). Relative size not to scale.

Bentham (1748–1832), the 'spiritual founder' of University College London, left money for mourning rings in his will.

Rings were not the only form of *memento mori* jewellery. Two bone *memento mori* rosary beads have been recorded with the PAS. Both were found on the Thames foreshore, where the special environmental conditions allowed for their preservation. One (LON-78B66F), found in 2022 by mudlark Caroline Nunneley in the City of London, conveys the inevitability of death through a two-sided carving of a human head: one side displays the face of a woman (perhaps the Virgin Mary) wearing a late medieval headdress, and the other side is a skull.

The second bead (LON-806576) was found by another mudlark on the south side of the river in 2023 and shows a bearded man's face (thought to be Jesus or John the Baptist) on one side with a skull on the other. The beads are likely to have come from rosaries that were manufactured nearby at Paternoster Row by St Paul's Cathedral.

Finds such as these provide a poignant connection to their original owners, whose worlds were no less uncertain than our own, and who were all too aware of the fragility of life. The Carreghofa Ring now resides in the collections of Amgueddfa Cymru – Museum Wales, where it helps scholars and visitors to make that connection with the past.

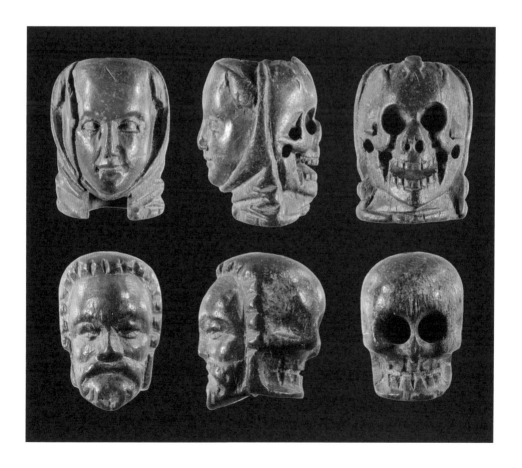

THE MAPLEDURWELL CIVIL WAR HOARD

A coin hoard deposited for safekeeping during the English Civil War – and recovered almost 400 years later by a Canadian visitor on a trip of a lifetime

HAMP-8B9913

OBJECT TYPE Coin hoard

MATERIALS Silver, ceramic (vessel)

DATE *c.* 1641–43 CE

LOCATION Mapledurwell, Hampshire

DISCOVERY METHOD Metal detecting

COLLECTION British Museum

CONTENTS OF HOARD

345 silver coins

German stoneware jug

OPPOSITE The 17th-century coin hoard found by Canadian visitor Darcy Fear in 2018.

BELOW One of the Charles I coins that helped to date the hoard.

TRANSATLANTIC HOLIDAY

In spring 2018, Darcy Fear 'crossed the pond' from western Canada to visit his family in northern Hampshire. It was his lifelong dream to go metal detecting in England, so he took the opportunity to join the Midweek Searchers on a detecting rally held on a farmer's field in the parish of Mapledurwell and Up Nately. Within five minutes of sweeping the area, he got a strong signal and dug down. He unearthed a few silver coins dating to the mid-17th century and ceramic potsherds, and then realised that he had found a hoard.

Darcy contacted Katie Hinds, the FLO for Hampshire at the time, to notify her of the find and seek advice. Since no professional archaeologists were employed by the rally organisers and many people knew where the coins had been found, a decision was taken by the organisers to lift the coins and potsherds in a single block of soil (weighing 30 kg!) and wrap it in clingfilm. Darcy was only in England for a short time on holiday, so he decided to bring the hoard in a car to the British Museum the very next day. There he met with conservator Pippa Pearce, who organised for British Museum scientists Daniel O'Flynn and Duncan Hook to X-ray the block before it would be micro-excavated in the Museum's labs. These experts were more commonly presented with Roman coin hoards to examine, so welcomed the chance to look at 17th-century finds, for a change.

Prior to flying back to Canada, Darcy was able to return to the Museum to view the work in progress. Working intensively on the hoard, British Museum conservator Duygu Çamurcuoğlu had extracted the coins and incomplete pottery vessel from the soil block in just one day as Pippa and her colleagues washed them. Compared to the heavily corroded base metal Roman coin hoards that the conservation team regularly dealt with, these silver coins were much easier to disaggregate and clean to a state where they could be readily identified – their primary objective for the Treasure process. The conservators carefully recorded the coins' locations within the block as they were extracted, so that Barrie Cook (Curator

BELOW Micro-excavation of the hoard at the British Museum.

BELOW Finder Darcy Fear delivering the hoard to Pippa Pearce at the British Museum.

of Medieval and Early Modern Coins at the British Museum) could determine more about the nature of their deposition. As expected, Barrie was able to confirm that the coins had been grouped and buried in a single event. He set to work on cataloguing them and Beverley Nenk (Curator of Later Medieval Collections at the British Museum) examined the earthenware vessel fragments.

The hoard consisted of 345 silver coins – a mix of English sixpences, shillings and halfcrowns, and one counterfeit shilling. The earliest coin was minted in the reign of Edward VI (r. 1547–53). Also present were 181 coins of Elizabeth I (r. 1558–1603), 33 of James I (r.1603–25) and 130 of Charles I (r. 1625–49). The later coins can be dated fairly precisely because they either have dates as part of their design or a different distinctive mint mark that was changed regularly as a means of currency control. From 1641 to 1643 coins were minted with the mark of a triangle in a circle, and these are the latest coins in the group, suggesting that it was buried at that time. All of this is consistent with the hoard having been deposited for safekeeping (and never retrieved) during the English Civil War.

HOARDS OF HOARDS

If one is to plot the number of hoards discovered by the periods in which they were hidden, there are two large spikes – one in the later Roman period and another in the mid-17th century. Some of the Roman hoards were placed in the ground for ritual or 'votive' reasons, but those from the second spike are inextricably linked to the turmoil of the English Civil War. This arose from Charles I's dispute with Parliament, formally starting when he raised his standard in Nottingham in 1642, and ending after his execution (on 30 January 1649) in 1651, with Parliamentary forces in control of the country and Charles's heir (the future Charles II) fleeing into exile in France. Tens of thousands of civilians were killed during this period of upheaval, and many ordinary people hid their wealth with the hopes of collecting it when things calmed down. Coin hoards whose latest issues

BELOW Basing House, where
Royalist soldiers were stationed
during the English Civil War, only
a few kilometres away from the
findspot of the hoard.

had the privy mark of the triangle in a circle
(as in the Mapledurwell Hoard) make up a
large proportion of the coin hoards buried
during the war, and were probably related
to the Royalist advances from the north-west
in 1642 and the south-west in 1643; both of
these regions of England are peppered with
unrecovered hoards, in the view of Edward
Besly (former Curator of Numismatics at
Amgueddfa Cymru – Museum Wales).

It is not just coins that were buried: in 2008
detectorist Arthur Haig uncovered in Nether
Stowey, Somerset (SOM-849CA3), a cache of
four silver spoons, a goblet and a bell salt,
all most likely hidden within an earthenware
vessel whose fragments were found alongside.
The latest object in the hoard, the goblet,
is dated by its marks to 1633. Nearby Stowey
Court was a Royalist garrison during the Civil
War and the silver items were probably buried
during this time.

UPHEAVAL IN HAMPSHIRE

The ruins of Basing House, a large brick
Tudor palace, lie around 4 km to the west
of the findspot of the Mapledurwell Hoard.
In 1642 it was garrisoned for the king by
its owner John Paulet, the 5th Marquess of
Winchester. It occupied a strategic position,
commanding the road from London through
Old Basing and to the west. Between 1642 and
1645 it withstood three sieges by Parliamentary
forces until it was finally taken by Oliver
Cromwell, its contents looted and a number
of the non-combatants slaughtered. Although
there is no obvious direct connection between
the Mapledurwell Hoard and these actions
at nearby Basing House, soldiers were clearly
present in the area around the time the hoard
was buried, and there was a high level of
violence and disruption locally.

At the time it was buried the hoard had a
face value of more than £13, which was several

months' pay for a soldier or over a year's pay for a labourer. The Mapledurwell Hoard is not massive in the number of coins it contains compared with other hoards from this period (1,200 silver coins believed to have been buried during the Civil War were found in 2016 in Ewerby, Lincolnshire), nor in their total value, but it is still larger than most – usually worth less than £10 each, according to Edward.

The broken stoneware jug, whose bottom half the coins had filled, bears a decorative medallion in the form of a ten-petalled rosette. When complete, the vessel would have had the image of a bearded face above the medallion, towards the neck. These jugs, sometimes known as Bartmann (German for 'bearded man') or 'Bellarmines' – the latter name mocking Cardinal Robert Bellarmine, a fierce critic of Protestantism – were produced in high numbers at Frechen, Germany, and were a common 17th-century import to England and elsewhere.

An interesting aspect of the coins from the hoard is that several of them show signs of having been deliberately scratched with long straight lines across the face of the monarch. Whether this was an attempt by a Parliamentary supporter to 'deface' the coins and show displeasure with the ruler is uncertain. Other coins are pierced, presumably for suspension, though their inclusion in the hoard implies that they still functioned as currency.

With the local museums unable to take on the Mapledurwell Hoard, it was acquired by the British Museum. Despite the number of Civil War hoards that have been found, the Museum had historically only acquired selected coins from them, and this is the first time a Civil War hoard in its entirety has made its way into the Museum's collection. It is on display in the Museum's Money and Medals gallery, where Darcy, who still occasionally detects on his visits to England, has been able to see it whenever he likes.

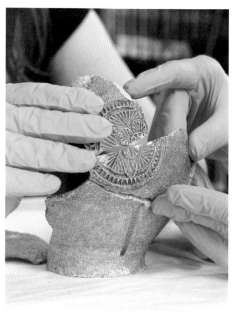

BELOW A complete Bartmann jug in the British Museum. The Mapledurwell vessel would have had a similar bearded face on the neck, which was broken off.

TOY COACH
FROM LONDON

A crumpled metal ball found by a London mudlark unfolds to reveal a 17th-century child's toy vehicle that was the Meccano or LEGO set of its day

LON-81D1C7	
OBJECT TYPE	Toy
MATERIALS	Lead alloy
DATE	1550–1600 CE
LOCATION	London
DISCOVERY METHOD	Metal detecting

LENGTH	39 mm
WIDTH	65 mm
THICKNESS	19 mm
DIAMETER	18 mm

OPPOSITE Two views of the toy coach after it was unfolded by the finder.

BELOW The toy coach as found, crumpled into a ball.

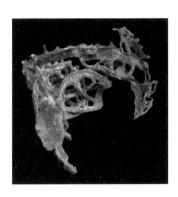

METAL BALL

Andy Johannesen is a regular on the Thames foreshore, using his metal detector (and eyes) to locate lost items from the past. In March 2009 he came across an intriguing ball made from lead scraps. Unsure of what it was, he began to unfold the metal parcel to learn more. This is not generally advised for crushed or folded metal finds, but in this case, Andy did not know whether the item was of any archaeological interest, and he undertook the disassembly of his strange sphere as carefully as possible. To his amazement, its parts formed an openwork toy coach, which he subsequently reassembled and recorded with Kate Sumnall, then FLO for London.

Around the mid-16th century, coaches suddenly became more common and fashionable as a means of transport, which is reflected in their survival as toys. Andy's toy coach would have been assembled from eight component parts – the Meccano or LEGO set of its day! Mirroring sides were formed from metal plates. To this would be added the front panel, the back panel, the roof and four wheels. Of these, the two main sides (with horses) remain, along with two complete wheels (including axles and axle loops) and the front panel with coach driver; the roof, back panel and two wheels are lost.

The toy coach found by Andy resembles others found in London and the Low Countries, where they survive thanks to the river mud – preserving items not only from oxidisation, but also from accidental damage. In this case, somewhat ironically, the fact that the coach was squashed into a ball helped to preserve it as most other examples survive only as isolated parts – the occasional horse, coach fragment or wheel. We can only wonder why Andy's toy coach was crumpled and thrown away. Maybe it was broken, perhaps by a child in a fit of anger, and then screwed up, possibly even deliberately repurposed as a ball. Maybe the object was then purposefully delivered to the Thames – though perhaps (as a ball) it was accidentally lost. Indeed, the mystery of its deposition is just as fascinating as the object that now survives.

BELOW Drawing of a 17th-century
coach by Rembrandt, *c.* 1660–63.

OVERLEAF The Thames foreshore
in the City of London.

POST-MEDIEVAL AND MODERN

BELOW Lead-alloy frying pan (its handle now lost) with fish, 17th century, LON-1318C1 (top); lead-alloy mirror, 17th century, LON-60302A (bottom).

BELOW Lead-alloy watch, 17th century, LON-1143DD (top); miniature stoneware jug, 15th/16th century, LON-DE0B6F (bottom).

TOYS

Other toys have been found by mudlarks on the Thames foreshore. Toy timepieces are relatively common, mostly represented by their faces. Flora Dunster recovered from the City of London foreshore a 17th-century lead-alloy watch face with its hours in Roman numerals, telling the time as 6 o'clock, surrounded by a floral border (LON-1143DD). Toy cups, pots and plates, as well as cooking utensils, have also been found. A tiny 15th- or 16th-century imported Rhenish-style stoneware jug (LON-DE0B6F), decorated with stamps and with moulding around the neck suggesting rope, was found by a mudlark at Wapping. A 17th-century lead-alloy miniature frying pan (LON-1318C1), sadly now missing its handle,

was found by Stefanie Clothier at Rotherhithe. Within the pan are two fish in high relief, placed on their sides, head to tail across the pan within a field of moulded pellets, which Stuart Wyatt (London FLO), who recorded the item, suggests are to represent 'hot bubbling fat or perhaps herbs and berries'. A lead-alloy toy mirror with an openwork design and scrollwork was found on the City of London foreshore (LON-6032A). Within the rectangular opening would have been a sheet of metal that served as the mirror (when made, these lead-alloy toys were much shinier than they now are after weathering).

As a group, these post-medieval playthings show that the toys children play with today, 300 years on, are not substantially different.

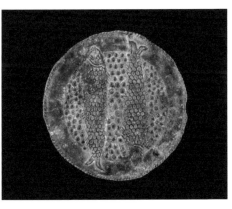

DUTCH CLOTH SEALS

Humble lead seals bear witness to the international cloth trade that drove the English economy and brought Dutch refugees to Colchester

KENT-95E90E	
OBJECT TYPE	Cloth seal
MATERIALS	Lead
DATE	1500–1800
LOCATION	Wingham, Kent
DISCOVERY METHOD	Metal detecting
THICKNESS	3 mm
DIAMETER	28 mm

OPPOSITE AND BELOW Two-part cloth seal from Haarlem, found at Wingham, Kent, KENT-95E90E. The front half (opposite) has the arms of Haarlem and reads '+HAER[LEMS] GOET' (goods from Haarlem). The other half (below) has the number 20, for the length of the cloth in Dutch ells; the imprint of the woven fabric to which the seal was attached is also visible.

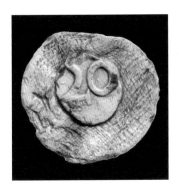

CLOTH TRADE

During the Middle Ages, England led the way in producing wool for cloth. By 1280 almost 26,000 sacks of wool were exported from England, reaching a peak of over 45,000 in the early 1300s. Much of this wool was sold to the Low Countries (modern-day Belgium and the Netherlands), where it was woven into bolts of cloth. Some of this cloth was returned to England to be dyed, often by London-based dyehouses positioned close to the River Thames, and then exported again. During the later medieval period, especially from the mid-14th century and peaking during the mid-16th century, exports of cloth 'finished' in England were becoming just as important as exports of raw wool. Since the cloth trade was driving the economy and was a major source of taxation revenue for the Crown, in London and other large English towns it became essential to protect it through regulation. This regulation is evidenced by many lead cloth seals commonly found through metal detecting and mudlarking. They were affixed to commercially produced cloths as part of a complicated system of industrial regulation and taxation. The first reference to the marking of cloth by the *alnager* (a Crown or bishop-appointed official) is in 1328, but most found seals date from the 16th to early 18th century. Cloth seals give archaeologists and historians crucial information about the development of the trans-national cloth trade, and the people and manufacturing centres it involved.

LEAD SEALS

Blank seals were cast in stone moulds and later stamped with an individual privy or merchant's mark, denoting the integrity of the merchant and the quality of his goods, or with a government-issued ligature or royal device. They are often hard to read, even when well preserved – sometimes they are off-struck, weakly struck or struck multiple times, and others have suffered post-depositional damage from being in the ground or river. Seals come in three main forms: single-part, with a central hole attaching it to cloth; two-part, one half with a projecting rivet that passed through a hole in the other when the two halves were

BELOW Cloth-seal mould from London. Such moulds provide important evidence on the production of seals.

BELOW Sheep in the early 14th-century Luttrell Psalter. Medieval England was a huge exporter of wool to the Low Countries where it was made into cloth.

folded, then sealed together; and four-part, like two-part but with two further elements that increased the space to record information.

Seals were issued by many individuals involved in the cloth-making process, and therefore lengths of cloth could have multiple seals upon them. The late Geoff Egan, PAS National Finds Adviser and an expert in all sorts of medieval and later finds, noted that many single-part seals found in London bear dyers' privy marks, normally based on their initials. Two-part seals can also have merchant's marks or personal heraldic devices, whether of the manufacturer or of a guild official (known as a searcher or warden) who checked it – some seals have the word 'searched', and the words 'faultie' [sic] or 'defective' are occasionally recorded. Gary Bankhead, also an expert in cloth seals, has noted that most 16th- and 17th-century two-part lead cloth seals found on the Thames foreshore are dyers' seals, attributed to the London Dyers' Company. Seals can also have numbers related to the statutory lengths or weights for different kinds of cloth, and even name the type of cloth. Some give the names of towns and counties, which is especially important information for archaeologists and historians. Four-part seals seem to be a 17th-century innovation; the two inner lobes are often impressed with the mark of an excise official and/or the tax paid for its export.

ENGLAND AND THE LOW COUNTRIES

Cloth seals give important information about the medieval and later cross-Channel cloth trade. Most were affixed to textiles imported into England from France, Germany and the Low Countries. A two-part cloth seal from Haarlem (modern Netherlands) was found by a detectorist at Wingham, Kent (KENT-95E90E). On one side is the arms of the city with the legend '+HAER[LEMS] GOET' (goods from Haarlem). The other side has '20', for the measured length of the cloth in Dutch ells. Other known seals have lengths 19½, 20½, 40½ and 56½. The woven cloth imprints preserved in the soft lead on the reverse side of Haarlem seals show that fine fabrics in a variety of weaves were made there. Between 1580 and 1585 many Flemish weavers moved to Haarlem, which became a finishing centre for linens. The clear waters near the Kennemerland coast were suited to bleaching cloths. These fine fabrics were known in England as 'holland cloth'.

Only one part survives of a two-part cloth seal discovered by Tyndall Jones while detecting on cultivated land at Patching, West Sussex (SUSS-7EA464). It shows the arms of Turnhout (modern-day Belgium) with part of the legend 'TVR[NOVT]'. The other side would have had St Peter holding two keys, as on an example from Wonston, Hampshire

BELOW Fine linen 'holland cloth' laid
out in the sun to dry after bleaching,
near Haarlem in the 17th century.
Jacob van Ruisdael, *Bleaching
Ground in the Countryside near
Haarlem*, 1670 (detail).

(HAMP-19B0F2), which was kindly donated
to Winchester Museum Service by the finder.
Turnhout was the main centre of the Kempen
tick-weaving industry in the mid-16th century
and traded cloths were known as 'Turnhout
ticks', often used for bedding.

Bobby Baker was detecting on ploughed
land at Hurstbourne Priors, Hampshire
(ESS-D0B806), when he came across a cloth
seal from Gouda (modern-day Netherlands).
One side shows a double-headed eagle, the
emblem used by the dyers' guild in several
towns in and around the Low Countries.
The other side has the remnants of the word
'[G]OV//[D]A'.

The Dutch were also producing cloth in
England. They arrived as religious refugees
to Colchester in 1565 and 1570, fleeing
persecution as Protestants in the Spanish
Catholic-controlled Low Countries, but quickly
became successful manufacturers of the
so-called 'new draperies'. Geoff Egan noted
that the high quality of their bays and says

(both coarse woollen fabrics), maintained by
stringent searching procedures, led rival textile
producers to counterfeit the Dutch immigrant
community's special seals to take advantage
of the high reputation of their products: in
1632, one cloth worker was fined £1,000 (about
£185,000 in today's money) for using fake
Dutch migrant seals to sell his produce. An
impressive complete two-part cloth seal issued
in the name of English weavers of Colchester,
to distinguish their products from those of
Dutch immigrants, was found by Corneliu
Thira on the Thames foreshore in London
(PUBLIC-DC9AF2). One side depicts the arms
of Colchester with the date 1618, and the other
has the inscription '[E]NG/[LISH][*COL]*/
CH[ESTE]R/SAYE/1618'. As a belated
response to the success of the Dutch, the local
English weavers established a new corporation
of their own in 1618. But their cloth seals were
still designed to look like those of the Dutch
immigrant community, evidence of how well
respected its textiles had become.

HAMP-19B0F2

Half of a two-part cloth seal from
Turnhout (modern-day Belgium)
depicting St Peter holding two keys.
The missing half of the seal would
have looked like SUSS-7EA464
below.
Wonston, Hampshire
Length: 28 mm
Width: 25 mm
Thickness: 1 mm

a. Image of St Peter holding two keys
b. Impression of woven cloth seal was
attached to

SUSS-7EA464

Half of a two-part cloth seal with arms
of Turnhout (modern-day Belgium).
The other side would have had the
image of St Peter holding two keys,
as in HAMP-19B0F2 above.
Patching, West Sussex
Diameter: 23 mm
Thickness: 1 mm

a. Remnants of inscription:
'TVR[NOVT]' (Turnhout)
b. Impression of woven cloth
the seal was attached to

ESS-D0B806

Cloth seal from Gouda (modern-day
Netherlands)
Hurstbourne Priors, Hampshire
Diameter: 26 mm
Thickness: 4 mm

a. Double-headed eagle emblem
of dyers' guild
b. Remnants of inscription:
'[G]OV//[D]A' (Gouda)

PUBLIC-DC9AF2

Complete two-part cloth seal issued
in the name of English weavers of
Colchester
Thames foreshore, London
Length: 60 mm
Diameter: 24 mm
Thickness: 3 mm

a. Arms of Colchester with the year
1618
b. Remnants of inscription:
'[E]NG/[LISH][*COL]*/CH[ESTE]R/
SAYE/1618' (English Colchester
Saye 1618)

cm

THE HACKNEY HOARD OF DOUBLE EAGLES

A jar of American gold coins found in a north London garden leads back to a Jewish family fleeing the Nazis, and British internment camps on the Isle of Man

PAS-867115	
OBJECT TYPE Coin hoard	
MATERIALS Gold	
DATE OF DEPOSITION 1938–40 CE	
LOCATION Hackney, north London	
DISCOVERY METHOD Gardening	
COLLECTION Hackney Museum and private collections	

CONTENTS OF HOARD
80 gold coins
Glass jar
Wax paper

DISCOVERY

Britain is a land packed with archaeology, so amazing discoveries are sometimes made by members of the public completely by chance. Such was the case in 2007 when a care worker in Hackney, north London, assisting several residents in digging a fishpond in the back garden of their shared housing, unearthed a glass Kilner jar holding 80 American gold coins, wrapped in bundles of ten in wax paper. The finders contacted the London Museum, where Kate Sumnall, then FLO for London, took possession of the coins and reported them to the local coroner as potential treasure under the Treasure Act 1996.

AMERICAN DOUBLE EAGLES

The coins were all of a type called the 'double eagle', with a nominal face value of $20. The standard weight of a double eagle was 33.44 g and they were made of 90% gold and 10% copper alloy: a modern British gold sovereign, for comparison, weighs 7.98 g and is 91.7% gold. Double eagles were minted between 1850 and 1933. Varying numbers were made each year but overall there were millions produced at mints across the USA, and as such they are not rare coins.

The original design of the double eagle had a Liberty head (the Roman goddess Libertas) depicted in profile on the obverse and, on the reverse, a 'displayed' eagle with a shield across its chest bearing the stars and stripes of the American flag, gripping a clutch of arrows in one talon and an olive branch in the other. In 1907 the coins underwent a dramatic redesign by famed sculptor Augustus Saint-Gaudens with the obverse featuring a full-figured 'Liberty Lighting the Way' and the reverse showing an eagle in flight. The Hackney Hoard contained coins minted between 1854 and 1913, so it included examples of both types.

The Kilner jar that held the coins was determined by glassware specialist Karen Wehner to be of post-1932 manufacture. This helped in providing the earliest possible date for the burial of the hoard.

OPPOSITE American gold 'double eagle' $20 coins from the hoard.
BELOW Ian Richardson holding one of the coins from the hoard.

INVESTIGATION

The discovery of the Hackney Hoard kickstarted an investigation into its origins. This was not only a matter of historical curiosity, but one of legal importance. Since the coins were less than 300 years old, the only way they could be classed as Treasure (and claimed as Crown property) would be if they passed all three tests of the old 'common law' criteria, which required that the finds be: made substantially of precious metal (i.e., gold or silver); hidden with an intention of deliberate recovery; and their original owner or their heirs unknown. The coins clearly passed the first two tests, but the third was another matter. Owing to their relatively recent age, the amount of wealth they represented, and the fact that they were found in the back garden of what had once been a private house, identifying the owner initially seemed possible. However, despite research commissioned by the coroner into the history of the property in Hackney, no obvious claimant could be found initially.

In 2010 the coroner opened the inquest into the case and then immediately paused it to allow news of the discovery to be broadcast, with an appeal for anyone with information on the original owner of the coins to come forward. Thankfully, Stephen Selby, a north

London antiquarian, saw the media reports and connected the recent discovery to a story in the *Times* news archive about a remarkably similar inquest in 1952. The *Times* story detailed how a find of American gold coins at the same address had been awarded by the coroner to a former resident, Martin Sulzbacher, and this proved key in unlocking a fascinating and tragic story behind the gold coins found in 2007.

Martin, a German Jewish banker, had escaped from Nazi Germany with his immediate family just before the infamous Kristallnacht, when on the night of 9–10 November 1938 the Nazi regime unleashed a coordinated campaign of violence against German Jews. He settled in north London with his parents, brother and sister-in-law, establishing himself as a seller of Jewish books. He managed to smuggle some of his savings out of Germany (in the form of gold coins) at a time when that country forbade emigrating Jews from taking any wealth with them.

At the start of the Second World War, the British government took stock of more than 70,000 UK residents of German and Austrian origin and, concerned about potential fifth-column activity, set up tribunals (often made up of only a single magistrate and a clerk) to classify each individual according to the likely threat they posed to national security. Initially, only 569 people were deemed enough of a risk to warrant immediate detention, and the rest were given freedom of movement. That changed drastically in May 1940, with Germany triumphant on all fronts and a cross-Channel invasion seemingly a realistic proposition. German and Austrian (and eventually also Italian) men living in restricted areas along the southern and eastern coasts of England, and anyone whose loyalty could not be absolutely guaranteed, were then rounded up for internment. Even though

a. Lid was still sealed when the jar was unearthed
b. Kilner glass jar, of a type manufactured after 1932

c. Wax paper for wrapping coins in bundles
d. American 'double eagle' gold coins, minted between 1854 and 1913, wrapped in bundles of ten

Martin Sulzbacher was Jewish, he was one of these detainees. He was originally housed in a camp on the Isle of Man but on 1 July 1940 was put on the SS *Arandora Star* for transport to Canada. This ship was torpedoed by a German U-boat in the Irish Sea and more than 800 of its passengers and crew were lost. Martin, along with 500 others, was rescued. He was shortly put aboard another vessel, the SS *Dunera*, for a two-month voyage to Australia for internment in a camp several hundred miles west of Sydney. The internees on the *Dunera* were so poorly treated by the British soldiers guarding them that the officer in charge was court-martialled upon arrival in Australia.

During this time the Luftwaffe began its campaign of bombing British cities. On the night of 13 October 1940, the home in Hackney

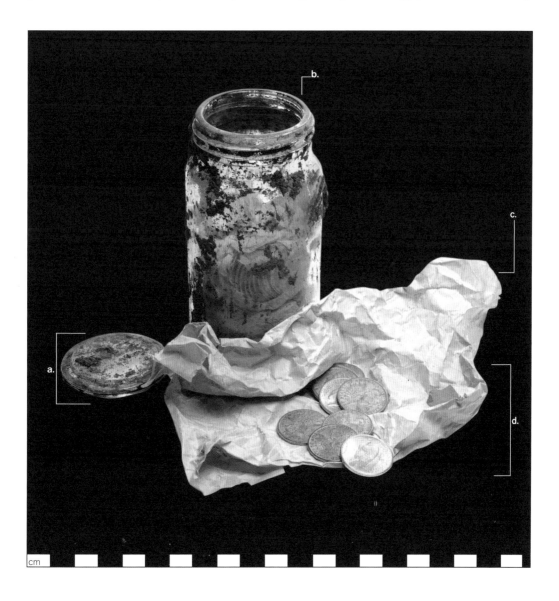

BELOW London County Council map recording extensive bomb damage for the neighbourhood where Martin Sulzbacher lived in Hackney, and where most of his family died in the Blitz on 13 October 1940.

where Martin had been living was completely destroyed, tragically killing his father, mother, sister, brother and sister-in-law, who had all been allowed to stay in London. Martin himself did not return to Britain until late 1941, and was not fully released from custody until the spring of 1942, when he went back to the site of his former house and found it still covered in rubble. He learned from a neighbour that prior to the bombing his family had withdrawn the contents of his safe-deposit box and hidden the coins. Although Martin hired workers to search among the debris, no trace of the coins was found. He moved to Golders Green in north London and rebuilt his life.

It was only in 1952, when the site of the bombed-out home in Hackney was being cleared for redevelopment, that the initial discovery of 82 gold coins was made. Martin was successfully able to argue in the coroner's court that they belonged to him, though he gave up hope that the rest of the coins would be found. He passed away in 1982.

These details of Martin Sulzbacher's life were provided by his son, Max Sulzbacher, who was living in Jerusalem at the time of the 2007 discovery and travelled to London to meet with British Museum staff and share his father's story. They are corroborated by Martin's internment record at the National Archives, and by newspaper reports and correspondence from the coroner to the Keeper of Coins and Medals at the British Museum in 1952. The coroner for the 2007 discovery agreed that Max, as Martin's heir, should take possession of the coins. Max kindly donated one of the coins, along with the wax-paper packaging and the Kilner jar, to the Hackney Museum. He also provided a reward for the finders. The rest of the coins were sold at auction, and the proceeds were used to repair Sulzbacher family graves in north London.

Staff from the British Museum and University College London, with the kind assistance of a volunteer detectorist, carried out an archaeological scoping exercise on the site of the 2007 discovery to see if they could locate any further material that had been buried by the family for safekeeping during the war, but nothing more was revealed.

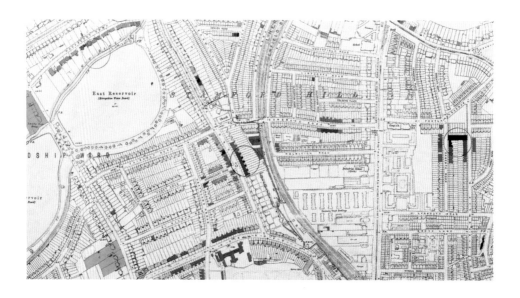

POST-MEDIEVAL AND MODERN

BELOW Martin Sulzbacher's Second
World War internment record in the
UK National Archives.

BOTTOM The SS *Dunera*, on which
Martin Sulzbacher was deported
from the UK to Australia for
internment in 1940.

MALE ENEMY ALIEN—INTERNMENT—REFUGEE

S 194

(1) Surname (*block capitals*) .... SULZBACHER

RETURNED TO U.K.

Forenames .... Martin 9- FEB

Alias .... re- INTERNED

(2) Date and place of birth .... 5-5-1896 Frankfurt. Reclassified '6

(3) Nationality .... German. Release auth. Cert 18.
28.2.42.

(4) Police Regn. Cert. No. 684085

Home Office reference, if known S/94427.

Special Procedure Card Number, if known ....

(5) Address prior to Internment .... RELEASED
8 MAR 1942

O/A/1

(6) Normal occupation .... Banker.

Nil.

Sailed for Australia
in s.s. "DUNERA"
on 10th July, 1940.

rove, Chelsea. Date .... 6-2-40.

No.

15m 9/39 (7701) 315zz/876 15m 10/39 4076 G & S 704 [OVER]

BEST PRACTICE

The Portable Antiquities Scheme (PAS) records archaeological finds made by the public to advance knowledge, tell the stories of past communities and further public interest in the past. It is a partnership project, managed by the British Museum (in England) and Amgueddfa Cymru – Museum Wales (in Wales), working with more than 100 partners across both countries.

Finders in Scotland, Northern Ireland and UK Crown Dependencies should make themselves aware of local laws and any linked guidance available. Public searching for archaeology is restricted in many countries across Europe and other parts of the world, so it is important to check national and local laws if you intend to look for finds abroad.

This section provides information about the PAS and the accompanying law of Treasure, which was last updated in 2023. It also reproduces the 2017 *Code of Practice for Responsible Metal Detecting in England and Wales*, which was agreed by the leading archaeological, landowner and metal-detecting organisations in the UK and has useful practical information for detectorists. Some but not all of this guidance is relevant to other types of searching, such as mudlarking, beachcombing and fieldwalking. See the 'Useful Websites' section for sources of information specific to other search methods, and for web addresses of the online resources mentioned in the text, including the PAS website and database, UK government agency resources and archaeology, landowner and metal-detecting organisations.

ADVICE FOR FINDERS OF ARCHAEOLOGICAL OBJECTS AND TREASURE

THE OBJECTIVES OF THE PORTABLE ANTIQUITIES SCHEME:

- Transform archaeological knowledge through the recording and research of public finds, to enable the stories of past peoples and their landscapes to be told.
- Share new knowledge about archaeological finds made within communities, so that people might learn more about their past, their archaeology and their history.
- Promote best archaeological practice among finder communities, so that the past is preserved and protected for the future.
- Support museum acquisition of finds made by the public, so that these can be saved for future generations and enjoyed by local people.
- Provide long-term sustainability for the recording of new finds, so that these discoveries can contribute to the rewriting of our histories.

AM I LEGALLY OBLIGED TO REPORT ALL MY FINDS?

No. The Portable Antiquities Scheme (PAS) is entirely voluntary, but by recording finds with the PAS you are contributing to our knowledge of Britain's past. However, you must report material that constitutes Treasure, or that you believe may be Treasure (see 'The Treasure Act 1996', opposite).

ARE YOU ONLY INTERESTED IN SEEING FINDS MADE BY METAL-DETECTOR USERS?

Not at all. We would like to see archaeological objects found by anyone. The focus of the Scheme is to record finds made by the general public.

WHAT TYPES OF ARCHAEOLOGICAL FINDS WOULD YOU LIKE TO RECORD?

We would like to see everything that you have found – not just metal objects. We try to record all items made before about 1540, but selectively record more modern finds. Your local Finds Liaison Officer (FLO) will decide what to record on the PAS database.

WHAT TYPE OF INFORMATION ABOUT MY FINDS DO YOU WANT?

We would like to record details of the objects that you have found, including written descriptions of each find along with their weight and measurements. We will also photograph your finds. Most importantly, we need to record where they were discovered (their findspot), which gives us key archaeological information. As there is always pressure on FLO staff time, we will only undertake to identify and record important artefacts for which findspot information is provided. Findspots should be recorded as precisely as possible (the nearest 1–10 m or 8–10-figure National Grid Reference), obtained using a handheld GPS device or similar.

HOW LONG WILL THIS TAKE?

Your FLO will borrow your finds for a period of time, determined by the type of find and the resources available, while they research and record them. You will be issued with a receipt while they are in our care. This should also indicate when your finds will be returned.

WILL MY FINDS BE TAKEN AWAY FROM ME?

No. We only want to record information about your finds. Museums may sometimes be glad to have the opportunity to acquire non-Treasure finds, but this will only happen if you and the landowner agree.

WHAT WILL I GAIN FROM REPORTING MY FINDS?

Your local FLO will be able to offer you:

Finds identification (either personally, or after consulting a specialist) and recording.
• Advice on conservation and storage of your finds.
• Advice on the Treasure Act 1996.

WHO WILL HAVE ACCESS TO THE INFORMATION ABOUT MY FINDS?

Our aim is to make as much of the information available as possible while protecting your personal details and archaeological sites from damage. We will publish details of the finds you show us on the PAS database, but the findspots of objects will not be identified more precisely than 1 km and with the relevant parish or community name; the most sensitive findspots will not be identified as accurately as this. This data is made available to third parties, such as Historic Environment Records and researchers, who must agree to follow the Scheme's terms and conditions for publishing data online.

DO I NEED PERMISSION BEFORE I START SEARCHING WITH MY METAL DETECTOR?

Yes. As outlined in the 2017 *Code of Practice for Responsible Metal Detecting in England and Wales* (see pp. 256–57) you must have the landowner's permission to search, and it is useful to have a written agreement with the landowner (not only the tenant) regarding the ownership of any finds. All land in England and Wales, including the foreshore, is owned by someone (whether a person, organisation or government body), so do not assume you may detect without securing that permission. It is prohibited to search or disturb protected sites, such as Scheduled Monuments, and it is important to avoid damaging preserved archaeology.

CAN THE REPORTING OF FINDS LEAD TO THE AREA BECOMING A SCHEDULED MONUMENT, MEANING THAT I CAN NO LONGER DETECT THERE?

Only sites of national importance are scheduled (which means it is illegal to use a metal detector on them without permission from Historic England or Cadw). It is rare for detector finds on their own to lead to a site being scheduled or otherwise protected.

I HAVE BEEN DETECTING FOR MANY YEARS AND HAVE A LARGE COLLECTION OF FINDS. AM I EXPECTED TO HAVE THIS MATERIAL RECORDED?

We would be very glad to know about all your finds, no matter how long ago you found them, as long as you know where the items were found. It is best to discuss the logistics of recording a large collection with your local FLO.

SHOULD I CLEAN MY FINDS?

Most of your finds will need no treatment other than dry storage. For further information about caring for non-Treasure finds refer to our Conservation Advice for Finders (available on the PAS website – finds.org.uk/conservation/index). Finds that may be potential Treasure cases should not be cleaned before being reported.

THE TREASURE ACT 1996:
INFORMATION FOR FINDERS OF TREASURE

WHO OWNS TREASURE?

Treasure belongs to the Crown until it is disclaimed or acquired by a museum (landowners will normally have best title to all other finds). Finders and landowners are not able to sell Treasure finds; rather, they may claim a reward (see further below), paid at the discretion of the Secretary of State for the Department for Culture, Media and Sport (DCMS). The aim of the Treasure Act is to ensure the most important archaeological finds are acquired by museums for public benefit.

WHAT OBJECTS QUALIFY AS TREASURE?

The following finds are Treasure under the Act if found on or after 24 September 1997 (in all cases except those otherwise highlighted):

1. Any object that is not a coin, that is more than 300 years old when found, and has metallic content of which at least 10% by weight is precious metal (gold or silver).
2. A single prehistoric object (up to and including the Iron Age), any part of which is precious metal (if found on or after 1 January 2003).
3. Groups of at least two base metal prehistoric objects from the same find (if found on or after 1 January 2003).
4. Groups of at least two coins that are more than 300 years old and contain more than 10% by weight precious metal (gold or silver), and groups of at least 10 coins of any metal that are more than 300 years old, and (in both cases) are from the same find. The following will normally be regarded as coming from the same find: hoards, groups of similar coins in the same place, and votive or ritual deposits. Finders should be aware that finds may have become scattered since they were originally deposited in the ground.
5. Any object, whatever it is made of, that is found in

the same place as, or had previously been together with, another object that is Treasure. This might include the vessels for coin hoards, items in a burial, or other items in a hoard that are not gold or silver.

6. Any object that would previously have been Treasure Trove (under the common law in place prior to the Treasure Act) but does not fall within the specific categories given above. These are objects that are made substantially (more than 50%) of gold or silver, deliberately hidden with the intention of recovery and whose owners or heirs are unknown.

7. An item or group of objects made of metal and more than 200 years old that provides an exceptional insight into an aspect of national or regional archaeology, culture or history, a) because it is a rare example of its type, b) because of the location in which it was found, or c) because of its connection with a particular person or event (but only if found on or after 30 July 2023).

WHAT OBJECTS DO NOT QUALIFY AS TREASURE?

Treasure does not include unworked natural objects, including human and animal remains (even if they are found in association with Treasure), and objects from the foreshore and the sea that are Wreck (the latter, usually from beaches, should be reported to the Receiver of Wreck). If you are in any doubt, it is always safest to report your find: you can find contact details at gov.uk/government/groups/receiver-of-wreck.

WHAT SHOULD I DO IF I FIND SOMETHING THAT MAY BE TREASURE?

You should show your find to your local FLO, or the relevant Treasure Registry (in England, the British Museum, and in Wales, Amgueddfa Cymru – Museum Wales), who will confirm whether it is likely to be Treasure or not. You must report all finds of Treasure to the Coroner for the district in which the finds were made, either within 14 days of discovering it or within 14 days of the day on which you realised that the find might be Treasure (for example, as a result of having it identified). The obligation to report finds applies to everyone. If you fully notify the FLO or relevant Treasure Registry within this period with all required information about a find, either in person or by letter, telephone or email, you will have been considered to have met this obligation. Your FLO (in Wales, the Treasure Registry) will then report the find to the Coroner on your behalf. Coroners will not usually want you to report finds to them directly as they generally do not have a place to store finds.

HOW DO I KNOW IF A FIND IS OF OUTSTANDING NATIONAL OR REGIONAL SIGNIFICANCE?

You may have an idea yourself, or others (such as fellow detectorists, FLOs, curators, researchers and antiquities dealers) may suggest that the find is exceptionally significant. If you suspect that you have made an important find it is best that you contact your local FLO or the relevant Treasure Registry for advice. They will be happy to give you a first response from images, advising you on how best to proceed. Advice will also be taken from relevant colleagues and finds experts in coming to a decision about whether to progress your find under the significance-based criteria. Please note that these

deliberations might take some time as further research will be necessary. If the expert opinion believes a find is of outstanding national or local significance a report will be prepared for the Coroner, who will ultimately decide if the find is Treasure.

WHERE WILL I HAVE TO TAKE MY FIND?

Your local FLO or relevant Treasure Registry is normally the main point of contact for Treasure finds. You will be given a receipt when you deposit the find. Your find may be sent to another institution (usually the British Museum or Amgueddfa Cymru – Museum Wales) as part of the Treasure process.

WHAT INFORMATION DO I NEED TO PROVIDE?

You will need to provide information about exactly where you made the find (the findspot), a legal minimum of within 10 m, but ideally within 1 m, and information about the circumstances of discovery. In public communications about the find, only a parish (England) or community (Wales) name will be given, while a more general location description may be used for particularly sensitive finds. It is strongly recommended that you and the landowner should keep the find-site location confidential and avoid sharing information on social media.

WHAT IF I DO NOT REPORT A FIND OF POTENTIAL TREASURE?

The penalty for not reporting a find that you believe (or there is good evidence for believing) to be Treasure, without a reasonable excuse, is imprisonment and/or a fine. Failure to report a find because you did not at first recognise that it may be Treasure will not get you into trouble, but you should report it once you realise this.

WHAT HAPPENS AFTER THE FIND IS REPORTED TO THE CORONER?

If the institution or individual receiving the find on behalf of the Coroner believes that the find may be Treasure, they will inform the British Museum or Amgueddfa Cymru – Museum Wales. Once all the relevant details about the find (contact information for finder and landowner, findspot, date of find) are provided, a report will be prepared for the Coroner by a suitable expert or experts, describing the find and recommending whether (and on what basis) it meets the criteria for Treasure. For those finds which are subsequently deemed to fall outside the criteria for Treasure, the Coroner will be informed and the item returned to the finder/landowner. If the find appears to meet the criteria for Treasure, appropriate museums will be asked if they would like to acquire the find for public benefit. If not, the Secretary of State will disclaim it. When this happens, the Coroner will notify the landowner that the object is to be returned to you after 28 days unless the landowner objects. If the landowner objects, the find will be retained by the relevant Treasure Registry on behalf of the Crown until you and the landowner have resolved any dispute. It is important to note that Treasure finds remain Crown property until they are disclaimed or acquired.

WHAT IF A MUSEUM WANTS MY FIND?

The Coroner will hold an inquest to decide whether the find is Treasure based on the written report and other evidence gathered as necessary. If the find is declared to be Treasure then it may be valued remotely, unless the Treasure Valuation Committee (TVC) wishes to see it or an objection is raised by any interested party (finder, landowner, acquiring museum). This amount is the reward and is equal to what a museum will need to raise to acquire the find. However, the UK government wishes to encourage finders and landowners to consider donating their finds (therefore waiving their right to this financial reward) and gives certificates to all those who do. There is no obligation to do this.

HOW IS A FAIR MARKET VALUE FOR A TREASURE FIND ARRIVED AT?

The TVC, which consists of independent experts, values all finds that museums wish to acquire. The TVC will commission a valuation from one or more experts drawn from the antiquities or coin trades. You, the landowner and the acquiring museum will have the option to comment on this valuation, and/or to send in a separate valuation for the TVC to consider. The TVC will inspect the find and arrive at a valuation. If you are then dissatisfied with the recommendation there is an opportunity to provide evidence to support your claim and to ask the TVC to reconsider the case. If you are still dissatisfied, you can then appeal to the Secretary of State.

WHAT IF THE CORONER, THE NATIONAL MUSEUM OR THE HOST ORGANISATION RESPONSIBLE FOR TAKING IN FINDS LOSES OR DAMAGES MY FIND?

They are required to take reasonable steps to ensure that this does not happen but, if it does, you should be compensated as if the find was being acquired.

WHO IS ELIGIBLE TO RECEIVE A SHARE OF THE REWARD?

This is set out in detail in the Treasure Act Code of Practice. To summarise:
- The finder who has obtained permission to be on the land from its owner, and acted in good faith.
- The landowner.
- Sometimes the person who occupies the particular site as a tenant of the owner may also receive reward, subject to the landowner's agreement (unless this is precluded by the terms of the tenancy agreement).

- Where pre-existing written agreements exist between finder or rally organiser and the landowner, these terms will take precedence and be followed.

WHO IS NOT ELIGIBLE TO RECEIVE A SHARE OF THE REWARD?

- Any person involved in an archaeological project who makes a Treasure find.
- A finder or a landowner who has acted in bad faith, and not in accordance with the Treasure Act Code of Practice, may expect a reduced share of the valuation, or none at all.

HOW LONG WILL IT TAKE BEFORE I RECEIVE MY REWARD?

The target time for payment of an ex gratia reward is 18 months after the find is received by the FLO or relevant Treasure Registry and all the necessary details are supplied (provided no challenges to the valuation are made), although it may be necessary to exceed this period in cases such as large hoards of coins, where finds need cleaning for identification or scientific analysis, or in cases of finds that are particularly rare or complex.

FOR FURTHER ADVICE ABOUT TREASURE

Finders are strongly advised to review the Treasure Act Code of Practice (3rd Revision), which provides further information about the Act and the Treasure process. This can be found at finds.org.uk/documents/treasure_act.pdf.

SUMMARY OF THE LAW (ACROSS THE UK) AND LINKS FOR FURTHER INFORMATION

- England: Finders must have the landowner's permission to search and avoid protected sites. Only Treasure must be reported by law. See finds.org.uk.
- Northern Ireland: Searching for archaeology is licenced and anyone finding archaeological finds must report them by law. See communities-ni.gov.uk/articles/ guide-metal-detecting-archaeology-and-law.
- Scotland: Finders must have the landowner's permission to search and avoid protected sites. They must report all finds by law. See treasuretrovescotland.co.uk.
- Wales: Finders must have the landowner's permission to search and avoid protected sites. Only Treasure must be reported by law. See museum.wales/treasure/.

CODE OF PRACTICE FOR RESPONSIBLE METAL DETECTING IN ENGLAND AND WALES (2017)

BEING RESPONSIBLE MEANS:

BEFORE YOU GO METAL DETECTING

- Not trespassing; before you start detecting obtain permission to search from the landowner, regardless of the status, or perceived status, of the land. Remember that all land (including parks, public open spaces, beaches and foreshores) has an owner, and an occupier (such as a tenant farmer) can only grant permission with both the landowner's and tenant's agreement.

Any finds discovered will normally be the property of the landowner, so to avoid disputes it is advisable to get permission and agreement in writing first regarding the ownership of any finds subsequently discovered.
- Obeying the law concerning protected sites (such as those defined as Scheduled Monuments, Sites of Special Scientific Interest or military crash sites, and those involving human remains), and those other sites

on which metal detecting might also be restricted (such as land under Countryside Stewardship or other agri-environment schemes). You can obtain details of these sites from several sources, including the landowner/occupier, your local Finds Liaison Officer or Historic Environment Record, or MAGIC or Cadw (see 'Useful Websites'), which will help to research and better understand the site. Take extra care when detecting near protected sites since it is not always clear where the boundaries of these lie on the ground.

- Familiarising yourself with the Portable Antiquities Scheme, including contact details for your local Finds Liaison Officer (England, finds.org.uk/contacts, telephone 0207 3238611, email info@finds.org.uk) or Treasure Administrator (Wales, telephone 029 20573374, email treasure@museumwales.ac.uk and trysor@amgueddfacymru.ac.uk), and its guidance on the recording of archaeological finds discovered by the public. Make it clear to the landowner that you wish to record finds with the Portable Antiquities Scheme. Ensure that you follow current conservation advice on the handling, care and storage of archaeological objects.
- Obtaining public liability insurance (to protect yourself and others from accidental damage), such as that offered by the National Council for Metal Detecting or the Federation of Independent Detectorists.

WHILE YOU ARE METAL DETECTING

- Working on ground that has already been disturbed (such as ploughed land or that which has formerly been ploughed), and only within the depth of ploughing. If detecting takes place on pasture, be careful to ensure that no damage is done to the archaeological value of the land, including earthworks. Avoid damaging stratified archaeological deposits (that is to say, finds that seem to be in the place where they were deposited in antiquity) and minimise any ground disturbance through the use of suitable tools and by reinstating any ground and turf as neatly as possible.
- Stopping any digging and making the landowner aware that you are seeking expert help if you discover something below the ploughsoil, or a concentration of finds or unusual material, or wreck remains. Your local Finds Liaison Officer may be able to help or will be able to advise on an appropriate contact. Reporting the find does not change your rights of discovery, but will result in far more archaeological evidence being recovered.
- Recording findspots as accurately as possible for all archaeological finds (i.e., to at least a 10-m square – an 8-figure National Grid Reference), using a handheld Global Positioning System (GPS) device while in the field or a 1:25000 scale map if this is not possible. Bag finds individually, recording the National Grid Reference on the bag with a waterproof/indelible marker.
- Archaeologists are interested in learning about all archaeological finds you discover, not just metallic items, because such finds contribute to knowledge.
- Respecting the Country Code: leave gates and property as you find them, dispose properly of litter, and do not damage crops, frighten animals or disturb ground-nesting birds.

AFTER YOU HAVE BEEN METAL DETECTING:

- Reporting all archaeological finds to the relevant landowner/occupier, and making it clear to the landowner that you wish to report archaeological finds to the Portable Antiquities Scheme, so the information can pass into the local Historic Environment Record. Both the Country Land and Business Association and the National Farmers Union support the recording of finds with the Portable Antiquities Scheme..
- Abiding by the statutory provisions of the Treasure Act 1996, the Treasure Act Code of Practice and wreck law. If you wish to take artefacts and archaeological material that is more than 50 years old out of the UK, you will require an export licence. If you need advice, your local Finds Liaison Officer will be able to help you.
- Calling the Police (101) and notifying the landowner/occupier if you find any traces of human remains or a likely burial. Human remains can only be disturbed further with a licence from the Ministry of Justice.
- Calling the Police or HM Coastguard and notifying the landowner/occupier if you find anything that may be a live explosive, device or other ordnance. Do not attempt to move or interfere with any such explosives.
- Calling the Police if you notice any illegal activity while out metal detecting, such as theft of farm equipment or illegal metal detecting (nighthawking). Further details can be found by contacting Historic England/Cadw or the 'heritage crime' contact within your local police force.

FINDING OUT MORE ABOUT ARCHAEOLOGY AND METAL DETECTING

- You can find out more about the archaeology of your own area from the Historic Environment Records maintained by local authority archaeology services (in England) and Heneb (The Trust for Welsh Archaeology), as well as the Heritage Gateway (in England) and Archwilio (in Wales).
- For further information about the recording and reporting of finds discovered by the public and the Treasure Act 1996, contact the Portable Antiquities Scheme (email your local Finds Liaison Officer or telephone 0207 3238611).
- For further information about how you can become involved in archaeology, contact the Council for British Archaeology (telephone 01904 671417). They can also supply details of local archaeology societies.
- You can find out more about metal detecting via the National Council for Metal Detecting, the Federation of Independent Detectorists or the Association for Metal Detecting Sport.

The text of the Best Practice section has been adapted from a Portable Antiquities Scheme leaflet that is available here: https://finds.org.uk/documents/file/pa-and-t-leaflet.pdf

USEFUL WEBSITES

PORTABLE ANTIQUITIES SCHEME (PAS):

PAS HOMEPAGE
https://finds.org.uk

FIND YOUR LOCAL FINDS LIAISON OFFICER (FLO)
https://finds.org.uk/contacts

CONSERVATION ADVICE FOR FINDERS
https://finds.org.uk/conservation/index

SEARCH THE DATABASE
https://finds.org.uk/database/search

**CODE OF PRACTICE FOR RESPONSIBLE
METAL DETECTING**
https://finds.org.uk/getinvolved/guides/codeofpractice

TREASURE ACT
Information about the UK Treasure Act 1996.
https://finds.org.uk/treasure

TREASURE ADMINISTRATOR WALES
museum.wales/treasure

UK GOVERNMENT AGENCIES AND RESOURCES:

ARCHWILIO
Database of Welsh archaeological and historical
information.
https://archwilio.org.uk/wp/

CADW
Historic environment service of the Welsh government.
https://cadw.gov.wales/

THE COUNTRYSIDE CODE
UK government statutory guidance for visitors
to the countryside.
https://www.gov.uk/government/publications/the-
countryside-code

**HISTORIC ENGLAND NATIONAL HERITAGE LIST
FOR ENGLAND (NHLE)**
Official register of all nationally protected sites
in England, including battlefields, listed buildings,
Scheduled Monuments, protected wrecks and
registered parks and gardens.
https://historicengland.org.uk/listing/the-list/

HERITAGE GATEWAY
Local and national records on the historic environment.
https://www.heritagegateway.org.uk/gateway/

**MAGIC (MULTI-AGENCY GEOGRAPHIC INFORMATION
FOR THE COUNTRYSIDE)**
Geographic information about rural, urban, coastal
and marine natural environments across Great Britain,
from multiple UK government agencies.
https://magic.defra.gov.uk/

PORT OF LONDON AUTHORITY (PLA)
The PLA administers the tidal Thames foreshore on
behalf of the Crown Estate as landowner. Permission
for mudlarking is granted through a foreshore permit
scheme: https://pla.co.uk/thames-foreshore-permits

The PLA Code of Practice for mudlarks is available here:
https://pla.co.uk/sites/default/files/2024-10/Foreshore-
permits-code-of-conduct.pdf

RECEIVER OF WRECK
The Receiver of Wreck receives reports of wreckage
of ocean-going ships and cargo of any age found on
seashores or in tidal waters:
https://www.gov.uk/report-wreck-material

TREASURE TROVE SCOTLAND
https://treasuretrovescotland.co.uk/

ARCHAEOLOGY AND DETECTING ORGANISATIONS:

COUNCIL FOR BRITISH ARCHAEOLOGY
Details of local archaeology organisations in your area,
and other opportunities for members of the public to get
involved in archaeology.
https://www.archaeologyuk.org/

HENEB: THE TRUST FOR WELSH ARCHAEOLOGY
A charity for public education in archaeology.
https://www.heneb.org.uk

ASSOCIATION FOR METAL DETECTING SPORT
https://www.amds.org.uk/

FEDERATION OF INDEPENDENT DETECTORISTS
http://www.fid.org.uk

NATIONAL COUNCIL FOR METAL DETECTING
https://www.ncmd.co.uk/

FURTHER READING

If you are interested in learning more about the objects featured in this book, the best starting point is the record created for each of them on the Portable Antiquities Scheme (PAS) database (finds.org.uk). These records can be searched by PAS reference number (e.g., NMS-12C4EF). These records are usually created by the Finds Liaison Officer (FLO) who recorded the object, sometimes in collaboration with British Museum or Amgueddfa Cymru colleagues, or with input from other experts. Other publications drawn upon by the authors of this volume are listed below. Additional publications relevant to each object are listed in the PAS database records.

PUBLIC FINDS

Roger Bland, 'A pragmatic approach to the problem of portable antiquities: the experience of England and Wales', *Antiquity*, vol. 79, no. 304 (2005), pp. 440–47.

Norma Dawson, *A Modern Legal History of Treasure* (Palgrave, 2023).

Richard Hobbs, *Treasure: Finding our past* (The British Museum Press, 2003).

Michael Lewis, 'A detectorist's utopia? Archaeology and metal-detecting in England and Wales', *Open Archaeology*, vol. 2 (2016), pp. 127–39.

Lara Maiklem, *Mudlarking: Lost and found on the River Thames* (Bloomsbury, 2019).

Malcolm Russell, *Mudlark'd: Hidden histories from the River Thames* (Thames & Hudson, 2022).

GENERAL FINDS

50 Finds series (Amberley, 2015–) [various authors].

Kevin Leahy and Michael Lewis, *Finds Identified: An illustrated guide to metal detecting and archaeological finds* (Greenlight, 2018).

Kevin Leahy and Michael Lewis, *Finds Identified II: Dress fittings and ornaments* (Greenlight, 2020).

Kevin Leahy and Michael Lewis, *Finds Identified III: Materials, manufacture and design* (Greenlight, 2024).

Mary-Ann Ochota, *Britain's Secret Treasures: Extraordinary finds uncovered by members of the public* (Headline, 2013).

PREHISTORIC

Alexandra Baldwin and Jody Joy, *A Celtic Feast: The Iron Age cauldrons from Chiseldon, Wiltshire*, British Museum Research Publication 203 (The British Museum, 2017).

Mary Cahill, 'A gold dress-fastener from Clohernagh, Co. Tipperary, and a catalogue of related material', in Michael Ryan (ed.), *Irish Antiquities: Essays in memory of Joseph Raftery* (Wordwell, 1998), pp. 27–78.

Michael Farley, 'A Bronze Age bracelet from The Lee', *Records of Buckinghamshire*, vol. 37 (1997), pp. 159–63.

Duncan Garrow and Neil Wilkin, *The World of Stonehenge* (The British Museum Press, 2022).

Jaime Kaminski, 'The "Near Lewes" Hoard', *Sussex Archaeological Collections*, vol. 161 (2023), pp. 1–29.

Stuart Needham, 'The Gold and Copper Metalwork', in Gwilym Hughes (ed.), *The Lockington Gold Hoard: An Early Bronze Age barrow cemetery at Lockington, Leicestershire* (Oxbow, 2000), pp. 23–47.

Stuart Needham, Keith Parfitt and Gill Varndell (eds), *The Ringlemere Cup: Precious cups and the beginning of the Channel Bronze Age*, British Museum Research Publication 163 (The British Museum, 2006).

Ron Pinhashi, Ian Armit and David Reich, 'Large-scale migration into Britain during the Middle to Late Bronze Age', *Nature*, vol. 601 (2021), pp. 588–94.

Vicki Score (ed.), *Hoards, Hounds and Helmets: The story of the Hallaton Treasure* (University of Leicester Archaeological Services, 2011).

ROMAN

Roger Bland, Sam Moorhead and Anna Booth, *The Frome Hoard* (The British Museum Press, 2010).

David Breeze (ed.), *The Crosby Garrett Helmet* (Cumberland & Westmoreland Antiquarian and Archaeological Society, 2018).

David Breeze and Christof Flügel, 'A military surveyor's souvenir? The Ilam Pan', in *Transactions of the Cumberland & Westmorland Antiquarian & Archaeological Society* vol. 21 (2021), pp. 43–62.

Sam Moorhead, *A History of Roman Coinage in Britain* (Greenlight, 2013).

Sam Moorhead, 'The Frome Hoard. How a massive find changes everything', in Bruno Callegher (ed.), *Too Big to Study? Troppo grandi da studiare?* (EUT Edizioni Università di Trieste, 2019), pp. 281–304.

Sam Moorhead and David Stuttard, *The Romans Who Shaped Britain* (Thames & Hudson, 2012).

MEDIEVAL

Barry Ager, 'The Carolingian cup from the Vale of York Hoard: origins of its form and decorative features', *The Antiquaries Journal*, vol. 100 (September 2020), pp. 86–108.

Charlotte Behr and Tim Pestell, 'The bracteate hoard from Binham: an early Anglo-Saxon central place?', *Medieval Archaeology*, vol. 58 (2014), pp. 44–77.

John Cherry, 'The medieval jewellery from the Fishpool, Nottinghamshire, hoard', *Archaeologia*, vol. 104 (1973), pp. 307–21.

Lloyd de Beer and Naomi Speakman, *Thomas Becket: Murder and the making of a saint* (The British Museum Press, 2021).

Geoff Egan and Frances Pritchard, *Dress Accessories 1150–1450: Medieval finds from excavations in London 3* (HMSO, 1991; repr. Boydell Press in association with Museum of London, 2018).

Chris Fern, Tania Dickinson and Leslie Webster (eds), *The Staffordshire Hoard: An Anglo-Saxon treasure* (The Society of Antiquaries of London, 2019).

Robin Fleming, *Britain After Rome: The fall and rise 400 to 1070* (Penguin, 2011).

David A. Hinton, *Gold and Gilt, Pots and Pins: Possessions and people in Medieval Britain* (Oxford University Press, 2005).

Richard Kelleher, *A History of Medieval Coinage in England* (Greenlight, 2015).

Kevin Leahy and Roger Bland, *The Staffordshire Hoard* (The British Museum Press, 2009).

John Naylor and Eleanor Standley, *The Watlington Hoard: coinage, kings and the Viking Great Army in Oxfordshire*, AD 875–880 (Archaeopress, 2022).

Leslie Webster, *Anglo-Saxon Art: A new history* (The British Museum Press, 2012).

Gareth Williams and Barry Ager, *The Vale of York Hoard* (The British Museum Press, 2010).

POST-MEDIEVAL AND MODERN

Edward Besly, 'Mapping conflict: coin hoards of the English Civil War', in John Naylor and Roger Bland (eds), *Hoarding and the Deposition of Metalwork from the Bronze Age to the 20th Century: A British perspective*, BAR British Series 615 (BAR Publishing, 2015).

Hazel Forsyth and Geoff Egan, *Toys, Trifles and Trinkets: Base-metal miniatures from London 1200 to 1800* (Unicorn Press/Museum of London, 2005).

Michael Lewis and Ian Richardson, *Inscribed Vervels: A corpus and discussion of late Medieval and Renaissance hawking rings found in Britain*, BAR British Series 648 (BAR Publishing, 2019).

Sarah Nehama, *In Death Lamented: The tradition of Anglo-American mourning jewelry* (Massachusetts Historical Society, 2012).

Ian Richardson. 'Stoke Newington's double eagles: the story of the "Hackney Hoard"', *Hackney History*, vol. 17 (2013), pp. 38–46.

Roy Strong, *Henry, Prince of Wales and England's Lost Renaissance* (Pimlico, 2000).

SOURCES OF QUOTATIONS

p. 58 'the handle from a chest of drawers': Cahill 1998, p. 29.

p. 71 'a pavement of bones': Score 2011, p. 103.

p. 99 'changes everything': Moorhead 2019, p. 281.

p. 107 'The line of the wall': Breeze and Flügel 2021, p. 56.

p. 137 'Hold now, O earth…': translation from *Beowulf* by Flora Spiegel.

p. 155 'which are most necessary…that we can all understand': translation from King Alfred's *Preface to Pastoral Care* by Flora Spiegel.

p. 213 'shrieked like a schoolgirl': Esther Addley, 'Metal detectorist unearths Tudor gold pendant linked to Henry VIII in Warwickshire', *The Guardian*, 31 January 2023, accessed November 2024: theguardian.com/culture/2023/jan/31/metal-detectorist-tudor-gold-pendant-henry-viii-katherine-of-aragon-warwickshire.

All other quotations are from personal communication with the authors.

ILLUSTRATION CREDITS

The publisher would like to thank the copyright holders for granting permission to reproduce the images illustrated. Every attempt has been made to trace accurate ownership of copyrighted images in this book. Any errors or omissions will be corrected in subsequent editions provided notification is sent to the publisher. Further information about the Museum and its collection can be found at britishmuseum.org. Registration numbers for British Museum objects are included in the separate list that follows. All images of British Museum objects are © 2025 The Trustees of the British Museum, courtesy of the Department of Photography and Imaging.

key: b=bottom; c=centre; l=left; r=right; t=top

2 Courtesy of Mark Didlick
6 Photograph © Mackenzie Crook
7 Suffolk County Council / Courtesy of the Portable Antiquities Scheme
8, 9, 10 Trustees of the British Museum
11 Courtesy of the Portable Antiquities Scheme
12 Norwich Castle Museum and Art Gallery
13 Trustees of the British Museum
14 National Museums Liverpool / Courtesy of the Portable Antiquities Scheme
15 Photo courtesy of Tom Redmayne
16 Trustees of the British Museum
17 Image © York Museums Trust
20, 21 Norwich Castle Museum and Art Gallery
22 John Sibbick / Ancient Human Occupation of Britain
23t, 23b Pathways to Ancient Britain
24, 25 Courtesy of the Portable Antiquities Scheme
26t Trustees of the British Museum
26b Photo by Stuart Wyatt
27 © Thames & Hudson / Photo Matthew Williams-Ellis
28, 29 National Museums Liverpool / Courtesy of the Portable Antiquities Scheme
30 © AncientCraft / Emma Jones. Replica by Dr James Dilley.
31 © Elizabeth Dale
32, 33 Courtesy of the Portable Antiquities Scheme
35 (top row, left and centre) West Yorkshire Archaeology Advisory Service / Courtesy of the Portable Antiquities Scheme
35 (top row, right) Courtesy of the Portable Antiquities Scheme
35 (second row, left) National Museums Liverpool / Courtesy of the Portable Antiquities Scheme

35 (second row, centre) Leicestershire County Council / Courtesy of the Portable Antiquities Scheme
35 (second row, right) West Yorkshire Archaeology Advisory Service / Courtesy of the Portable Antiquities Scheme
35 (third row, left) Birmingham Museums Trust / Courtesy of the Portable Antiquities Scheme
35 (third row, right) Courtesy of the Portable Antiquities Scheme
35 (bottom row, left) Surrey County Council / Courtesy of the Portable Antiquities Scheme
35 (bottom row, centre and right) Courtesy of the Portable Antiquities Scheme
36 Wessex Archaeology
37 Courtesy of the Portable Antiquities Scheme
40, 41 Trustees of the British Museum
42t LVR-Landesmuseum Bonn, photo: Juergen Vogel
42b, 43 Trustees of the British Museum
44t, 45 Courtesy of Keith Parfitt
46, 47 Trustees of the British Museum
48l Courtesy of Bob Greenaway
48r Trustees of the British Museum
49 Birmingham Museums Trust / Courtesy of the Portable Antiquities Scheme
50 © Shropshire Council
51 Trustees of the British Museum / Photo by Colin Davison
52 Trustees of the British Museum
53 Barbican House Museum, The Sussex Archaeological Society
54, 55 Trustees of the British Museum
56 Courtesy of Jonathan Needham
58 National Museums Liverpool / Courtesy of the Portable Antiquities Scheme
59 Courtesy of Jonathan Needham

60 Photo by Nicola Ferguson, reproduced by permission of Billy Vaughan
61 Courtesy of the Portable Antiquities Scheme
62 Norwich Castle Museum and Art Gallery
64 Shutterstock
65l Illustrated by Jason Gibbons, © Norfolk County Council
65r Trustees of the British Museum
68 Leicestershire County Council Museums
69, 70l, 70r Trustees of the British Museum
71t Leicestershire County Council Museums
71b, 72, 73b University of Leicester Archaeological Services
73t Leicestershire County Council Museums
74, 75 Image courtesy of the Potteries Museum & Art Gallery, Stoke-on-Trent
76 Courtesy of the Portable Antiquities Scheme
77t Image courtesy of the Potteries Museum & Art Gallery, Stoke-on-Trent
77b Courtesy of the Portable Antiquities Scheme
78 Wessex Archaeology
79 Illustration by Alexandra Baldwin
80, 81, 82t, 82b Trustees of the British Museum
83 Wessex Archaeology
84, 85 Lincolnshire County Council / Courtesy of the Portable Antiquities Scheme
86 Shutterstock
87l, 87c Lincolnshire County Council / Courtesy of the Portable Antiquities Scheme
87r Trustees of the British Museum
89tl, 89tr, 89cl, 89cr Lincolnshire County Council / Courtesy of the Portable Antiquities Scheme

89b Surrey County Council / Courtesy of the Portable Antiquities Scheme

92 Image courtesy of York Museums Trust – Public Domain

94l, 94r Courtesy of Mark Didlick

95, 96 Trustees of the British Museum

97 Image © York Museums Trust

98 South West Heritage Trust

100t Trustees of the British Museum

100b South West Heritage Trust

101, 102t, 103t Trustees of the British Museum

102b South West Heritage Trust

103b Shutterstock

104, 105 Christie's Images / Bridgeman Images

106 Johnny Shumate

107 Trustees of the British Museum

108–9 Shutterstock

110, 111 Trustees of the British Museum

112t PA Images / Alamy Stock Photo

112b Colchester and Ipswich Museum Service / Courtesy of the Portable Antiquities Scheme

113 Photo by Sally Worrell, UCL

114–15 Shutterstock

116 Trustees of the British Museum

117 Courtesy of Rossen Iantchev

118l, 118r, 119 Trustees of the British Museum

120 Courtesy of the Portable Antiquities Scheme, photography by Eve Andreski

122 Courtesy of the Portable Antiquities Scheme

123 Courtesy of the Portable Antiquities Scheme, photography by Eve Andreski

124t Lydney Park Estate

124b, 125 Courtesy of the Portable Antiquities Scheme, photography by Eve Andreski

128, 129, 130, 131, 133 Norwich Castle Museum and Art Gallery

134 Trustees of the British Museum

135 Norwich Castle Museum and Art Gallery

136, 138–39 Birmingham Museums Trust

140t Trustees of the British Museum

140b Birmingham Museums Trust / Courtesy of the Portable Antiquities Scheme

141 Birmingham Museums Trust

142 Staffordshire County Council

143t, 143b Trustees of the British Museum

144t Birmingham Museums Trust / Courtesy of the Portable Antiquities Scheme

144b Staffordshire County Council

145 Birmingham Museums Trust

146, 147 Norwich Castle Museum and Art Gallery

148 Photo courtesy of John Rainer

149t Courtesy of the Portable Antiquities Scheme

149c Norfolk County Council

149b Norwich Castle Museum and Art Gallery

150, 151, 152l, 152r Trustees of the British Museum

153 Credit: Ian Wallman

154, 155 Suffolk County Council / Courtesy of the Portable Antiquities Scheme

156 © Ashmolean Museum, University of Oxford; AN1836. p135.371, bequeathed by Colonel Nathaniel Palmer, 1718.

157t Trustees of the British Museum

157c © Ashmolean Museum, University of Oxford; AN1869.20, Presented by Reverend Wilson, 1869.

157b With kind permission of Salisbury Museum ©; SBYWM:2000.9

159t Photograph Eleanore Cox, Portable Antiquities Scheme

159 (second from top) Image courtesy of York Museums Trust – Public Domain

159 (third from top) © Bonhams 1793 Ltd R180

159b Leicestershire County Council / Courtesy of the Portable Antiquities Scheme

161 Image courtesy of York Museums Trust – Public Domain

162 Treasure Trove Productions, Channel X North, Lola Television

163 MS Hatton 20, fol. 1r, The Bodleian Libraries, University of Oxford

164, 165, 166t, 166b, 167, 168, 169tl, 169tr, 169b, 170–71, 174, 176–77 Trustees of the British Museum

178 Detail of the Bayeux Tapestry – 11th century. City of Bayeux

179 Trustees of the British Museum

180, 181 Oxfordshire County Council / Courtesy of the Portable Antiquities Scheme

182 Shutterstock

183 MS Cotton Claudius D. II, fol. 116; from the British Library archive / Bridgeman Images

184, 185, 186 Courtesy of the Portable Antiquities Scheme

187 MS Arundel 157, fol. 71v; from the British Library archive / Bridgeman Images

188–89 © Thames & Hudson / Photo Matthew Williams-Ellis

190 Leicestershire County Council Museums

192t Society of Antiquaries of London, UK / Bridgeman Images, SOA1066157

192c Image courtesy of York Museums Trust – Public Domain

192b Courtesy of the Portable Antiquities Scheme

193l Image courtesy of York Museums Trust – Public Domain

193r Lincolnshire County Council / Courtesy of the Portable Antiquities Scheme

194t Courtesy of the Portable Antiquities Scheme

194b Trustees of the British Museum

195t Courtesy of the Portable Antiquities Scheme

195b Trustees of the British Museum

196 Courtesy of Ian Morrison

197t Public domain / The Metropolitan Museum of Art, New York, 1975,1,110. Robert Lehman Collection, 1975

197b With thanks to Polesworth Abbey and Teresa Gilmore

199t Courtesy of the Portable Antiquities Scheme

199c, 199b Trustees of the British Museum

200, 201 Courtesy of the Portable Antiquities Scheme

202t MS Royal 18 E I, fol. 172; from the British Library archive / Bridgeman Images

202b Photo by Colin Torode

203t, 203b Courtesy of the Portable Antiquities Scheme

204, 205 Kent County Council / Courtesy of the Portable Antiquities Scheme

206t York Museums Trust / Courtesy of the Portable Antiquities Scheme

206b National Museum Wales / Courtesy of the Portable Antiquities Scheme

207l, 207r Kent County Council / Courtesy of the Portable Antiquities Scheme

208l © National Portrait Gallery, London; NPG 668

208r Kent County Council / Courtesy of the Portable Antiquities Scheme

209 Photo © Curtis Miller

212, 213 Birmingham Museums Trust

214t Courtesy of the Portable Antiquities Scheme

214b By permission of the Church Commissioners for England / © National Portrait Gallery, London.

By permission of the Archbishop of Canterbury and the Church Commissioners; on loan to the National Portrait Gallery, London; NPG L.246

215l Cotton Titus D IV, fol. 12v; from the British Library archive / Bridgeman Images

215r Birmingham Museums Trust

216–17 College of Arms MS Westminster Tournament Roll, 1511, membranes 25–26; reproduced by permission of the Kings, Heralds and Pursuivants of Arms

218, 219 Norwich Castle Museum and Art Gallery

220–21 Somerset County Council / Courtesy of the Portable Antiquities Scheme

221l © Royal Collection Enterprises Limited 2024 | Royal Collection Trust; RCIN 404440

221r Trustees of the British Museum

222 Royal MS 10 E IV, fol. 254r; from the British Library archive / Bridgeman Images

223t Birmingham Museums Trust / Courtesy of the Portable Antiquities Scheme

223b Trustees of the British Museum

224t National Museum Wales / Courtesy of the Portable Antiquities Scheme

224c Suffolk County Council / Courtesy of the Portable Antiquities Scheme

224b Kent County Council / Courtesy of the Portable Antiquities Scheme

226t National Museums Liverpool / Courtesy of the Portable Antiquities Scheme

226b Bristol City Council / Courtesy of the Portable Antiquities Scheme

227 Courtesy of the Portable Antiquities Scheme

228, 229, 230t, 230b Trustees of the British Museum

231 Francis Joseph Baigent and James Elwin Millard, *A History of the Ancient Town and Manor of Basingstoke in the County of Southampton; with a brief account of the Siege of Basing House, AD 1643–1645*, 1889

232l, 232r, 233 Trustees of the British Museum

234, 235 Courtesy of the Portable Antiquities Scheme

236 Trustees of the British Museum

237tl, 237tr, 237bl Courtesy of the Portable Antiquities Scheme

237br London Museum / Courtesy of the Portable Antiquities Scheme

238–39 © Thames & Hudson / Photo Matthew Williams-Ellis

240, 241 Kent County Council / Courtesy of the Portable Antiquities Scheme

242t Add MS 42130; from the British Library archive / Bridgeman Images

242b © London Museum; MOL.81.234

243 Kunsthaus Zürich, The Ruzicka Foundation, 1949; R 32

245t Winchester Museum Service / Courtesy of the Portable Antiquities Scheme

245 (second from top) Sussex Archaeological Society / Courtesy of the Portable Antiquities Scheme

245 (third from top) Colchester and Ipswich Museum Service / Courtesy of the Portable Antiquities Scheme

245b, 246 Courtesy of the Portable Antiquities Scheme

247, 248 Trustees of the British Museum

249 Courtesy of the Portable Antiquities Scheme

250 Detail of London County Council bomb damage map, The London Archives, City of London; ref. LCC/AR/TP/P/038/021

251t The National Archives, ref. HO396/151

251b Image courtesy of the National Archives of Australia. NAA: A11666, 63

272 Courtesy Ash Solly

BRITISH MUSEUM OBJECT INFORMATION

26t 1987,0202.1023, 1987,0202.1024

40, 41, 43 2003,0501.1, acquired through the Treasure Act with contribution from Art Fund (as NACF), Heritage Lottery Fund and British Museum Friends

46, 47 2020,8005.1

65r 1994,1003.1, purchased with contribution from Art Fund (as NACF)

80, 82 2007,8034.1-158, acquired through the Treasure Act

87r 1857,0715.1

95 1925,0610.1-4, 1925,0610.7-9

96 1879,0710.1, donated by Sir Augustus Wollaston Franks

107 1814,0705.1

110, 111 2005,1204.1, joint acquisition between the British Museum, the Potteries Museum and Art Gallery (Stoke-on-Trent) and the Tullie House Museum and Gallery (Carlisle); purchased with contribution from Heritage Lottery Fund

116 2020,8006.1

118l 1998,0401.1

118r 1946,1007.1, acquired as Treasure Trove

119 1812,0613.1, donated by Henry Brooke

157 1993,0102.1

164–69 2009,4133.1-693 and 2009,8023.1-69, jointly acquired with the York Museums Trust through the Treasure Act with contribution from Art Fund, National Heritage Memorial Fund, British Museum Friends, York Museums Trust and Wolfson Foundation

170 AF.541, bequeathed by Sir Augustus Wollaston Franks

192b 2021,8010.1

193r 2013,8006.1, acquired through the Treasure Act

194t, 195t, 199b 2010,8023.1, acquired through the Treasure Act

199c 1967,1208.6, acquired as Treasure Trove

223b 2000,0701.1, acquired through the Treasure Act

228–32 2019,4126.1-344, purchase funded by the Archibald Bequest

233 1854,0321.4

236 Oo,9.112, bequeathed by Richard Payne Knight

ACKNOWLEDGMENTS

Our first thanks go to the many finders who have reported their finds to the Portable Antiquities Scheme (PAS), especially those who have done this with the primary motivation of sharing their discoveries with archaeologists so we can all learn more about the past. Secondly, we thank those who have studied, researched and recorded those finds, which has led to the creation of the PAS records that we then shaped for this book. Most archaeological finds made by the public in England and Wales have been recorded by local PAS Finds Liaison Officers (FLOs), with support from colleagues in museums and universities, but an increasing number has been produced by finder communities, interns and volunteers. We therefore would like to thank the many people – probably several thousand each year – who have contributed to bringing the past alive by reporting, identifying and recording public finds.

We are very grateful to a 'panel of experts' who have provided us with much more help than we anticipated in ensuring that what we said about the finds in this book was as accurate and current as possible. Some of their names appear in the text, but others are present only silently – like the people who made and used the items we discuss! They are: Kurt Adams, Sophie Adams, Barry Ager, Nick Ashton, Gary Bankhead, Charlotte Behr, Gail Boyle, Andrew Brown, Anni Byard, Mary Cahill, John Cherry, Barrie Cook, Adam Daubney, James Dilley, Julia Farley, Hazel Forsyth, Eleanor Ghey, Teresa Gilmore, Martin Henig, Richard Hobbs, Sian Iles, Ralph Jackson, Andy Johannesen, Jody Joy, Amal Khreisheh, Rachel King, Kevin Leahy, Simon Maslin, Sam Moorhead, John Naylor, Stuart Needham, Keith Parfitt, John Pearce, Pippa Pearce, Tim Pestell, Ben Roberts, Andrew Rogerson, Vicki Score, Naomi Speakman, Kate Sumnall, Corneliu Thira, Rob Webley, Leslie Webster, Ben Westwood, Neil Wilkin, Sally Worrell and Stuart Wyatt.

We are also indebted to all the others who provided invaluable assistance with the stories, facts and images in this book: Jo Ahmet, Adrian Ailes, Cyril Askew, Estelle Baker, David Balfour, Frank Basford, Heather Beeton, Roger Bland, Anna Booth, Dot Boughton, Laura Burnett, Natalie Buy, Clive Cheesman, Penny Coombe, Eleanore Cox, Erica Darch, Mark Didlick, Amy Downes, Mélodie Duverger, Geoff Egan, Ben Elliot, Stuart Elton, Darcy Fear, Jason Gibbons, Bob Greenaway, Rebecca Griffiths, Andrew Haigh, Katie Hinds, Rossen Iantchev, Sian Iles, Aedan Jones, Meghan King, Helen Leaf, Ian Leins, Glenn Lister, Mark Lodwick, James Mather, Curtis and Ruth Miller, Faye Minter, Ian Morrison, Beverley Nenk, Emma O'Connor, Dennis O'Neill, Ben Paites, Adam Parker, Joe Perry, Laura Perucchetti, Lydia Prosser, Peter Reavill, Anja Rohde, Jessica Romano, Sabrina Ruffino, Wendy Scott, Stephanie Smith, Ash Solly, James Spark, Max Sulzbacher, Natalie Sutcliffe, Colin Torode, Pete Wakeman, Karen Wehner, Susie White, David Williams, Gareth Williams, Andrew Woods and Danielle Wootton.

We are grateful to Claudia Bloch and Laura Meachem at the British Museum for their help and support throughout: Claudia for facilitating the arrangement with Thames & Hudson in the first place and for keeping the project chugging along; Laura for her persistence and thoroughness in sourcing permission for many of the (old) photographs we wanted to use and for finding new ones.

We would like to thank the team at Thames & Hudson for partnering with us and putting so many of their resources into the book. Ben Hayes has been the patient and calm champion that we needed. Designer Agatha Smith worked wonders combining (often borderline resolution) photographs, artwork and text to create a beautiful product, with production controller Celia Falconer. Flora Spiegel and India Jackson invested an incredible amount of time and energy in improving and polishing the text, helping to bring together these varied stories and many voices into a cohesive volume. We are very lucky to have been gifted the right team to work on this 'labour of love'.

Finally, we want to acknowledge the patience and understanding of our families while we spent evenings and weekends working on this book, and thank them for their encouragement – thank you Emma, Emily, Sophie, James, Janina, Peggy and Teddy.

NOTE TO FINDERS

Wherever possible we have credited finders by name, but only when we were able to obtain permission to do so. Errors and omissions can be corrected in future reprints if written notification is sent to the publisher, or to the Portable Antiquities Scheme Central Unit at the British Museum via email at treasure@britishmuseum.org. We are grateful to all finders for reporting their discoveries and would like them to be recognised for this.

BRITISH MUSEUM
Head of Publishing: Claudia Bloch
Editorial Assistant: Laura Meachem

THAMES & HUDSON, LTD
Commissioning Editor: Ben Hayes
Senior Editor: Flora Spiegel
Assistant Editor: India Jackson
Designer: Agatha Smith
Art Direction: Tristan de Lancey
Production: Celia Falconer

INDEX

AUTHOR BIOGRAPHIES

Michael Lewis is Head of Portable Antiquities and Treasure at the British Museum and a visiting professor at the University of Reading and the University of Helsinki. He is known for his research on medieval finds associated with religion and everyday life and is co-author of *The Story of the Bayeux Tapestry* (with Dave Musgrove).

Ian Richardson is the Senior Treasure Registrar at the British Museum and Secretary to the Treasure Valuation Committee. He has a particular interest in post-medieval archaeology – and especially vervels!

Mackenzie Crook is an actor, director, screenwriter and author. He wrote, directed and starred in the BAFTA-winning television series *Detectorists* and is himself a keen detectorist.

Alice Roberts is an anatomist, television presenter and the author of fourteen books on popular science, history and archaeology. She is Professor of Public Engagement in Science at the University of Birmingham.

ON THE COVER Ringlemere Cup, PAS-BE40C2 (front centre); Wiltshire farmland, Getty Images / 500px Prime (front above); metal detectorist searching a ploughed field, Tahreer Photography / Getty Images (back).

ENDPAPERS Staffordshire Hoard, WMID-0B5416 and WMID-399670.

FRONTISPIECE Roman sceptre-head bust from the Ryedale Hoard, YORYM-870B0E.

OVERLEAF Detectorist Ash Solly visiting his Tudor signet ring (KENT-D29B09; see pp. 204–09) on display at Hampton Court.

First published in the United Kingdom in 2025 by
Thames & Hudson Ltd, 181A High Holborn, London WC1V 7QX
in collaboration with the British Museum

First published in the United States of America in 2025 by
Thames & Hudson Inc., 500 Fifth Avenue, New York, New York 10110

Beneath Our Feet: Everyday Discoveries Reshaping History
© 2025 The Trustees of the British Museum / Thames & Hudson Ltd, London
Text © 2025 The Trustees of the British Museum
Foreword © 2025 Mackenzie Crook
Foreword © 2025 Alice Roberts
Images © 2025 The Trustees of the British Museum, unless stated otherwise on pp. 260–62
Design © 2025 Thames & Hudson Ltd, London

All Rights Reserved. No part of this publication may be reproduced or transmitted in any form or by any means, electronic or mechanical, including photocopy, recording or any other information storage and retrieval system, without prior permission in writing from the publisher.

British Library Cataloguing-in-Publication Data
A catalogue record for this book is available from the British Library

Library of Congress Control Number 2024952298

ISBN 978-0-500-02752-3

Impression 01

Printed in China by Shenzhen Reliance Printing Co. Ltd

For more information about the Museum and its collection, please visit **britishmuseum.org**

Be the first to know about our new releases, exclusive content and author events by visiting
thamesandhudson.com
thamesandhudsonusa.com
thamesandhudsonusa.com.au

Dedicated to all public finders who have reported
their discoveries to the Portable Antiquities Scheme
and shared the history beneath our feet with the
world, and to the staff who make that happen.